南京大学研究生"三个一百"优质课程建设项目建设成果

English for Academic and Cultural Communication:
Selected Readings of *Four Books*

新编博士生思政学术交流英语：
中国传统文化译介

李 寄　雒少锋　陈 萱　编著

南京大学出版社

图书在版编目(CIP)数据

新编博士生思政学术交流英语：中国传统文化译介 / 李寄，雒少锋，陈萱编著. —南京：南京大学出版社，2023.6
ISBN 978-7-305-26265-4

Ⅰ. ①新⋯ Ⅱ. ①李⋯ ②雒⋯ ③陈⋯ Ⅲ. ①四书—英语—翻译—研究 Ⅳ. ①B222.1②H315.9

中国版本图书馆 CIP 数据核字(2022)第 212092 号

出版发行	南京大学出版社
社　　址	南京市汉口路 22 号　　邮　编 210093
出 版 人	金鑫荣

书　　名	新编博士生思政学术交流英语：中国传统文化译介
编　　著	李　寄　雒少锋　陈　萱
责任编辑	董　颖

照　　排	南京紫藤制版印务中心
印　　刷	南京京新印刷有限公司
开　　本	787×1092　1/16　印张 14.5　字数 309 千
版　　次	2023 年 6 月第 1 版　2023 年 6 月第 1 次印刷
ISBN	978-7-305-26265-4
定　　价	48.00 元

网　　址	http://www.njupco.com
官方微博	http://weibo.com/njupco
微信服务号	njuyuexue
销售咨询	(025)83594756

＊版权所有，侵权必究
＊凡购买南大版图书，如有印装质量问题，请与所购图书销售部门联系调换

前言 PREFACE

博士生英语作为英语课程学习的最高阶段,教什么、如何教一直是从事这一课程教学教师面临的首要问题。南京大学在这一领域进行了二十多年的不懈探索,为中国外语教学界贡献了南大方案。在对学术交流英语教学优化提档的同时,我们一直致力于探讨解决中国学人在对外交往中"中国文化失语症"的痼疾。本书就是这一方面的最新成果。教材分两个部分:一、学术交流英语;二、中国传统文化交流。

对于学术交流英语,我们不拟作面面俱到的铺陈,而是挑选了我们认为对于当下学术交流英语最基础、最必要、最有特色的专题。第一单元以学术交流英语电子邮件的写作为主题。该单元详尽介绍了英语电子邮件格式和语言上的标准和要求,并提供了电子邮件的常用套语,还展示了学术交流英语电子邮件的范文,供读者参考学习。第二单元以学术发言讲稿为主题。不仅介绍了相关的格式、文体的标准和要求,而且着重介绍了利用视觉辅助手段加强学术发言汇报的吸引力的技巧。第三单元以国际学术会议交流为主题。介绍了会议之前、之中、之后的种种注意事项,强调了如何把握国际学术会议的机会进行学术社交,深度参与国际交流的可行性和重要性。第四单元以提升英语表达的基本功为主题。鉴于英语不是绝大多数读者的本科专业,缺乏英语表达的系统训练,我们对于"结构、衔接、用词、文体"这几个英语表达的要素进行了介绍,希望读者借此对于英语表达有系统的把握。四个单元提纲挈领,突出重点,旨在通过上述标准、要求、范文、实例的学习和课后练习的操练,让读者能够熟练掌握英语学术交流的几个最重要方面,从而提高自己的英语学术交流能力,拓展自己的国际学术圈,为今后科研走向世界打下坚实基础。

对于中国传统文化交流,我们同样避开了常见的面面俱到的介绍,而是选取了中国传统文化的核心部分——《四书》及其英译作为本书的内容。《四书》指朱熹编辑作注的《论语》《孟子》《大学》和《中庸》。这一组儒家经典伴随着元明清的科举考试,成为中国传统文化的核心经典,塑造了中国人的精神世界,对于周边国家的文化也颇有影响。不仅如此,《四书》还随着其被翻译为各国语言而影响力波及全球,使得域外人士透过这部书了解了中国人的精神和心灵、中国人的人格和品性、中国人的观念和习惯。《四书》是中国文化走向世界的重要起点,是中国这个古老文明与世界文明交汇的重要契机。而在所有外国文字对《四书》的介绍中,英义翻译所占比重最大,受众最广,研究最盛,因此成为我们研究和教学的重点所在。本书注重英译,另有一层想法。通过系统地梳理《四书》英译中外大家的译本,理解翻译的基本要点,特别是中国文言翻译的一些核心理念和技巧。为了完成这一任务,本书在选择译本方面颇多用心。

我们参照中国经典整理的汇校集释的方法,采用了一个英译作底本,另外数个译本作参照文本的编写呈现方式。底本和参照本都是《四书》英译史中各个时期东西方最有代表性的译本。以《论语》为例,我们选择了韦利的译本作底本。该译本在史学和诗学上均有很高的造诣。参照本有理雅各译本(该译本是西方里程碑式的经典译本)、辜鸿铭译本(华人的第一个译本,其翻译的独特性极具争议)、安乐哲和罗思文译本(该译本代表了当代西方汉学翻译的最高水平)、林戊荪译本(该译本是当代中国的标准译本)。本书收录的《四书》译本体现了不同地区、不同时期的不同宗教、学术身份和背景的译者对于《四书》的各具特色、精彩纷呈的诠释和翻译。我们尤其重视选入具有代表性的华人译者的译本。在过去的有关研究中,这些译本的特色和重要性没有得到彰显。通过本书的编选和英译专题,可以看得出华人译者在《四书》以及中国古代思想典籍的翻译中地位特殊,成就巨大,贡献突出。我们希望读者通过本书的阅读和学习,能够取前贤之长,在中国传统经典英译方面取得更大的成就。

此外,除了对《四书》中英文本的字句疑难点作详尽注释外,我们在每个单元的最后一部分附上了《四书》英译专题。英译专题有两个主题。一是《四书》英译名家简论。收录的名家有理雅各、韦利、安乐哲、辜鸿铭、林戊荪、陈荣捷、刘殿爵。虽然都以译者为题,我们的论述尝试了尽可能多的角度——译者的专业/职业身份、目的语读者、译本的经典性和标准性、语体和文体、读者导向。这基于我们的认识:译学即人学。我们希望展示译本背后每一位性情各异、追求不同、成就也不同的译者。二是《四书》暨中国古代思想典籍的翻译策略和方法。以往的论述大多围绕着直译意译的二元套路,我们尝试突破这样的套路,引入释译(paraphrase)和统一(unity)的概念和术语。

因为篇幅的限制,本教程除了选录《大学》《中庸》全文外,我们用主题摘录的方式编选了《论语》《孟子》。这样做是为了更好地体现《论语》《孟子》思想的体系,便于读者从总体上了解孔孟的思想,更好地把握《四书》作为一个整体的互文互释。

我们编写本教程有促进中西文化交流、学术研究与翻译教学的多重考虑。读者对于同一原本的多个译本的校勘比照,对于译者的知人论世,有助于了解在东西文化交流过程中中国经典外译不可避免出现的误读甚至歪曲、碰撞甚至冲突;有助于了解中西文化从"半推半就"式的相互适应到相互交融式的"相亲相近"。正是在上述中西文化碰撞和交融中,中国经典产生了新的意义,中国经典才真正属于整个世界。同时,我们可以了解中国经典走向世界的艰难过程中,东西先贤筚路蓝缕、披荆斩棘的智慧、勇气和坚韧;增强我们在他们搭起的学术和思想的高台上添砖加瓦、更上一层楼的能力、信心和勇气。用心研读这些跨越古今、融汇中西的经典译作,温故而知新,切问而近思,还有助于培养21世纪具有中国灵魂、世界视野的君子人格。此外,本书编选《四书》译本代表了中国古代思想典籍英译的最高水平。通过对这些译本的研读,从译介体例设计、篇章布局、段落句子的安排到术语以及普通语汇的翻译,细心揣摩,举一反三,有助于今天的学者提高中国古代思想典籍的英译能力以及跨语际交流对话的能力。每个单元还都附有汉译英和英译汉的练习,以便读者在研读赏鉴之余,亲自尝试翻译,悟仁道和译道。我们还编写了开放式的思考题、讨论题,供学习者思辨、讨论、践行。诚如《中庸》所言,博学之,审问之,慎思之,明辨之,笃行之。

    本教程的编写基于编者在南京大学博士学术交流英语的教学成果。在多年试用之后,本教程被列入南京大学研究生"三个一百"优质课程建设项目。本书在编写时,根据党的二十大精神对具体内容做了一些调整。本教程的第二部分作为"东哲西释——《四书》英译精读精讲精练"还被列为南京大学通识课和南京大学悦读经典课,而这两类课程是南京大学近年来教学改革的标志性成果。后者于2018年获得高等教育国家级教学成果一等奖。因此,本教程同样适用于本科阶段的教学。本教程的编写和出版得到了多位师友的鼎力支持和无私帮助,恕不一一鸣谢。

编者
2023年6月

CONTENTS

Part One   English for Academic Communication

Unit One   Email Writing for Academic Purposes ·················· 003

Unit Two   Writing the Text for Academic Presentation Slides ·················· 014

Unit Three   Networking at Academic Conferences ·················· 025

Unit Four   Structure, Coherence, Diction and Style ·················· 035

Part Two   English for Cultural Communication

   —Selected Readings of *Four Books*

Unit Five   Confucius on "Benevolence"—Selected Readings of *The Analects of Confucius* (1) ·················· 047

Unit Six   Confucius on "Filial Piety"—Selected Readings of *The Analects of Confucius* (2) ·················· 057

Unit Seven   Confucius on "Being a Gentleman"—Selected Readings of *The Analects of Confucius* (3) ·················· 066

Unit Eight   Confucius on "Governance"—Selected Readings of *The Analects of Confucius* (4) ·················· 079

Unit Nine   Confucius on "Rites and Music"—Selected Readings of *The Analects of Confucius* (5) ·················· 091

Unit Ten   Confucius as a Man—Selected Readings of *The Analects of Confucius* (6) ·················· 102

Unit Eleven　*The Great Learning* (1) ········· 116

Unit Twelve　*The Great Learning* (2) ········· 129

Unit Thirteen　*The Doctrine of the Mean* (1) ········· 146

Unit Fourteen　*The Doctrine of the Mean* (2) ········· 163

Unit Fifteen　*The Doctrine of the Mean* (3) ········· 178

Unit Sixteen　Mencius on "Benevolent Government"—Selected Readings of *Mencius* (1) ········· 198

Unit Seventeen　Mencius on "Nourishing the Vast, Flowing Passion-Nature"—Selected Readings of *Mencius* (2) ········· 210

References ········· 221

Part One

English for Academic Communication

Unit One
Email Writing for Academic Purposes

With the rapid development of the Internet, email has the tendency of replacing the traditional form of correspondence—letter writing. Though people may prefer to communicate through the more informal and more convenient channel of social media, email remains a very popular form of communication in the academic circle, because it is fast, economical, and carries a certain degree of formality.

In this unit, you will be able to find the general principles of email writing, including the format and some guidelines of language use.

1.1 Format

Usually an email includes the subject line, the beginning, the body, and the ending.

1) The subject line

The subject line is crucial. It can determine whether your email will be opened or responded immediately by your recipient, rather than set aside for future reading.

It should be relevant in some way to recipients, so that they will have the interest to read it. It should also be specific. You can think from recipients' perspective. Imagine you are writing to an editor, trying to discuss a problem in a research article. If you simply put "Research article" in the subject line, it will not make any sense, since the editor may receive dozens or even hundreds of similar emails each day. It will be helpful if you can specify the name or the key words of the research article in the subject line.

If you only have a quick notice to announce in an email, you can even use the subject line to contain the whole message, so as to save the recipient's time in opening the email. For example: *April 9th meeting shifted to the Office Meeting Room. Same time. EOM.*

EOM stands for "End of message". And this indicates to the recipient that he doesn't have to open the email.

2) The beginning

At the beginning of an email, you need to address your recipients. If you know their names, make sure you spell correctly. Any spelling mistake in names can leave a very bad first impression. If you do not know whether they are male or female, you can simply avoid using "Mr, Mrs, Ms", and "Miss". Use their titles or their full names instead.

The word *Dear* is safe to use before the title *Professor*, *Dr* and the full name, even though Chinese students may fear that it contains too much intimacy. In fact, words like "Respectful" or "Honorable" are literal translations of the Chinese equivalents. They sound too foreign and unnatural to a Western ear.

Remember, do not use "Hi", the abbreviation "Prof.", or just the surname to address people. They are too informal.

3) The body

Instead of stating your own name, you can begin by giving the reason for writing. If there was previous contact, mention it briefly so as to remind the recipient who you are. For example, you can write:

You may remember we met last year at...

After that, organize the content of your email logically, including only the necessary information. For example, the following sender is requesting a delay of submission of a research paper. Instead of giving detailed description of the paper and the explanation for the delay, the sender simply writes:

Dear Conference Organizers,

I would like to request a delay in submission of manuscript #: 00231 until 3 May. I hope this does not cause any inconvenience.

Thank you in advance.

Best regards,
Ida Smith

If you have more than one request, clarify your requests by giving them numbers and keeping them short. You also need to provide all the relevant information the recipient needs to assess your request. For example, if you want to get an internship in a professor's lab, apart from explaining how you get this information and why you are writing, you also need to give a short summary of your research area emphasizing how it is related to the professor's area, as well as where you could add value. If you already have funding, or your tutor may be familiar to the professor, do mention it. A letter of recommendation from your tutor and references from other people are also welcome.

If the message you want to convey is complicated and you have to write a long email, try to make it easy for the reader. You can achieve this by using bullets, boldface or highlighted words or white space between items. Or you can use link words to show logical connections or important points. Make sure you will not write the whole message in one long paragraph. This also applies to emails with multiple requests. If a request is long, make sure you number it. You can even provide a summary of all the requests at the end. This will increase the chance of getting your requests replied.

4) The ending

English speakers differ in their acceptance of formality in the ending of an email. Expressions such as "Sincerely yours" or "Yours sincerely" are acceptable to Indian speakers of English, but sound too formal or even archaic to people in the UK or US. A more neutral and more commonly used final salutation is "Best regards". Note that you can put a comma or no punctuation after it.

Before this final salutation, there is often another standard phrase, such as "Thank you in advance", or "I look forward to hearing from you". But try to avoid using too many standard phrases as salutations at the end. They are too formal and too time-consuming to read.

At the very end of your email, you need to provide your signature. It should contain all the necessary information your recipient needs to know about you, such as your full name, your position, your department and university, and your phone number.

1.2 Language

Apart from the format of email, language use is another very important factor in successful email writing. It will be explored from the following three aspects.

1) Reduce ambiguity

Conciseness is a merit in email writing. However, it cannot be achieved at the cost of precision. Pronouns, modifiers and expressions of time are often sources of ambiguity. Therefore, you need to be as specific as possible in using them. Always be on alert for ambiguity. You can simply spell out which noun a pronoun refers to, which noun an adjective modifies, or which time zone you are speaking of when readers are in different parts of the world.

2) Decide the level of formality

In email writing, the style you adopt is dependent on whom you are writing to. In general, writing to professors in your academic field should be formal, even though they may have been informal and friendly. You should also avoid mixing levels of formality, such as using language of chatrooms or text message style in a formal email. Some abbreviations or acronyms are a case in point, such as "Dunno" for "don't know", "rgds" for "regards", and *thx* for *thanks*. The use of these informal expressions will make you sound not so serious or in a hurry.

3) Be polite

Chinese people are known for their politeness in treating friends from both home and abroad. But surprisingly, many Chinese students or even scholars are deemed impolite in their English communication with experts overseas. One reason is the tone they adopt. They tend to use very direct expressions such as simple sentences when making requests, without adding any cushion to soften the tone. One possible reason is that they have never attached any importance to the learning of more polite expressions. Thus they will sometimes sound more aggressive than intended. For example, instead of saying "I need it now", you can say, "I appreciate that this is a busy time of year for you but I really do need it now."

Besides, language that indicates the recipient is the guilty party should be avoided, like "As clearly stated in my previous email, ...", or "You have ignored the fact that..."

Another way of showing more courteousness is to use modal verbs. Expressions such as "Could you please...", "May I remind you..." can be added to your requests to sound more polite.

1.3 Useful Expressions in Email Writing

1) Initial salutation

Dear all / Hi all / Hi everybody / To all members of the XXX group

Hi / Hello / Good morning / To whom it may concern / Dear Sir / Madam

2) Phrases before the final salutation

Say hello to… / Please send my regards to…

Happy New Year to everyone. / Have a great Thanksgiving! / Best wishes for the holiday and the new year!

3) Giving main reasons for a message

I am writing to you because… / Your address was given to me by…

You may remember that we met at the conference in Beijing… / As I mentioned on the phone / Further to our conversation yesterday…

4) Asking favors / giving help

I am writing to you in the hope that you may be able to help me. / Please could you… / I was wondering if… / I would be extremely grateful if you could… / It would be very helpful for me if… / I would like to ask your advice about…

5) Making inquiries

Could you please tell me…? / I would like to know… / Could you possibly send me…? / I look forward to receiving… / Any information you could give me would be greatly appreciated.

6) Replying to inquiries

In response to your questions: / Here is the information you requested: / As requested, I am sending you… / With reference to your request for… / Could you tell me exactly why you need…?

7) Telling recipients they can ask for further information

Please feel free to email, fax, or call if you have any questions. / If you need any further details, do not hesitate to contact me. / Should you have any questions, please let us know.

8) Asking for and giving clarification

I'm not sure what you mean by... / What exactly do you mean by...? / Sorry, what's a "xxx"?

What I meant by xxx is... / My point is that... / In other words... / So my question is... / Sorry about the confusion, what I actually meant was...

9) Apologizing

Sorry. I haven't replied sooner. / Please accept our apologies for not getting back to you sooner. / I apologize for the late reply. / Sorry, but I have only just read your message.

10) Sending attachments

I'm attaching... / Please find attached... / Attached you will find...

Sorry. I couldn't read your mail—it just has a series of strange characters. / I receive your email, but I'm afraid I can't open the attachment.

1.4 Examples of Different Types of Emails

1) Sample emails: Application of a visiting scholar's appointment

> Dear Dr. Smith,
>
> I am an associate professor of the English Department at XYZ University, China. I'm writing to you about the possibility of a visiting scholar's appointment in your department in the fall semester, 2024. With your help, I would have a fruitful stay and get remarkable achievements in my research. I also hope that my expertise in the field of Australian literature could make significant contributions to your work and that we could initiate some projects for future collaboration between our two departments.

> I will be provided by XXX Council with all the travel and living expenses.
>
> Enclosed please find a CV of my education, research, teaching experiences, publications, translations and letters of recommendation, which, I hope, will meet your requirements.
>
> Thank you for your consideration. I am looking forward to a favorable reply from you soon.
>
> Best regards,
> Ming Fan

2) Sample emails: Submitting journal articles

A cover letter is often needed when you submit your article to a journal. In this letter or email, you should **explain why your work is perfect for their journal** and why it will be of interest to the readers of this journal. You can also use this great opportunity to highlight to the journal editor what makes your research new and important.

> Dear Editor,
>
> My name is Wei Ying. I am submitting the attached article entitled "Implications of the Output Hypothesis to EFL Learners in China" on behalf of my colleagues (Dr. Ning Jiang, and Yuanbing Chen) for publication by *Modern Language Journal*.
>
> We believe that the three aspects of this paper will make it interesting to the general readership of your journal. First, we report the empirical findings of a well-designed experiment from the perspective of Output Hypothesis. Secondly, we compare results obtained from our research to previous researches that are relevant. Thirdly, we show that some crucial factors may influence the findings of research along the same line. This work demonstrates that under certain circumstances, the Output Hypothesis is proved effective in enhancing EFL learners' oral and written performance.

Neither the entire paper nor any part of its content has been published or considered elsewhere. All authors have read the final version of this manuscript and approved submitting it to your journal. I have attached the manuscript in its final form, as well as consent to publish from my colleagues.

Thank you very much for your consideration of this submission to your journal.

Sincerely yours,
Dr. Wei Ying

3) Sample emails: Application for financial support

To which it may concern,

I am a Ph.D. candidate of the School of XXX studying industrial and environmental regulation in China. I learned from your website that the theme of the XXX Conference is the discussion of latest policy developments to reduce the environmental impacts of industry, bringing together participants from all the countries. I take a great interest in attending this conference for the opportunity to exchange views on policies in this field with participants from around the world.

I noticed that you would provide financial assistance for a speaker from China since the organizing committee is interested in China's particular experience in industrial pollution control policy development and implementation. The paper I am preparing is just on this issue, for I have had five years of experience working in a governmental institution in charge of environmental policy-making for XXX Province. I will send you my abstract and a copy of my CV to the email address you provided for paper submission. I would be very happy if you could accept my abstract and support my attendance.

I am looking forward to your favorable reply.

Best regards,
Lei Wang

4) Sample emails: Attending conferences

Dear Sir / Madam,

I learned from a colleague of mine that the 21st International Conference of XXX will be held at your university in April, 2024. Since I have been undertaking research on XXX for many years, I am very much interested in attending this conference.

I should be very much obliged if you could kindly keep me posted of the updated information of this conference, such as topics, invited speakers, and the deadline for the submission of papers.

Attached you will find my CV. If there are special requirements concerning the eligibility of the attendance, please kindly let me know.

I am looking forward to hearing from you soon.

Best regards,
Meiling Li

Exercises

1. Read the following email and decide what problems it has and how you can improve it.

Dear Secretariat of the 5th XTC Ph.D. Symposium,

My Supervisor and I would like to register for the XTC Symposium but we couldn't find any registration form in your website. I would be very grateful to you if you could suggest me the best way to register for the event. Moreover, would it be possible to pay the registration fee by credit card? Finally, is the preliminary program available for download? Thank you very much in advance for you kind cooperation.

Best regards

2. Work in pairs, and complete the following exercise step by step.

1) Write a complete email to a professor in your field requesting an internship in his / her laboratory / department. It should contain all the necessary parts of an email.

2) Exchange your email with your partner. Give some feedback on your partner's format and language.

3) Write a reply to your partner's email. You can choose to accept or decline his / her request.

3. Work in groups, and complete the following exercise step by step.

1) Read the following email of approval of Bob Zhang's request to attend a seminar.

2) Discuss with each other what information is necessary and should be included in Bob's email.

3) Try to write this email from the standpoint of Bob, and then compare your version with each other.

4) Choose the best version in your group and share it with the whole class.

Dear Mr Bob Zhang,

I am pleased to inform you that the board has approved your request to attend the XXX Seminar in London, England on the 16th of May. You will be our company's representative at this 3-day event.

Among other employees of the organization, you are a worthy candidate for attending this seminar. The board has based your selection on your qualifications and experiences. In addition, you have also shown your own interest in being a part of this event. Your enthusiasm has been taken into consideration by the authorities for the approval of your request.

It is going to be a great learning experience for you. It will certainly be an important upgrade for your CV. The company wants you to share your learning once you return to the office. We are going to organize an official workshop so that you can impart the knowledge gained at the seminar to other employees of the company. This training session is going to be valuable for the overall progress of the organization.

All your travel and accommodation expenses will be reimbursed by the company. You may take your spouse along on the trip. However, the company will not be responsible for any extra expenses.

Kindly contact Mr John of the HR Department for further details.

Daniel Reed
CEO of XUU Company

Necessary information in Bob's email:

Unit Two
Writing the Text for Academic Presentation Slides

With your paper and slides at hand, you may think writing the text for your presentation is a waste of time. Or you may even feel it is inconvenient, because all you have to do is just to cut and paste parts of your paper onto the slides and read them during the presentation. But in fact, both of the two opinions are wrong.

This unit will inform you why you need to write down the text for your presentation, what language style you should choose, and how you could write a good presentation.

2.1 The Basic Requirements of a Good Presentation

There are many advantages of writing out the text for your presentation slides. For one thing, the script will make it easy for you to identify flaws in the content, the language, and the order of presenting your slides. You may even question the necessity of some slides. Then you can revise them accordingly. For another thing, you can send your revised version to your friends or your professors and ask them to help you improve it. Also, when you are practicing your presentation, the script can help you spot words difficult to pronounce, terms you need to explain, and decide whether the amount of time you spend on each point is balanced. Last but not least, before the presentation, you can upload the script onto your smartphone and use it as a memory aid while doing the presentation.

A common mistake of writing the text for presentation is to copy from the paper. As far as language style is concerned, the English used in an academic speech lies in between the extremely formal academic writing and the extremely informal conversational English. To be more accessible to the audience, the academic speech tends to use shorter sentences, less formal language, fewer hard facts like exact dates or numbers, and more interesting facts and even stories.

Therefore, it is important to be concise. This can be done by cutting abstract words such as "thing", "activity", "task", "phenomenon", and "criteria". For example, instead of saying "Another thing we wanted to do was...", you can say "We also wanted to...". And you can say "Let's see how we analyzed the samples" instead of saying "Regarding the analysis of the samples, we analyzed them using..."

Contrary to writing research papers, in speech you can use more verbs than nouns, because verbs can make your sentences shorter and more dynamic. The following sentences are some examples.

X is meaningful for an understanding of Y = X will help you to understand Y

When you take into consideration = When you consider

This gives you the possibility to do X = This means you can do X / This enables you to do X

2.2 How Could You Make a Good Presentation?

To write a good presentation, you need to know how to begin, transition and end it, how to present the methodology, results and conclusion, as well as how to make the presentation attractive to the audience and how to maintain this attraction. The following section will be arranged in this order.

2.2.1 How to Begin, Transition and End Your Presentation

1) Beginning

The most common way to begin is to tell your audience what you plan to do in your presentation and why, although this opening can be too plain. You can use some other techniques to attract the audience's attention.

For instance, if your study is about soil erosion, you can begin with a dramatic statistic.

Ten thousand tons of soil are lost through erosion in my country every year. This means that fertility is lost and desertification ensues.

Or you can use a statistic that relates directly to the audience and get them to imagine something.

Imagine that this room was filled with soil. Well, after a single rainstorm on a small field in my country, three quarters of the soil would have disappeared.

If your study is about sports, you can mention something topical, such as anecdotes in the recent Beijing 2022 Olympics. Likewise, if you are studying new developments in science and technology, you can mention some recent breakthroughs in your field that are well-known. If your research is on literary theories, you can begin your presentation by talking about some recent films or best-sellers that are related to the theories. If your study is about language learning, you can start by talking about your own personal language learning experiences, especially setbacks or successes related to your study. The personal stories of your best friends will achieve a similar effect.

Whatever technique you choose, make sure you can connect with the audience. You can be creative and try out different techniques until you find the best approach. But before using it at the conference, you can try it out on your roommates or classmates to see its effectiveness in capturing their attention.

2) Transition

When reading a research paper, readers can reread if they get lost. When listening to a presentation, however, the audience have to rely on the speaker to give them guidance. Apart from giving the audience a general map or agenda, the speaker also needs transitions between slides. They are like taking turns in following the direction. You need to make it very clear whenever you take a turn.

You can use signpost language such as "firstly", "secondly", ... or words like "And now we are going to explore the most important factor of...".

You can also ask a rhetorical question, "Have you ever wondered why...? Well, this is what I'm going to present..."

Sometimes it is a good strategy if you just turn off the screen and write something on the whiteboard or present something orally. This will definitely regain the audience's attention.

It will also be helpful to the audience if you summarize what you have told them so far at each turn. You can say, for instance, "Having looked at..., let's now turn to...". This repetition gives the audience a chance to check their understanding.

When you move on to the next section, you need to explain how it relates to the previous one. By doing this, you will make it easier for the audience to follow you, giving them an opportunity to relax and letting the previous information sink in.

3) Ending

There are several ways to end your presentation.

For instance, if you want your final slide to be memorable, you can take some time to find or create a proper picture. It can be taken from something related to your key findings, or to the topic you have just talked about, or a cartoon that sums up your message.

You can also end by giving interesting statistics. They should be related to the audience in some way. If necessary, you can multiply them to get a number that is powerful and impressive.

Whether you have any difficulty in explaining your results or not, you can end your presentation by asking for help or feedback from your audience. Their response may turn out to be valuable or insightful.

Whether you are confident or not about your research findings, you can always end by talking about your future work. If your presentation is convincing, you may get invitations of cooperation. If you have pointed out the limitation of your work, you may get suggestions from the audience about how to improve it.

However, when you end your presentation, try to make your final slide interesting. If you want to express your gratitude in the end, avoid simply writing "Thank you", because it is too common to be interesting. Be creative. Let it come out from the image of a cute animal or a bunch of flowers. And this may add some color to your presentation.

2.2.2 How to Present Your Methodology, Results and Conclusion

1) Methodology

Methodology is usually the hardest part for the audience, so clear explanations are fundamental. If technical explanations are unavoidable, you can simplify them and give concrete examples first. You do not need to go into detail. Only mention what the audience really need to know in order to make sense of what you have done.

For example, if you have a complex process/procedure to describe, do not cut and paste the whole diagram from your paper. Break up the whole process into several slides, with each slide explaining one step. Or you can show only the key steps, and explain why you are not describing the whole process.

You can make a very technical explanation more interesting if you describe it like a story. You need to exclude nonessential details, such as difficult equations, formulas and calculations. They are difficult to explain and confusing. If they are really important, you can talk about how they relate to your study briefly, and give details in a handout.

You also need to use more active verbs. The following examples demonstrate two different versions of the report of methodology. You can decide which one is more effective for oral presentation.

Version 1: The study comprised 120 patients with various levels of... The inclusion criteria covered ages between 30 and 60 years... Patients were not included if any of the following conditions were found to be present: ...

Version 2: We selected 120 patients that... We decided to study patients with an age range between 30 and 60, as those are the types of people who tend to opt for... treatment. They had various levels of... For obvious reasons we excluded any patients who had had any of these conditions 【 *shows a list on the slide* 】.

You can see that in the first version, impersonal subjects are adopted more often than personal subjects. When the latter is used, a passive voice is employed. By contrast, both subjects and active voice are used throughout the second version. And this makes it more like telling stories.

Active voice gives energy and dynamism to the description, but it can be used interchangeably with passive voice to add variety to the language, especially when the recipient of the action is relevant to the audience. In this sense, the first version is alright if not too technical.

2) Results and Discussion

You do not need to present all of your results, which could be too much information to the audience and can be easily forgotten. Just focus on the key ones, such as: what you found, whether it was what you expected, what it means, and why the audience should be interested.

When discussing your results, you will often need to talk about graphs, figures, tables, etc. A rule of thumb is: the easier a figure is to understand, the less time you will have to spend on explaining it. When explaining, keep it short. For example, when explaining and commenting on a graph, do not talk about the information that can be easily worked out by the audience themselves. Just interpret the curve and point out what lessons can be learned from it. Highlight what the audience need to know and talk about the implications.

When talking about your results, use the strategy of "hedging". That is, do not sound overconfident, arrogant or critical of others. Try to leave your discussion open to other interpretations. The following are some ways of hedging:

● Replacing strong verbs such as "prove" and "demonstrate" with less strong verbs such as "suggest", "imply" and "indicate".

● Replacing absolute adverbs such as "definitely", "certainly", "surely", "undoubtedly", "indisputably" with more tentative adverbs such as "probably", "possibly", "likely".

● Supplementing expressions such as "No data exist in the literature on this topic" or "This is the first time that such a result has been achieved" with phrases such as "to the best of our knowledge", "as far as I know", "I believe", "I think".

● Hedging strong affirmations using modal verbs such as "would", "might", "may", "could".

When interpreting your results, be polite and open to other possibilities. Do not leave the impression that yours is the only way of interpretation. Conferences are a good place to exchange ideas. If you encourage discussions or even debates on your results, you may benefit from these ideas with different perspectives.

If your results were unexpected, do not hide them. Be frank. You can try to explain them in an interesting way. Even when you have "negative" results that seem inexplicable, you can be upfront with them. Sometimes negative results in science, like in medical research, may actually save lives, thus benefiting the community. You can tell your audience what you plan to do to solve the problem, or ask them for help or suggestions. And this may turn out to be a great opportunity for collaboration in the future.

3) Conclusion

A good conclusion can remind your audience of your most important points and leave them with a positive final impression. And this will encourage them to read your paper and contact you in the future. To write a good conclusion, you need to be brief and to the point.

The conclusion should be short. It usually takes up about 10% of the total time of presentation. So if the presentation is 10 minutes, the conclusion is about 1 minute, which is about three to four sentences. So you need to be very brief, otherwise no one can remember your message. Therefore, you only need to include the key findings in your conclusion.

Also, the conclusion should be to the point. Your final slide should only give useful or essential information to your audience. You can catch people's attention by using words like "to sum up" or "in conclusion". You can use short phrases instead of complete sentences to give people the take-home message. You can re-use a picture or a statistic that is related to your key points or major findings. Or you can ask for feedback or talk about future work.

To sum up, whatever you do, try to make the conclusion memorable.

2.2.3 How to Make Your Presentation Attractive and Maintain This Attraction

1) Title

The title of your presentation is like an advertisement for a product. If it is interesting, it can attract more people to your presentation. So you can choose not to use the title of your research paper, and choose nontechnical titles. The following are two examples:

A Pervasive Solution for Risk Awareness in the Context of Fall Prevention in the Elderly	Stop Your Grandmother from Falling!
An Investigation into the Perpetuation of the Classic Stereotypes Associated with Lawyers	Lawyer Stereotypes vs Reality: Spot the Difference

You can see which one is more effective in presentation.

For titles of slides, we typically have Introduction, Methodology, Results, Discussion and so on. But in fact, they can be changed into more interesting alternatives, such as:

Methodology→ How? / Don't try this at home

Results→ What did we find? / Not what we were expecting

Discussion→ So what? / Why should you care?

Future work→ What next? / Men at work

Thank you→ That's all folks. / See you in Bangladesh.

2) Minimum Text

People love pictures more than texts. Long texts on slides will surely put your audience to sleep or divert their attention to something else. Therefore, it is wise to use minimum text on your slides. To achieve this, you can write complete sentences only when necessary, use shorter words or phrases and shorter quotations, and avoid references. But beware—when use acronyms, abbreviations, contractions and symbols, only choose the well-known ones to avoid misunderstanding. If you introduce new ones, they are very easily forgotten. You can just stick to the full words.

Bullets are useful to divide long texts into sections. But do limit yourself to six bullets per slide with a maximum of two levels of bullets. Too many bullets or levels of bullets will kill the interest of your audience.

If possible, use images instead of texts to illustrate your point. As shown in a 2012 TED talk "Talk Nerdy to Me" by Melissa Marshal, a faculty member at Penn State University then, texts are not as effective as images in expressing the same idea. She contrasted a text description with an example slide by Genevieve Brown, a Ph.D. candidate at Columbia University at the time, pointing out the latter is more effective with adequate explanation of the presenter.

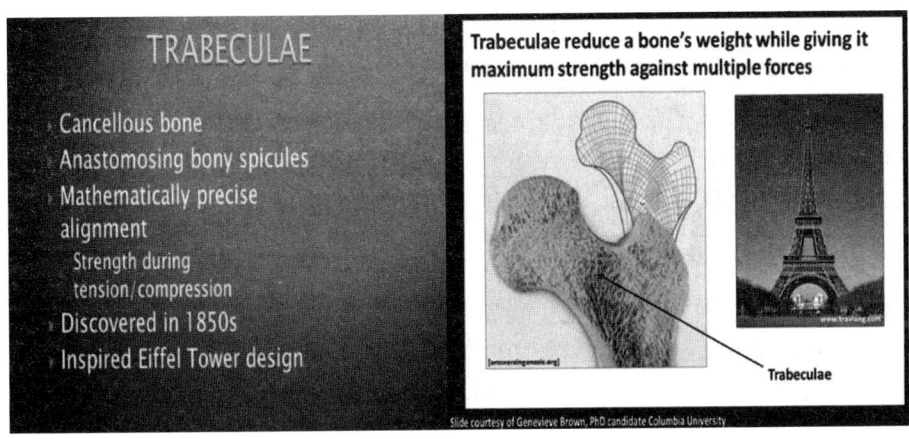

The reason behind this is actually related to the next point—visual aids.

3) Visual Aids

Humans are visual animals. You can use visual aids to capture the attention of your audience. Visual aids include images, photos, figures, charts, and graphs.

A visual aid is necessary if it adds value for the audience, relates to what you are saying and looks good. It can be used to help your audience understand. This can only be achieved if the visual aid is simple. Complex visual aids such as intricate graphs, pie charts with many slices or bar charts with a dozen columns will only confuse your audience. So try to keep your visual aids simple.In your presentation, less is more.

The same principle applies to the use of animation. It is useful only when your presentation is very long. For shorter conference presentations, it is not desirable. Anyone who has been to a conference before may have seen all the animations available (fading in, peeking in, dissolving, flying in etc.). They are no longer attractive. Worse still, they may not convert from your laptop to the conference PC. In a nutshell, however interesting an animation is, it does not disguise a bad presentation.

4) Moments of High Attention

Moments of high attention are usually at the beginning and end of a presentation. Presenters need to make good use of these moments. If the audience are attracted at the beginning, you can maintain their attention by having continuous eye contact; sometimes you could even consider blanking the screen. When you come to the end of the presentation, you can also give such signals so as to regain their attention.

To maintain the audience's attention, you can also repeat important facts and explanations. People tend to pay more attention to things they hear more than once. Of course, you can vary the tone and tempo of your voice when repeating these things to attract more attention.

You can also include examples or analogies that the audience can relate to personally, or curious facts and things that stand out. Things people can relate to tend to be more accessible, and hence easier to notice. The same is true of facts that are unusual.

As an endnote, it is very important to write down the text for your presentation. It is a good opportunity to sell the ideas you have written in your conference paper and to impress those who want to publish it and those who want a cooperation with you. The effort you put into writing it will pay off in the end.

2.3 Useful Expressions

1) Introduction

Good morning. Thanks for coming...
I am a Ph.D. student / researcher at...
I am part of a team of 10 researchers and most of our funding comes from...

2) Agenda / Outline

In this presentation I am going to... / I would like to discuss some findings... / introduce a new model of... / review / describe / argue...

3) Transition

First, let me start by looking at... / In a few minutes, I am going to tell you about... /

Having considered…, let's go on and look at… / This brings me to my next point…

4) Results

This chart illustrates… / For the sake of simplicity, I have included only essential information. / The curve rises rapidly, then reaches a peak, and then forms a plateau.

5) Discussion and conclusion

What these results prove is… / It seems probable from these results that… / A possible explanation is… / What we are planning to do next is…

6) Ending

We're very close to the end now, but there are a couple of important things that I still want to share with you. / And this brings me to the end of the presentation. So, just to recap… / If you would like more information, please feel free to email me. This is my email address.

Exercises

1. Revise the following sentences to make them more concise.

1) X was used in the calculation of Y.

2) Symbols will be defined in the text at their first occurrence.

3) This will be completed in the month of December for a period of six days.

4) The task of analysis is not a straightforward operation and there is a serious danger that…

5) The analyses performed in this context highlighted among other things the fundamental and critical importance of using the correct methodology in a consistent and coherent manner of conduction.

6) The method lends itself most amiably to being solved by…

7) The installation of the system is done automatically.

8) This has exerted an influence on X.

9) I'll give an explanation about how…

10) From a financial standpoint, it makes more sense to…

2. Choose a research article related to your field of study. Read it carefully and write an opening to its presentation. Then share it in class.

Title: _____

Opening: _____

---

3. Work in a group of four. Choose a research article from the top-notch journals in your field. Read the article and write a presentation based on your reading and discussion. Your discussion should focus on what to report for each section, what language style to choose, what to write in the opening and the ending. Then do your presentation in class with PPT slides.

Unit Three
Networking at Academic Conferences

Academic conferences are not just where you can have your voice heard and your research results publicized; they are also a great opportunity for you to meet people. These people include renowned professors you may want to study under, and authors of key books in your field, hiring managers that you might want to work for, as well as graduate students who are pursuing their degree courses, and those who one day may become the scholarly circle of yours. Who knows? Some of them may become your co-authors, or people who review your journal submissions. So why not leverage these conferences for networking?

In this unit, you are going to learn how to network before, during and after academic conferences.

3.1 Before the Conference

It is essential for you to make good preparation before the conference. The preparation includes deciding on the people you would like to network with, getting your materials ready for your own presentation and your networking, and getting your language ready.

3.1.1 Decide Whom You Are Going to Meet

If you want to meet big names, you need to be prepared that they may be too busy to notice you. You can impress them by reading their publications carefully and getting to know as many of their interests and hobbies as possible. This information will be useful when you get the chance of talking to them. Or you can choose to network with those not so famous but sharing research interests with yours. These people have the potential to set up collaborations with you or give you useful feedback on your work.

One way to help you decide is to look through the conference program and find the names of people you want to meet. You can find information about them from their personal pages on the website of their institute. If you cannot find too much information, read the abstract they provide for the conference to know their research interest. Try to find things you might have in common. This may become a good place to start your networking.

After you have decided whom to network with, find a photograph of them so you will be able to identify them in a room from a distance. Then you can send them an email before the conference to set up a meeting. Tell them you would be interested in meeting them. The following is the general structure of the email:

1) Say how you know about them.
2) Briefly introduce yourself.
3) Show what you do relates to what they do.
4) Indicate how long the meeting might last.
5) Suggest a possible meeting place and time, but show flexibility.

If you worry that your email may not even be opened, you can try a more traditional means—a phone call. This may actually help you stand out in today's app-dominated world.

Before you make the call, make sure what you want to say and how you will say everything in proper English. You can write these down as notes to help you. During the call, you can take some notes so as to check later for better understanding or for remembering the key points.

If possible, find out more information about people you are calling: their level of English, their accent, their speech rates etc. Then prepare some appropriate phrases for encouraging them to slow down in case they speak too fast. You can also prepare answers for possible questions they may ask you.

3.1.2 Get Your Materials Ready

These materials include hard copies of your research paper, handouts for your presentation, your résumé, business cards, as well as your formal clothes.

You never know who you are going to come across at conferences. But whoever you meet, if you want them to attend your presentation and give you some advice, it will be necessary to prepare enough handouts of your presentation. If you meet some professors whom you want to study under, you may even need to prepare hard copies of your important research papers and copies of your résumé. Of course, most of these materials can be stored in electronic form in your computer, so that you can send them to people conveniently if you run out of hard copies.

You also need to print enough business cards that will last you the entire event. You can add your social media information and even a photo to your card to make it easier for others to remember you and to keep in touch. But avoid giving out your cards without engaging in a truly valuable conversation first. A good time to exchange cards is when you do not have enough time to talk with someone. If you have promised people something, remember to write some notes on the back of the card as a reminder.

Another important preparation is your outfit. Do prepare outfits that look professional. Attending conferences is not like having a vacation. You may encounter your fellow attendees on the plane, at the train station, even in a taxi waiting line. If you happen to meet someone important in your casual wear or dirty shirts, you will feel embarrassed. Therefore, you should always dress professionally during your travels and throughout your stay at the conference. After all, your appearance matters, since you represent your school and your organization.

3.1.3 Get Your Language Ready

To achieve successful networking, you need to get your language ready. And this includes different versions of your self-introduction, introductions about your research, topics and expressions of small talk, and also topics and expressions to avoid in communication.

First of all, you need to prepare different versions of your self-introduction, which can be used depending on the time available and whether the occasion is formal or informal, as well as the audience. When introducing yourself in a formal occasion, such as a presentation, you can have a starter related to the theme of your presentation. It can be a fact, a group of statistics, a recent experience, or a question to arouse the curiosity of your audience and grab their attention. Then you can move on to present yourself, keeping in mind the purpose — to communicate your expertise to the audience so as to gain trust and convey reliability. If you need to formally introduce yourself to one person or a group of people, you need to state your name clearly and emphatically before you introduce your job title, your experience, or your educational degree and certification level. If you only need an informal introduction, you can consider your purpose and only keep the information most relevant to the particular audience.

Second, you need to know how to introduce your own work. The purpose here is to tell the audience your expertise quickly and effectively. So you need to explain what drew you to your research by telling a research story. Since not everyone is familiar with your research, you need to craft slight variations for different audiences. However, you need to be succinct so that you can convey the information in minutes. The information included should be neither too detailed to bore your listeners nor too brief to confuse them. Here is a sample pattern:

My name is XXX, and I work for / I am a(an)... I primarily design / do research in..., and I come to this conference to... with hopes of...

Third, you can prepare some topics of small talk. Academic conferences are not always about big, serious topics. There are chances for you to engage in informal small talk. Frequent topics include the weather, the food, other people's presentations, the location and how the conference has been organized, latest technologies, as well as topics related to family, work, sport, film, music, etc. If you can learn some expressions related to these topics, you will feel more confident and relaxed when networking.

Last but not the least, you need to know that some topics are to be avoided as a result of cultural differences. For example, many people from English-speaking countries feel embarrassed about topics related to their age, income, weight, religion, marital status, payment for a certain item, etc. Try to choose some safe topics instead, such as those related to your research field and your major, as well as broad topics like dialects of the same country and things people do for fun.

Likewise, some expressions with cultural bearings should be used with caution. For instance, Chinese people do not use phrases like "I'm sorry" or "Excuse me" as often as their counterparts in other countries. However, they are more inclined to express their concerns about other people's health by suggesting that they should wear more clothes or drink more water. To people from English-speaking countries, these suggestions may imply that they are not adult enough to make such decisions by themselves. Therefore, we need to consider these cultural differences and adjust our language accordingly.

3.2 At the Conference

At the conference, there are many opportunities for you to network. You may meet people after a presentation, at social functions like meals, poster sessions, and exhibits areas. We will first describe these opportunities and then introduce some useful strategies for successful communication.

3.2.1 Opportunities

1) A good time to network is immediately after the presentation. You can come up to the presenters, express your interest in their work by asking a few pertinent questions, or even offer your suggestions. If they find your questions good enough, they may want to discuss

with you further. Then you may set up a time for meeting. Don't forget to take along your business cards.

2) Many of the opportunities for networking at social functions during the conferences have something to do with eating. After all, everybody has to eat. You may meet early-risers at breakfast, because they have to make a presentation or attend one at the scheduled time. If you see people with a conference badge or agenda, go and ask if you can join them.

Between paper sessions, there are often mid-morning and mid-afternoon breaks. This is a good chance to chat with people casually as they are grabbing coffee or water. Introduce yourself. Ask whether they have a presentation to give, or ask them to come to yours.

You may also schedule informal lunch or dinner with people you want to meet. If they are engaged elsewhere, they may ask you to join their group for the meal. Don't miss the chance to pass out your business cards.

Even at a formal banquet, you still have time to talk to people. But one thing to note is your etiquette or table manners at meals. Some basic rules include: chewing with your mouth closed, taking small bites of food so as to handle conversations with ease, talking to people on both sides of you, etc. You can read relevant materials on etiquette beforehand. When in doubt, wait and watch what other people are doing.

3) Apart from social functions involving eating, poster sessions are also a good time to network. You can talk to the author on a one-to-one basis. Sometimes you can even go beyond the topic being presented. But beware not to monopolize the poster-session author's time. If you see others waiting to chat, you can invite others to join the conversation, or simply stand down politely.

4) Another good place for you to network is the exhibits area of a conference. Here you can learn directly from people who supply the products on display. You have a chance to flip through the materials on display, and even have access to free copies. You may also have the opportunity to meet with or learn the names of key individuals of these companies which produce the products. If you can have the business card of a key person, you will know who to contact when you need information or a job.

Wherever you network with people at conferences, do ask them to come to your presentation or poster session. The more people you meet, the more chances you will have to discuss your work either face-to-face or via email. You can simply do this by saying:

I am doing a presentation at... p.m in Conference Room 209. It would be great if you could come.

You can then give them your business card, with the topic, the time and the location of your presentation written on the back.

3.2.2 Strategies for Successful Conversations

During your interaction with people, there are certain strategies for you to achieve a successful conversation.

1) Try to maintain a positive attitude. When you talk with others, avoid complaining. Make sure you make only positive comments about the conference—its location and organization. When you are discussing their research, be polite and refrain from giving negative comments and bragging about how you did something better. Focus on what you like of their work. Find common ground. This is because people respond better to positive-thinking people and are more likely to listen to them. And this makes it possible for future collaboration.

2) Try to avoid dominating the conversation, especially with someone who could potentially help you. You can speak for a few seconds, and encourage your interlocutors to speak. And then they may pass the "ball" back to you, like in the game of *ping-pong*. If you continue to talk for a long time without showing an interest in the other's opinion, you may leave the impression that you are only interested in yourself, and the other is only a means to your end. You can take the focus off yourself by transferring their original question back to them, or by asking them if they have had a similar experience.

3) Show interest. When you show interest in people, it will give them a feeling of importance and recognition. You can do this by asking questions that your interlocutors might be pleased to answer. For example, questions beginning with "how", "where", "why", "when" and "what", such as:

> How did you decide on this research topic?
> When are you doing your presentation?
> Where are you staying?

When you listen to the answers, try to show some reactions like nodding, or comments such as "really" or "right". But avoid saying the word with an emphatic tone, because this will have just the opposite effect: showing your disbelief.

4) Be polite. Being polite means both showing some agreement and expressing your

disagreement strategically. Unlike writing an email, you do not have the time to reflect on the language you use in a face-to-face communication. You may end up sounding rude or abrupt. One strategy is to show some agreement with what your interlocutor is saying before expressing your own point of view. Here are some examples:

> I agree with you, but I also believe that...
> I know exactly what you mean, but another viewpoint / interpretation could be...

When you do have disagreement, you can express it diplomatically. That is to say, you need to hedge your language and soften your tone. One way is to omit words like "but", "nevertheless", and "however". Words like these tend to put your interlocutors on the defensive. Or you can admit your ignorance first before expressing different views. For example:

> Oh really? I may be wrong, but I'd always thought that...
> I didn't know that. What I heard / read was that...

5) Interrupt people with courtesy. In a formal or informal discussion, you may wish to get your point of view across. Then you can interrupt with a friendly tone:

> Sorry to interrupt you, but...
> Can I just make a point?
> Just a minute, before I forget...

If your interlocutors keep talking without giving any useful information, you can politely interrupt by reminding them of the time frame that you arranged by saying:

> Well, I don't want to take up any more of your time. I hope to see you at the dinner tonight.
> Well I think we've covered all the questions... but would it be OK if I email you when I need any further clarifications?
> Well, it was nice talking to you. I'll catch up with you later.

3.3 After the Conference

If you have collected a lot of business cards during the conference, one thing you need to do immediately is to make some notes on the back of these cards, as mentioned earlier. You can include information such as the name of the conference, the year, and your promises to each other. For example, you may have volunteered to send them a paper or a link to a website, or they may have promised you something. Don't forget to complete the actions you promised as soon as you get home.

About a week later, you can remind them of their earlier promises if they haven't taken any action. You can do so by following them on their blogs, LinkedIn, Facebook account or by contacting them through WeChat. Or you can use the more formal and more traditional approach: sending them an email.

In the email, you need to remind the people you are writing to who you are, what you discussed, and what decisions were reached or what offer was made. Besides, you can also express gratitude about the help they have given you and ask what you can do for them. A typical sample email is as follows:

Dear Professor Li,

I am a graduate student in Chinese Literature from Chengdu University.

Thank you very much for sparing the time to meet me last Friday. Your comments on my thesis were especially useful.

As I mentioned at our meeting, if by any chance you could accept me as a Ph.D. candidate of yours, I would be very grateful. My CV is attached.

I am also attaching a paper which I am currently writing that you might find of interest. Please don't hesitate to ask me if there is anything I can do for you.

Once again, thank you for all your help. I do hope we will meet again.

Best regards,
Ping Wang

3.4 Useful Expressions

1) Joining a group of people

I don't really know anyone else here. Do you mind if I join you? / Is it OK if I listen in? / Sorry. I was listening from distance and what you are saying sounds really interesting.

2) Introducing yourself

Hi, I'm XXX from the University of YYY. / Excuse me, could I just have a word with you? I am from... / Sorry. I have not introduced myself—I'm XXX from YYY. / Pleased to meet you. I'm XXX. /Excuse me. I listened to your presentation this morning.

3) Introducing your work

I am investigating new ways to... / I am doing some research into... / My team and I are doing a research on...

4) Making positive comments

I really enjoyed the first presentation yesterday. / The trip to... was very interesting. / I really appreciate what the organization committee has done for us here.

5) Giving others a chance to talk

Thanks. XXX. I see there are others waiting to talk to you. Here is my card; I'll call you next week about... / Well, it's been really interesting talking to you. I'll see you around.

6) Apologizing for something

Sorry, I didn't catch your name. / Sorry, how do you pronounce your name?

Sorry, I tend to be too direct when I speak in English. / I'm so sorry I didn't mean to sound rude. / I'm sorry, but I really don't have time at the moment. / I'm sorry, but I just need to have a look at my notes and I'll catch up with you later.

7) Finding an excuse to leave

Sorry. I just need to make a phone call. / Sorry. I just need to go to the bathroom. / Just a moment. I need to think.

Exercises

1. Imagine you are a doctoral student in XXX University majoring in Computer Science. You are going to attend an international conference next week in Tokyo. You want to meet Professor Robinson Smith, a keynote speaker at the conference, and have a talk with him. You happen to get his contact information from your supervisor, and you plan to give him a phone call beforehand. Make some notes below for your telephone conversation, and role-play it with your classmates. You can refer back to the structure of the email and make some adaptations.

_____
_____
_____

2. Work in a group of 3 to 5. Write two versions of introduction of you and your research. One version is detailed and more formal, targeted at interlocutors you plan to have future collaboration. The other version is brief and less formal, targeted at people you meet at informal contexts at conferences. Then compare your writing with that of your group members and discuss whose versions are better.

Version 1:

_____
_____
_____

Version 2:

_____

3. Role-play in a group of five. The different roles include: A famous professor in your field of study, a researcher having different viewpoints from this professor, a Ph.D. student who supports the view of this professor, a researcher in another field of research, and a conference organizer. Suppose you five happen to sit at the same table for the conference dinner. Try to initiate a conversation with each other. Pay attention to courtesy and manners.

Unit Four
Structure, Coherence, Diction and Style

This unit will deal with the fundamentals of English expression, especially English writing. It is understood that most of readers of the book are not English majors, so it is important for them to have a good mastery of these basic skills of English composition.

4.1 Structure

4.1.1 Sentence Combination

Simple sentences are easy to write. However, if a paragraph has nothing but simple sentences, it will most likely be choppy, disconnected and monotonous. Neither the writer nor the reader will be satisfied. To avoid the problem, writers need to vary the complexity of sentences where necessary. Here we introduce two important techniques that help form sentences of greater complexity, coordination and subordination.

Coordination is the use of coordinating conjunctions and connective adverbs to form compound sentences. Through coordination, we show that certain ideas or items form a series and are of equal importance. When we coordinate, we use such words as "and", "but", "for", "or", "nor", "so", or "yet". On the other hand, subordination combines simple sentences by making one or more clauses dependent on a main clause, thus forming a complex sentence. Through subordination, we show that one idea is less important than another. When we subordinate, we use conjunctions like "when", "although", "since", "while", "because", or "after". Subordination and coordination are devices mature writers use frequently. These devices not only help to demonstrate the logical relationships between ideas, they also create the meaningful content of the sentences. When combining sentences, you need to keep the following points in mind:

1) Both coordination and subordination can be used at the same time, thus forming compound-complex sentences.

2) Usually, there are more than one way to combine sentences and you are supposed to choose the one that suits your purpose best.

3) Very often, the relationships among ideas in a sentence will be clearer when subordination rather than coordination is used. Therefore, loose compound sentences, especially those linked by "and", "so" or "but", can often be converted into complex sentences.

4) Loose, stringy compound sentences, especially those carelessly linked by "and", should be carefully avoided. They can sometimes be contracted to a few words or just one phrase.

5) A paragraph packed with long and complex sentences may give readers too much difficulty in understanding and therefore deprive them of the interest in reading. So shorter sentences are combined to form longer ones ONLY when necessary.

4.1.2 Sentence Expansion

As is known to all, there are five basic English sentence patterns upon which all English sentences are built. In actual texts, however, they are often too simple to express complicated ideas and messages and more often than not they need to be expanded. Simple sentences are expanded mainly by adding details and using specific diction. For example, when readers come across the sentence "A man was walking on the street", they may not be satisfied with the amount of information contained in the sentence. They may raise such questions as:

How old was the man?

What kind of man was he?

When was he walking on the street?

How was he walking, slowly or hurriedly?

Where was he walking—on the side street or a main street?

To make the sentence more meaningful and vivid, it might be expanded in the following ways:

1) A middle-aged man with gray hair was walking slowly on the street with an obvious intention to find a job.

2) A young man waiting to go to college was strolling on the main street, looking in shop windows and sometimes just stopping and looking around.

3) At midnight, a tall man with a scar on his face was rushing through the deserted side street.

Structurally, the major sentence expansion techniques are as follows:

1) Using word modifiers such as adjectives and adverbs:

a. Jane is singing a song. → Jane is singing a popular song.

b. The secretary answered the phone. →The secretary answered the phone politely.

2) Using phrase modifiers

● Prepositional phrases.

a. The book is popular. → The book is popular with young people.

b. All the products are new. → All the products on display are new.

● Nonfinite phrase modifiers

a, They came into the room. → They came into the room laughing and talking.

b. This is the way. → This is the way to solve the problem.

c. I hate the people. → I hate the people losing their temper.

d. He decided to leave. → Exhausted and hungry, he decided to leave.

3) Clause modifiers

a. My friend was too tired to carry on the work. → My friend, who hadn't slept for two days, was too tired to carry on the work.

b. The robbers left the spot. → When the police arrived, the robbers had already left the spot.

c. The rain was heavy. → The rain was so heavy that they had to cancel their picnic.

4.2 Sentence Variety

1) Variety in Sentence Pattern and Length

In order to add variety and interest to your sentences, you need to continually vary the structure and the length of the sentences you write. If all your sentences are about the same length with similar structure, you may bore your reader. The following are two of the basic ways to achieve sentence variety:

● **Variety in sentence patterns.** A sentence may be simple, compound or complex. Remember to use varied sentence patterns, that is, all three kinds of sentences in writing.

● **Vary in sentence length.** The excessive use of short sentences makes a piece of writing sound choppy and childish. On the other hand, the excessive use of long and complicated sentences will make the reader breathless and bored. The best policy is to have short and brisk sentences stand among the long ones.

2) Variety at the Sentence Beginning

Instead of always starting a sentence with the subject, you have the following choices.

a) Infinitives

To succeed in the course, you must attend every class.

To get good seats, we went to the game early.

b) Prepositional phrases

On either side of the room, there are two bunk beds.

After watching the sunset, we left the country.

c) Adverbs and adverbial clauses

Softly, the boy spoke to her.

Because they make more money than I do, they think they are superior.

d) Absolute phrases

His eyebrows raised high in resignation, he began to examine the letter.

The sun having set, we sat quietly in the darkness.

e) Inversions

Rap, rap, rap, came the knock on the door.

4) Use the following at some point in a sentence.

a) Present participle phrases

The doctor, hoping for the best, examined the X-rays.

Jogging in the morning, I increased my energy level.

b) Past participle phrases

The room, swept every day, is always very clean.

Mary, amused by the joke, later told it to a friend.

c) Appositives

A city of ancient origins, Varna lies on the Black Sea Coast.

d) Adjectives or adjective phrases

Mr. Boyd, angry and sad, began to defend his reputation with strong arguments.

The boys returned to the camp, wet and dirty.

3) Variety in elements in a sentence

In a sentence, elements can be conveniently divided into three items: words, phrases and clauses. If you continually use words in writing, your writing will be monotonous and sloppy. Try to make use of phrases, also called collocations or chunks of idiomatic expressions, which are characteristic of English. As to clauses, there are actually only three kinds of clauses—nominal clauses, adjective clauses and adverbial clauses. A proper use of these clauses will make your writing fluent and idiomatic.

4.3 Expletive Constructions: "There be" and "It be"

"There be" and "It be" patterns are called "expletive constructions" in English grammar. In expletive constructions, "there" does not refer to any place. It simply indicates that something exists. In a similar way, the "it" in "It be" construction is not a pronoun referring to a specific object. It is just an "empty" word that fills the subject position of a sentence, but it does not function as the actual subject. A good command and skillful use of the English expletive constructions will make your writing varied and idiomatic.

4.4 Coherence

A good piece of writing must have both unity and coherence. Once you have achieved unity by eliminating all materials that do not support the main idea of a paragraph, you must decide next how the material you keep will be arranged in the paragraph. With several sentences at hand, for instance, you need to decide the organization of them.

Coherence belongs to the category of connection and organization, which means a smooth and logical movement from one sentence to the next in a paragraph. In general, there are two main ways to achieve coherence. The first is to use transition signals to show how one idea is related to the next; the second is to arrange your sentences in a logical order.

Transition signals are words or phrases that join one idea to another: These words or phrases may help introduce an additional idea (e.g. "and", "furthermore", "in addition"), an opposite idea (e.g. "but", "yet", "however", "on the other hand", "on the contrary"), an alternative (e.g. "otherwise", "or"), an example (e.g. "for example", "for instance"), or a conclusion (e.g. "in conclusion", "in summary", "to summarize").

In addition to using transition signals, internal logic between sentences also plays an important role in bringing coherence to paragraphs. The two most common kinds of logical order in English rhetoric are chronological order and order of importance. The former refers to the way of organizing ideas according to their occurrence in time. The latter requires the arrangement of ideas from the most important to the least or just the opposite.

Some guidelines to help you achieve coherence on the basis of logical order within a paragraph are presented below.

1) Discuss the events (in a story) or the steps (in a process) in order of occurrence.

2) Use chronological transition signals to indicate the sequence of events or steps.

3) Discuss your points in order of importance, discussing the most important point either first or last.

4) Use transition signals showing order of importance to guide your reader from one point to the next and to indicate your most important points.

4.5 Diction and Style

By diction it means the choice of words for the expression of our thoughts. Style means the proper use of words, i.e. the right words in the right places. Diction is based on the usage of the best speakers and writers of the present time. Concerning such usage, we can learn much from modern unabridged English dictionaries by observing the standing of various words we use. Abridged "pocket-sized" editions and ordinary electronic dictionaries are fine and convenient to be carried about, but they will not do for the thoughtful work. However, we must also remember that an unabridged dictionary contains all the words in the language, including obsolete words and meanings as well as comparatively recent slangs. So the fact that a word appears in the dictionary does not warrant our using unless it is in good standing.

Correctness of diction requires that each word chosen be in good use. Good use demands that words have a present, national, and reputable standing in the language.

a) A word is in present use if it is used in modern speech or is found in contemporary literature.

b) A word is in national use, when it is employed not merely in certain professions and trades or in particular geographical sections but by a majority of the people throughout the nation.

c) A word is in reputable use if it occurs in the speech of cultured persons and in the writings of the best authors.

Unless a word satisfies all three of these requirements, it is not in good use.

To produce a good piece of writing, it is important to express our thoughts with **accuracy, clarity and force**. Furthermore, out of the large number of words in good use we should choose those that convey our meaning best. In making such a choice, we should be guided by the principle of **effectiveness. Effectiveness** in diction requires that words be selected for their **exactness, appropriateness and expressiveness.**

1) To be **exact**, a word must fit precisely the idea for which it stands. If we write "A man moved across the street" when what we have in mind to say is "An aged beggar tottered over the cobblestones", we vaguely suggest our meaning, but we do not definitely express it. "Man", "moved" and "street" are general words, whereas "beggar", "tottered" and "cobblestones" are specific words. Specific words are essential to the exactness of expression. They are far more suggestive than general terms in that they tend to arouse in the mind of the reader vivid mental pictures.

2) Our diction is **appropriate** when it is properly adapted to our subject and to the understanding of our audience. Simple language is usually the best, though in the discussion of technical subjects for educated persons, we may rightly employ whatever technical words the subject may demand. Dialogues in narrative writing will properly contain colloquial words, and, if the characters are illiterate or speak somewhat carelessly, even slang words.

3) Many words have two degrees or levels of meaning. One consists of what the word literally says. This we call its denotation. In addition, the word may have acquired through long use an implied, or associated meaning, so that it suggests much more than it specifically denotes. This we call its connotation. The **expressiveness** of a word or phrase depends upon both its denotative and its connotative meaning. For example, the words "house" and "residence" denote the same object as does the word "home", but they are far less expressive. "home" means both "house" and "residence" and arouses within each of us associations and memories that cluster around it.

Exercises

1. Analyze the following paragraph and find out why and how simple sentences are expanded.

Time spent in a bookshop can be most enjoyable, whether you are a book-lover or merely there to buy a book as a present. You may even have entered the shop just to find shelter from a sudden shower. Whatever the reason, you can soon become totally unaware of your surroundings. The desire to pick up a book with an attractive dust jacket is irresistible, although this method of selection ought not to be followed, as you might end up with a rather dull book. You soon become engrossed in some book or other, and usually it is only much later that you realize you have spent far too much time there and must dash off to keep some forgotten appointment—without buying a book, of course.

2. The following paragraph is not coherent. Rewrite it by arranging the sentences in logical order.

I had a terrible morning today. In the middle of a class, I discovered I had left my physics assignments in my locker. I tripped over a curb on my way to my political science class and tore my raincoat. At the end of the class, the professor would not let me go to lunch on time. I slept so late that I did not have time to eat any breakfast. I had not turned in my assignments, and he wanted to talk over this problem with me.

3. Correct the following sentences by replacing the wordy expressions with clearer, more concise words and phrases.

Example: Did my sister's homemade pie meet with your approval? → Did you enjoy my sister's homemade pie?

1) Our holidays occur during the same time that our golf club is holding its Summerfest Golf Tournament.

2) Our math teacher, on many occasions, has given us short, unexpected quizzes.

3) I cannot go to the game tonight because of the fact that I have to work overtime.

4) We cannot stay long at the party, but we will certainly put in an appearance.

5) Please avail yourself of the opportunity to join our operational planning committee.

6) He thinks that we can still register for the college ski trip, but I am of the opinion that the registration is now closed.

7) I know how you feel about our unfortunate loss, but I would like to say that I feel confident about our next game.

8) Mike's newly decorated family room is similar in character to my uncle's family room.

9) She is, beyond a shadow of a doubt, a first-rate actress.

10) We shall, in the near future, settle the overdue account.

4. Correct the following sentences by replacing the wordy expressions with clearer, more concise words and phrases.

1) She has only a small number of hockey tickets left to distribute.

2) I could not see any apparent reason for her refusal to join our study group.

3) For the purpose of clarity, please afford us an opportunity to ask pertinent questions.

4) The college registrar is at the present time in receipt of your application for the business program.

5) I suppose I can make allowances inasmuch as you offered to write the make-up test.

6) Until such time as she agrees to return our books, we will not allow her to use our locker.

7) My company will send you, at a later date, a catalogue of our products.

8) Cody seldom ever wears neckties.

9) I have come to the conclusion that smoking in airplanes should be forbidden.

10) My birthday is celebrated late in the month of December subsequent to Christmas.

5. Rewrite the following sentences and eliminate redundancies in them.

1) I know that my work is not yet agreeable and satisfactory, but don't forget, I am a new beginner.

2) Heinz tried to change my mind about our marketing strategy, but my position on this subject is firm and fixed.

3) The department store gave out free gifts, which was a new innovation in its promotional campaign.

4) Sergeant Cooper was engaged in secret and covert activity for the RCMP.

5) Cleveland's quick response prevented a serious crisis at our plant.

6) Anna Maria's statue of the Sixteenth-century monk is an exact replica of the one I saw in a French art museum.

7) Our company's commitment to equal opportunity is complete and total.

8) The high-flying kite is barely visible to the eye.

9) Our antique coffee grinder may be small in size, but it is very unique.

10) After our soccer team entirely eliminated the second place team from the playoffs, we were ready for the championship game.

6. Translate the following sentences into English. Remember to achieve variety in sentence elements.

1）他总是拒绝别人的施舍。

2）我们应当珍惜前人留下的文化遗产。

3）环境往往决定一个人的成就。

4）南京就是古代的金陵。

5）你不懂我的感受。

6）我想知道你们的英语水平。

7）做事的方法常常比事情本身重要。

Part Two

English for Cultural Communication
—Selected Readings of *Four Books*

Unit Five
Confucius on "Benevolence"—Selected Readings of *The Analects of Confucius*（1）

"benevolence"(仁) is the core of Confucius' thought. There are many sayings in *The Analects of Confucius* that deal with "benevolence", but they are scattered thoughout the book and seem to differ in meaning, which makes it difficult to understand Confucius' thought of "benevolence". In this unit, we put the sayings of Confucius on "benevolence" together so that readers could have an overall picture of it. We think "benevolence" could be understood from the following perspectives: the connotations of "benevolence", the manifestations of "benevolence", and the methods of achieving "benevolence".

The following text is based on *The Analects of Confucius* translated by Arthur Waley, coupled with reference translations by James Legge, Ku Hung-ming, Roger T. Ames and Henry Rosemont, Lin Wusun.

Selected Readings of *The Analects of Confucius*（1） and Notes

1.3 The Master said, 'Clever talk and a pretentious manner' are seldom found in the Good①.

① "仁",韦利(Waley)译作 the Good。理雅各(Legge)译作 true virtue(真正的美德)。辜鸿铭译作 moral character(道德品性)。安乐哲(Ames)译作 authoritative conduct(可信靠的德行)。林戊荪译作 signs of being humane(仁德的表征)。【编者按语】good 也可指"善",韦利刻意用大写 G,特指"仁"。"仁"还常被译作 benevolence, humanity, humaneness, goodness, humanheartedness。

1.3 子曰:"巧①言令②色,鲜③矣仁！"
① 巧:本意是技艺高超,此处意为动听的、美好的。
② 令:本意是命令,作为形容词则有美好之意,此处带有贬义,一般理解为讨好的。
③ 鲜:少。

4.1 The Master said, It is Goodness that gives to a neighbourhood its beauty①. One who is free to choose, yet does not prefer to dwell among the Good—now can he be accorded the name of wise?

① "里仁为美",韦利译作 It is Goodness that gives to a neighborhood its beauty(只有仁才赋予居住地以美)。理雅各译作 It is virtuous manners which constitute the excellence of a neighbourhood(体现美德的行为举止构成社区的优点)。辜鸿铭译作 It is the moral life of a neighbourhood which constitutes its excellence(构成社区的优点的是其道德生活)。安乐哲译作 In taking up one's residence, it is the presence of authoritative persons(ren 仁) that is the greatest attraction(在选择居所时,有仁人为邻是最大的吸引力)。林戊荪译作 It is beautiful to have your mind set on achieving humaneness(人能一心于得仁,这是最美的)。【编者按语】"仁"理雅各在不同语境采用不同的英文词。而安乐哲始终用 authoritative 贯穿统一。对于核心术语,这是两种典型策略。各有利弊。林戊荪翻译依据的是钱穆的诠释。

4.1 子曰:"里仁①为美②。择不处仁,焉得知③?"

① 里仁:里,居住之处,古代为基层单位名称,做动词用时意思是居住,与什么为邻。仁,此处代指仁者。"里仁"一词,通常有两种解释:一种将"里"作为动词,即与仁者为邻。另一种则是将"里"解释为名词,意为有仁者之里。

② 美:现代语境中,"美"经常被理解为漂亮,但古代语境中,"美"与善、嘉等含义等同,此处意为善好。

③ 知:通"智"。

4.3, 4.4 Of the adage 'Only a Good Man knows how to like people, knows how to dislike① them', the Master said. He whose heart is in the smallest degree set upon Goodness will dislike no one.

① "恶",韦利译作 dislike(憎恶)。理雅各译作 practice of wickedness(恶行)。辜鸿铭译作 evil(邪恶)。安乐哲译作 do wrong(做恶事)。林戊荪译作 evil-doing(恶行)。【编者按语】韦利认为这两章应合二为一。

4.3 子曰:"唯仁者,能好①人,能恶②人。"

① 好:喜好。

② 恶:厌恶。

4.4 子曰:"苟志于仁矣,无恶①也。"

① 恶:坏的言行。

4.7　The Master said, Every man's faults belong to a set①. If one looks out for faults it is only as a means of recognizing Goodness.

① "人之过也,各于其党",韦利译作 Every man's faults belong to a set(每一个人的缺点都属于某一个团体)。理雅各译作 The faults of men are characteristic of the class to which they belong(人的缺点是他所属阶级所特有)。辜鸿铭译作 Men's faults are characteristic(人的缺点是典型性的)。Ames 译作 In going astray, people fall into groups(人们误入歧途,各自成群)。林戊荪译作 There are all types of people and all types of faults. Each one's fault can be traced to the type of people he belongs to(世上有形形色色的人,也有形形色色的错误。每一个人的过失都以群分,以类聚)。

4.7　子曰:"人之过也,各①于其党②。观过,斯知仁矣。"

① 各:每个,不相服从。
② 党:古为"黨",一般认为指小集团或朋党,此处指一个人生活所在的群体。

4.15　The Master said, Shen! My way has one (thread) that runs right through it①. Master Tseng said, Yes. When the Master has gone out, the disciples asked, saying What did he mean? Master Tseng said, Our Master's way is simply this: Loyalty, consideration.

① "一以贯之",韦利译作 one(thread) that runs right through it(有一根线索穿连)。理雅各译作 of an all-pervading unity(有一个贯穿始终的统一性)。辜鸿铭译作 There is one underlying connected principle(有一个潜在的关联的准则)。安乐哲译作 be bound together with one continuous strand(由一根连续的线连在一起)。林戊荪译作 there is one thing that pervades my teachings(有一样东西贯穿我的教导)。【编者按语】韦利和安乐哲采用了形象的文学性的译法,大概就是许渊冲所谓的深化和美化的翻译法。

4.15　子曰:"参①乎！吾道一以贯之。"曾子曰:"唯。"子出。门人问曰:"何谓也?"曾子曰:"夫子②之道,忠恕③而已矣。"

① 参:指曾参,后世尊称为曾子,鲁国人,为孔子晚年的重要弟子。
② 夫子:古代是对男子的敬称,后在儒家专指孔子,后世也将其作为老师的代称。
③ 忠恕:朱熹注为"尽己之谓忠,推己之谓恕"。

12.2　Jan Jung asked about Goodness. The Master said, Behave when away from home as though you were in the presence of an important guest. Deal with the common people as though you were officiating at an important sacrifice. Do not do to others what you would not like yourself①.

Then there will be no feelings of opposition to you, whether it is the affairs of a State that you are handling or the affairs of a Family.

Jan Yang said, I know that I am not clever; but this is a saying that, with your permission, I shall try to put into practice.

① "己所不欲,勿施于人",韦利译作 Do not do to others what you would not like yourself(不要对别人做你自己不喜欢的事)。理雅各译作 not to do to others as you would not wish done to yourself(不要对别人做你不愿别人对你做的事)。辜鸿铭译作 Whatsoever things you do not wish that others should do unto you, do not do unto them(任何你不愿别人对你做的事,也不要对他们做)。安乐哲译作 Do not impose upon others what you yourself do not want(你自己不要想的东西,不要强加给别人)。林戊荪译作 Do not do to others what you do not wish others do to you(不要对别人做你不愿别人对你做的事)。

12.2　仲弓问"仁"。子曰:"出门如见大宾①;使民如承大祭②;己所不欲,勿施于人;在邦无怨,在家无怨。"仲弓曰:"雍虽不敏,请事斯语矣!"

　　① 大宾:诸侯国之宾客,称为大宾。
　　② 大祭:古代祭天地、禘祭为大祭。

12.22　Fan Ch'ih asked about the Good (ruler). The Master said, He loves men. He asked about the wise (ruler). The Master said, he knows men. Fan Ch'ih did not quite understand. The Master said, By raising the straight and putting them on top of① the crooked, he can make the crooked straight. Fan Ch'ih withdrew, and meeting Tzu-hsia said to him, Just now I was with the Master and asked him about the wise (ruler). He said, By raising the straight and putting them on top of the crooked, he can make the crooked straight. What did he mean?

Tzu-hsia said, Oh, what a wealth of instruction is in those words! When Shun had all that is under Heaven, choosing from among the multitude he raised up Kao Yao, and straightway Wickedness disappeared. When T'ang had all that is under Heaven, choosing from among the multitude he raised up I Yin; and straightway Wickedness disappeared.

① "错",韦利译作 putting them on the top of(把……放在上面)。理雅各译作 put aside(放在一边)。辜鸿铭译作 put down(压制)。安乐哲译作 put into positions above(把……放在上面)。林戊荪译作 set them over(把……放在上面)。

12.22　樊迟问"仁"。子曰:"爱人。"问"知"。子曰:"知人。"樊迟未达。

子曰:"举直错①诸枉,能使枉者直。"樊迟退,见子夏曰:"乡②也,吾见于夫子而问'知';子曰:'举直错诸枉,能使枉者直。'何谓也?"子夏曰:"富哉言乎! 舜有天下,选于众,举皋陶③,不仁者远矣;汤有天下,选于众,举伊尹④,不仁者远矣。"

① 错:此处为动词,通"措",舍弃,置而不用。
② 乡:通"向",指刚才。
③ 皋陶:学界推定其为偃姓(一说为嬴姓),皋氏,名繇,字庭坚,生活在尧舜的时代,曾得到舜的推举为官,确立了中国最早的刑政制度,一般将其奉为中国司法之祖。
④ 伊尹:商朝的开国功臣,因被封为尹,故后世称其伊尹。伊尹富有雄才大略,他的部分思想被记载于《尚书》《史记》等文献中,对后世产生了较大影响。

13.19　Fan Ch'ih asked about Goodness. The Master said, In private life①, courteous, in public life, diligent, in relationships, loyal. This is a maxim that no matter where you may be, even amid the barbarians of the east or north, may never be set aside.

① "居处",韦利译作 in private life(在私人生活中)。理雅各译作 in retirement(在退隐之时)。辜鸿铭译作 in dealing with yourself(在自处时)。安乐哲译作 at home(在家)。林戊荪译作 in daily life(在日常生活中)。

13.19　樊迟问仁。子曰:"居处恭,执事①敬,与人忠;虽之②夷狄③,不可弃也。"

① 执事:做事。
② 之:到达。
③ 夷狄:古代中原地区之外的少数民族的代称。

13.27　The Master said, Imperturbable, resolute, tree-like, slow to speak①—such a one is near to Goodness.

① "刚、毅、木、讷",韦利译作 imperturbable, resolute, tree-like, slow to speak。理雅各译作 the firm, the enduring, the simple, and the modest。辜鸿铭译作 strong, resolute, simple。安乐哲译作 being firm, resolute, honest, and deliberate in speech。林戊荪译作 being staunch, resolute, modest and slow in speech。【编者按语】辜鸿铭,按照现代白话将"木、讷"理解为一个词,不妥。韦利将"木"译作 tree-like,看似生硬,体现了他诗人和文学翻译家的复合身份。

13.27　子曰:"刚①、毅②、木③、讷④,近仁。"

① 刚:直率而不虚与委蛇地行事。
② 毅:刚强果断。
③ 木:质朴。
④ 讷:说话谨慎,不轻易发表意见。

15.8   The Master said, Neither the knight who has truly the heart of a knight① nor the man of good stock who has the qualities that belong to good stock will ever seek life at the expense of Goodness; and it may be that he has to give his life in order to achieve Goodness.

① "志士",韦利译作 the knight who has truly the heart of a knight(真正有着骑士心肠的骑士)。理雅各译作 the determined scholar(意志坚定的学者)。辜鸿铭译作 a gentleman of spirit(有精神追求的绅士)。安乐哲译作 the resolute scholar-apprentice(意志坚定的学者-学徒)。林戊荪译作 those with public spirit(有着公共精神的人们)。【编者按语】韦利的翻译属于创造性翻译。

15.8   子曰:"志士①仁人,无求生以害仁,有杀身以成仁。"
① 志士:将某种高尚东西作为追求目标的士人。

15.9   Tzu-kung asked how to become Good. The Master said, A craftsman, if he means to do good work, must first sharpen his tools. In whatever State you dwell

Take service with① such of its officers as are worthy,

Make friends with such of its knights② as are Good.

① "事",韦利和理雅各译作 take service with(服务)。辜鸿铭、安乐哲和林戊荪译作 serve(服务)。
② "士",韦利译作 knights(骑士)。理雅各和林戊荪译作 scholars(学者)。辜鸿铭译作 gentlemen(绅士)。安乐哲译作 scholar-apprentices(学者-学徒)。

15.9   子贡问"为仁"。子曰:"工欲善①其事,必先利②其器。居是邦也,事其大夫之贤者,友其士之仁者。"
① 善:完善或圆满。
② 利:锋利,在此也可理解为使动用法,使……合宜或最佳。

15.23   Tzu-kung asked saying, Is there any single saying that one can act upon all day and every day①? The Master said, Perhaps the saying about consideration: 'Never do to others what you would not like them to do to you'.

① "终身",韦利译作 all day and every day(所有的日子以及每一个日子)。理雅各译作 for all one's life(终身)。辜鸿铭译作 throughout the whole life(终身)。安乐哲译作 until the end of one's days(到死为止)。林戊荪译作 as his life-long motto(作为他的终生座右铭)。

15.23 子贡问曰:"有一言而可以终身行之者乎?"子曰:"其恕^①乎! 己所不欲,勿施于人。"

① 恕:体谅,以自己推度他人。

15.34 The Master said, Goodness is more to the people than water and fire①. I have seen men lose their lives when 'treading upon' water and fire; but I have never seen anyone lose his life through 'treading upon' Goodness.

① "民之于仁也,甚于水火",韦利译作 Goodness is more to the people than water and fire(对于人来说,仁比水火更为重要)。理雅各译作 Virtue is more to man than either water and fire(对于人来说,美德比水火二者都更为重要)。辜鸿铭译作 Men need morality more than the necessities of life, such as fire and water(人们需要道德,超过日常生活所需的水与火)。安乐哲译作 Authoritative conduct is more vital to the common people than even fire and water(对于民众来说,仁甚至比水火更重要)。林戊荪译作 Humaneness is more vital to the common people than fire and water(对于民众来说,仁比水火更重要)。

15.34 子曰:"民之于仁也,甚于水火。水火,吾见蹈①水火而死者矣;未见蹈仁而死者也。"

① 蹈:踩、踏。

15.35 The Master said, When it comes to Goodness① one need not avoid competing with one's teacher.

① "当仁",韦利译作 When it comes to Goodness(当说到仁时)。理雅各译作 Let every man consider virtue as what devolves on himself(让每一个人把美德当成自己的责任)。辜鸿铭译作 When the question is one of morality(当这是一个道德问题时)。安乐哲译作 In striving to be authoritative in your conduct(在努力使你的行为具有权威性时)。林戊荪译作 Where humaneness is concerned(事关仁义时)。【编者按语】"当"有两解。一是作介词,当……时。二是作动词,承担。

15.35 子曰:"当①仁,不让②于师。"

① 当:承担、掌握。朱熹的注释为"当仁,以仁为己任也"。

② 让：该词有多义，此处为谦让，不争。朱熹认为，之所以不与老师谦让，原因是"盖仁者，人所自有而自为之，非有争也，何逊之有？"

17.6　Tzu-chang asked Master K'ung about Goodness. Master K'ung said, He who could put the Five into practice everywhere under Heaven would be good. Tzu-chang begged to hear what these were. The Master said, Courtesy, breadth, good faith, diligence and clemency①. 'He who is courteous is not scorned, he who is broad wins the multitude, he who is of good faith is trusted by the people, he who is diligent succeeds in all he undertakes, he who is clement can get service from the people'.

①"恭、宽、信、敏、惠"，韦利译作 Courtesy, breadth, good faith, diligence and clemency。理雅各译作 gravity, generosity, sincerity, earnestness, and kindness。辜鸿铭译作 earnestness, consideration for others, trustworthiness, diligence, and generosity。安乐哲译作 deference, tolerance, making good on one's word, diligence, and generosity。林戊荪译作 courtesy, tolerance, good faith, agility and generosity。【编者按语】先秦文言以单字词为主。抽象的概念词英译除了一一对应外，还可以用合成词或短语甚至从句对应。这是词的释译法。

17.6　子张问"仁"于孔子。孔子曰："能行五者于天下，为仁矣。""请问之？"曰："恭①、宽②、信③、敏④、惠⑤：恭则不侮，宽则得众，信则人任焉，敏则有功，惠则足以使人。"

① 恭：恭敬。
② 宽：宽宏大量。
③ 信：诚实不欺。
④ 敏：勤勉。
⑤ 惠：仁爱，给人好处，馈赠。

Exercises

1. Put the following sentences into English.

1）1.1 子曰："学而时习之，不亦说乎？有朋自远方来，不亦乐乎？人不知而不愠，不亦君子乎？"

2）1.9 曾子曰："慎终，追远，民德归厚矣。"

3）2.13 子贡问君子。子曰："先行其言而后从之。"

4）3.3 子曰："人而不仁，如礼何？人而不仁，如乐何？"

5）4.4 子曰："苟志于仁，无恶也。"

6）4.8 子曰："朝闻道，夕死可矣。"

2. Please check to see the various renditions of "仁" in English and comment on them—what underlies the different renditions.

3. Imagine you are going to lecture on Confucius to a group of international listeners. Prepare an abstract of about 300 words.

Supplementary Reading: James Legge as a Translator of Confucian Classics

作为标准的经典译本
——理雅各译《四书》

詹姆斯·理雅各(James Legge，1815—1897)是近代英国著名汉学家,曾任香港英华书院院长、伦敦布道会传教士,他也是牛津大学第一位汉学教授。他是西方第一个系统研究翻译中国古代经典的人。从1861年至1886年25年间,他将《四书》《五经》等中国典籍译成英语,以《中国经典》行世。理雅各与法国学者顾赛芬、德国学者卫礼贤并称汉籍西译三位翻译大师。

理雅各一生的突出成就是中国经典的英译。他的译本已经成为《四书》《五经》标准译本。所谓的标准译本,是指他的译本已经成为标杆,供后来的译者学习、效仿、回避、挑战和超越。同时成为研究者研究评判其他译本的参照或依据。他的译本甚至成为西方汉学家学习古代汉语和中国传统文化的重要教材。

本书的《中庸》英译即以理雅各的译本为底本,其他三部也以他的译本为参照文本。

理雅各译本的标准性首先体现在他确定的《四书》英译的翻译体例和文本构架已成为《四书》暨中国古代思想典籍外译的标准体例。在他之前的《四书》的马什曼、柯大卫译本体例还较为简陋。经过多年的研究探索,理雅各参考了东西方经典的诠释解经体例,确定了较为科学和全面的中国古代思想典籍的译本体例。以《论语》的英译本为例,理雅各译本正文排有中文原文以及译文和评述性注释。副文本包括长篇绪论、参考书目、索引。长篇绪论包括中国经典的由来和确认,中国经典书目,权威性文本的生成、注疏、传播,文字的异读,孔子的生平,孔子主要思想,孔子的影响,孔子的主要弟子及简介。参考书目包括主要的中文参考书目,翻译参考中文辞书,翻译参考的英译本及其他西文译本,外文参考书目。索引包括主题术语索引、专有名词索引,还有中文文本的全文汉字和词组索引。中英文对照与注释、绪论、参考书目、索引构成五位一体中国古代思想典籍外译的标准体例。后来的众多中外译者在翻译设计和译本编排上,各个项目和篇幅或有增减和调整,但整体上很少越出理雅各的翻译体例和文本构架。理雅各的翻译体例和文本构架事实上为中国古代思想典籍的外译树立了较高的学术门槛和学术标准,形成了融研究于翻译、以翻译促研究富有英国特色的汉学路径,对后来中国古代思想典籍英译产生了深远的影响。

理雅各译本的标准性还体现在译本与原作的高度对等,反映了译者忠实原文的翻译指导思想,信顺兼顾的翻译理念和以句子为单位的释译方法。比较《四书》汉语原文和理雅各的译文,再比较一下他的译文和其他中外众多译者的英译本,不难发现理雅各的译文在文本忠实度、在词句的对等上是很高的,即使按照今天的翻译标准去衡量。鉴于理雅各时代中国典籍英译译本忠实对等程度低,胡译乱译的情况还很普遍,理雅各译本确有正本清源之效。他提供的翻译标准也为后来的中国古代思想典籍的翻译立规示范。

然而,标准往往意味着平淡无奇,缺少特色。理雅各对标新立异似乎天然地反感。他的译文处处中规中矩,不越雷池。在用词上他几乎总是挑选标准的常规词。在句子结构上,他常常使用英语的常规结构。对于中国古代思想核心术语如"仁""德""道""天",他几乎总是采用西方文化的术语去对应,而不太顾及两种文化、两种思想在术语中体现的深刻差异。总之,理雅各的译文似乎少了什么——少了文采、少了灵气、少了节奏,更少了激情和诗意。而这些在《四书》中原本是并不缺乏的,在某些篇章中甚至是充盈激越的。厚重少文不仅由于理雅各严谨甚至拘谨的个性使然,似乎正是他的刻意追求。他似乎乐于掩身在圣哲的巨大身影后面,默默地做工,做一个隐身的话语转换者。正因为此,作为标准译本的理雅各译本或许近于至善,但远不是至美。而这又刺激了后来的中外译者去挑战,去超越,如辜鸿铭、韦利、庞德等人。

毋庸置疑,理雅各的《四书》翻译是中国古代思想经典外译的奠基之作。他的翻译倾注了宗教家的热忱和学者的渊博和严谨。他对中西文化交流的热忱态度和奉献精神,激励了后来一代代中国经典的中西翻译家继承他不朽的事业。他的堪称标准和标杆的《四书》翻译又使得儒学典籍的外译几乎一开始就成为中国经典外译的译介高台和学术高原。

Unit Six
Confucius on "Filial Piety"—Selected Readings of *The Analects of Confucius* (2)

Throughout its long history, China has developed a tradition of attaching great importance to filial piety (孝), which found its most comprehensive and convincing expression in Confucianism. For Confucianism, filial piety is an important ethical concept, which should be put into practice. The appearance of *Classic of Filial Piety* marked the cultimination in theory. However, the foundation for the Confucian concept of filial piety was laid in *The Analects of Confucius*. Confucius' sayings on filial piety are limited in number and scattered throughout the book. They can be roughly divided into three categories: the rationale of filial piety; the ways of being filial; the value and implications of filial piety. This unit is a collection of relevant sayings from these three areas.

Selected Readings of *The Analects of Confucius* (2) and Notes

1.2 Master Yu said, Those who in private life behave well towards their parents and elder brothers①, in public life seldom show a disposition to resist the authority of their superiors. And as for such men starting a revolution, no instance of it has ever occurred. It is upon the trunk② that a gentleman works. When that is firmly set up, the Way grows. And surely proper behaviour towards parents and elder brothers is the trunk of Goodness.

① "孝悌",韦利译作 behave well towards their parents and elder brothers(对父母和长兄恭谨有礼)。理雅各译作 being filial and fraternal(对父母孝顺、对兄长友爱)。辜鸿铭译作(A man) who is a good son and a good citizen(做好儿子和好公民的人)。安乐哲译作 someone who has a sense of filial and fraternal responsibility(有孝悌责任感的人)。林戊荪译作 one who is filial to his parents and respectful to his elder brothers(对父母孝顺、对长兄敬重的人)。【编者按语】理雅各的翻译采用了寻找对应词的方式。其他几位译者均采用了短语或从句的释译方式。

② "本",韦利译作 trunk(树干)。理雅各译作 what is radical(根本)。辜鸿铭译作 what is essential in the foundation of life(人生根基中的关键)。安乐哲译作 the root(树根)。林戊荪译作 the basics(基本的东西)。【编者按语】韦利是个诗人和译诗专家。"本"他译作 trunk(树干),对应于 the twigs(树枝;末),与下文的 grow(生长)呼应。"本"的翻译体现了他对译文文学性的追求。安乐哲译作 the root(树根),与下文的 take hold(扎根)和 grow(生长)呼应。

1.2　有子曰:"其为人也孝弟①,而好犯上②者,鲜矣;不好犯上,而好作乱者,未之有也。君子务本③,本立而道生。孝弟也者,其为仁之本与!"

① 弟:通"悌",指弟弟对兄长的敬爱。
② 犯上:上,指君主或在上位者;犯,冒犯。
③ 务本:务,专注、从事。本,根本。

1.6　The Master said, A young man's duty is to behave well to his parents at home and to his elders abroad, to be cautious in giving promises and punctual in keeping them, to have kindly feelings toward everyone, but seek the intimacy of the Good①. If, when all that is done, he has any energy to spare, then let him study the polite arts②.

① "亲仁",韦利译作 seek the intimacy of the Good(努力与仁亲近)。理雅各译作 cultivate the friendship of the good.(与好人培养友谊)。辜鸿铭译作 be intimate with men of moral character(与有道德品格的人亲密相处)。安乐哲译作 be intimate with those who are authoritative in their conduct(与那些言行具有权威性的人亲近)。林戊荪译作 befriend the humane(与好人做朋友)。

② "文",韦利译作 the polite arts(高雅的艺术)。理雅各译作 polite studies(高雅的研究)。辜鸿铭译作 literary pursuits(文学的追求)。安乐哲译作 study(研究)。林戊荪译作 wen(文)【编者按语】林戊荪译音,加脚注:The study of historical documents and the six arts, i.e. rites, music, archery, charioting, writing and arithmetic(历史文献和六艺——礼、乐、射、御、书、数的学习)。"文"作"六艺"解,出自朱熹的注。

1.6　子曰:"弟子①,入②则孝,出③则弟④,谨⑤而信,汎⑥爱众而亲仁⑦。行有余力,则以学文⑧。"

① 弟子:弟,为家中后生之男子。子,为儿子,该词代指弟弟和儿子。此外,《论语》中的弟子也指孔子的学生。
② 入:进入某处,根据此句背景,当为儿子进入父母所住的房屋。
③ 出:从某处出来,根据此句背景,当指从父母的房屋出来。

④ 弟:通"悌",即敬爱自己的兄长。
⑤ 谨:慎重,恭敬。
⑥ 汎:通"泛",广泛地。
⑦ 亲仁:该词有两种解释,一种认为亲近仁德,一种认为亲近仁德之人。
⑧ 文:朱熹认为,"文,谓诗书六艺之文"。

1.11　The Master said, While a man's father is alive, you can only see his intentions①; it is when his father dies that you discover whether or not he is capable of carrying them out. If for the whole three years of mourning he manages to carry on the household exactly as in his father's day, then he is a good son indeed.

① "其志",韦利译作"志向"(his intentions)。理雅各译作 the bent of his will(强烈的意愿)。辜鸿铭译作 what his father would have him do(他的父亲希望他做的事)。安乐哲译作 what he intends(他的父亲希望他做的事)。林戊荪译作 a person's aspirations(一个人的志向)。【编者按语】"其志"有两说。一说"父之志行"。辜鸿铭从此说,可能依据传统注疏中范祖禹"观父之志行"之说。二说"子之志行"。其他译者从此说。

1.11　子曰:"父在,观其志①;父没,观其行;三年无改于父之道,可谓孝矣。"

① 志:意愿。

2.5　Mêng I Tzu asked about the treatment of parents①. The Master said, Never disobey②! When Fan Ch'ih was driving his carriage for him, the Master said, Mêng asked me about the treatment of parents and I said, Never disobey! Fan Ch'ih said, In what sense did you mean it? The Master said, While they are alive, serve them according to ritual. When they die, bury them according to ritual and sacrifice to them according to ritual.

① "孝",韦利译作 the treatment of parents(对待父母的方式)。理雅各和林戊荪译作 filial piety(子女对父母的孝敬)。辜鸿铭译作 the duty of a good son(好儿子的责任)。安乐哲译作 filial conduct(xiao 孝)(孝行)。【编者按语】理雅各译"孝"为 filial piety 是经典译法。但 piety 本意主要指对神的虔敬。韦利和辜鸿铭作了中性处理。

② "无违",韦利译作 Never disobey!(永远不违拗!)。理雅各译作 It is not being disobedient(孝在于服从)。辜鸿铭译作 Do not fail in what is required of you(父母的要求要尽量满足)。安乐哲译作 Do not act contrary(不做相反的事)。林戊荪译作 Do not go against the rules(不要违反规则)。

2.5　孟懿子问孝,子曰:"无违。"樊迟御,子告之曰:"孟孙问孝于我,我对曰'无违'。"樊迟曰:"何谓也?"子曰:"生,事之以礼;死,葬之以礼,祭之以礼。"

2.7　Tzu-yu asked about the treatment of parents. The Master said, 'Filial sons' nowadays are people who see to it that their parents get enough to eat. But even dogs and horses are cared for to that extent. If there is no feeling of respect, wherein lies the difference?

2.7　子游①问孝。子曰:"今之孝者,是谓能养。至于犬马,皆能有养;不敬,何以别乎。"

① 子游:孔子重要弟子之一,姓言名偃,字子游,今江苏常熟人。

2.8　Tzu-hsia asked about the treatment of parents. The Master said, It is the demeanour① that is difficult. Filial piety does not consist merely in young people undertaking the hard work, when anything has to be done, or serving their elders first with wine and food. It is something much more than that.

① "色",韦利译作 demeanour(外在的行为或举止)。理雅各译作 countenance(表情;面容)。辜鸿铭译作 the expression of your look(脸色)。安乐哲译作 proper countenance(合适的表情)。林戊荪译作 having the right feeling(有正确的感情)。

2.8　子夏①问孝。子曰:"色难②。有事,弟子服其劳;有酒食,先生③馔④,曾是以为孝乎?"

① 子夏:孔子重要弟子之一,姓卜名商,字子夏,今河南温县人。
② 色难:此指侍奉父母时,表现出和颜悦色最为困难。
③ 先生:指比自己出生早的人,这里特指父母和兄长,与前面弟子相对。
④ 馔:准备饮食,此处指食用。

2.21　Someone, when talking to Master K'ung, said, How is it that you are not in the public service①? The Master said, The Book says: 'Be filial, only be filial and friendly towards your brothers, and you will be contributing to government.' There are other sorts of service quite different from what you mean by 'service'.

① "为政",韦利译作 be in the public service(从事公共服务)。理雅各译作 be engaged in the government(参政)。辜鸿铭译作 take part in the government of the country

(参与国家管理)。安乐哲译作 be employed in governing(从政)。林戊荪译作 become involved in government(参政)。

2.21　或①谓孔子曰:"子奚②不为政?"子曰:"《书》云:'孝乎惟孝,友于兄弟。'施于有政,是亦为政,奚其为为政?"

① 或:有人。
② 奚:为何。

4.18　The Master said, In serving his father and mother a man may gently① remonstrate with them. But if he sees that he has failed to change their opinion, he should resume an attitude of deference and not thwart them; may feel discouraged②, but not resentful.

① "几",韦利、理雅各和安乐哲均译作 gently(温柔地;婉转地)。辜鸿铭译作 seldom(很少;难得)。林戊荪译作 be gentle(要很婉转)。【编者按语】辜鸿铭的翻译似误。其他译者多用 gentle 和 gently,可见《论语》翻译的层累效应,即后来者对前人的仿效。
② "劳",韦利译作 feel discouraged(觉得泄气)。理雅各译作 should they punish him(如果父母惩罚他)。辜鸿铭译作 however much trouble they may give him(不管父母给他带来多少麻烦)。安乐哲译作 Although concerned(虽然他表示关切)。林戊荪译作 Do not feel bitter(不要觉得怨恨)。【编者按语】"劳"字的理解各译者差别极大。

4.18　子曰:"事父母几谏①。见志不从,又敬不违,劳而不怨。"

① 几谏:几,接近,差不多。谏,正也,指对尊长直言劝诫其改正错误。此处该词指以某种委婉的方式提出改正的意见,而非直言劝诫。

4.19　The Master said, While father and mother are alive, a good son does not wander far afield; or if he does so, goes only where he has said he was going①.

① "有方",韦利译作 go only where he has said he was going(只去他说过要去的地方)。理雅各译作 he must have a fixed place to which he goes(他必须去某个说好的地方)。辜鸿铭译作 he should let them know where he goes(他必须让他们知道他到哪里去)。安乐哲译作 be sure to have a specific destination(一定要有一个明确的目的地)。林戊荪译作 always let them know where you are(永远让他们知道你在哪里)。

4.19　子曰:"父母在,不远游,游必有方①。"

① 方:方所,要去的地方。

4.21 The Master said, It is always better for a man to know the age of his parents. In the one case such knowledge will be a comfort to him; in the other, it will fill him with a salutary dread①.

① "一则以惧",韦利译作 in the other, it will fill him with a salutary dread(另一方面,知道父母老去会让人感到出于善意的惶恐)。理雅各译作 as an occasion for fear(是忧惧的理由)。辜鸿铭译作 as a matter for anxiety(作为一件令人焦虑的事)。安乐哲译作 on the other, it is a source of trepidation(另一方面,这是恐惧的原因)。林戊荪译作 it is something to be anxious about(这也是令人担忧的事)。

4.21 子曰:"父母之年,不可不知也。一则以喜,一则以惧。"

11.4 The Master said, Min Tzu-ch'ien is indeed a very good son. No one can take exception to① what his parents or brothers have said of him.

① "间",韦利译作 take exception to(表示异议;反对)。理雅各译作 say of him different from(表示异议)。辜鸿铭译作 find in him different from(表示异议)。安乐哲译作 doubt(怀疑)。林戊荪译作 disagree with(不同意)。

11.4 子曰:"孝哉,闵子骞!人不间于其父母昆①弟之言。"
① 昆:通"兄"。

13.18 The 'Duke' of Shê addressed Master K'ung saying, In my country there was a man called Upright Kung①. His father appropriated a sheep, and Kung bore witness against him. Master K'ung said, In my country the upright men are of another sort. A father will screen② his son, and a son his father—which incidentally does involve a sort of uprightness.

① "直躬者",韦利译作 a man called Upright Kung(一个叫直躬的人)。理雅各译作 those who may be styled upright in their conduct(那些言行可以被称作正直的人)。辜鸿铭译作 men to be found who are upright(被发现是正派的人们)。安乐哲译作 someone who is called 'True Person'(称作"真人")。林戊荪译作 an upright man(一个正直的人)。【编者按语】"直躬者"韦利和安乐哲译作绰号。其他译者泛指一类人。

② "隐",韦利译作 screen(庇护)。理雅各译作 conceal the misconduct(遮掩不良言行)。辜鸿铭译作 to be silent(保持沉默)。安乐哲译作 cover for(遮掩)。林戊荪译作 cover up for(遮掩)。

13.18 叶公语孔子曰:"吾党①有直躬②者,其父攘③羊,而子证④之。"孔子曰:"吾党之直者异于是:父为子隐,子为父隐。直在其中矣。"

① 党:古代一级地方建制,五百户为一党。
② 直躬:一般指正直的人。
③ 攘:侵夺、窃取。
④ 证:告发。

19.18 Master Tsêng said, I once heard the Master say, Filial piety such as that of Mêng Chuang Tsu might in other respects be possible to imitate; but the way in which he changed neither his father's servants nor his father's domestic policy, that would indeed be hard to emulate①.

① "是难能也",韦利译作 that would indeed be hard to emulate(仿效他的确很困难)。理雅各译作 it is difficult to be attained to(这个境界很难达到)。辜鸿铭译作 men will find it difficult to do(人们很难做到)。安乐哲译作 it would be difficult indeed(能做到的确很难)。林戊荪译作 it will be difficult to follow his example(很难以他为榜样)。

19.18 曾子曰:"吾闻诸夫子,孟庄子①之孝也,其他可能也;其不改父之臣与父之政,是难能也。"

① 孟庄子:鲁国大夫。

Exercises

1. Put the following sentences into English.

1) 1.16 子曰:"不患人不己知,患不知人也。"

2) 2.24 子曰:"非其鬼而祭之,谄也。见义不为,无勇也。"

3) 3.20 子曰:"《关雎》,乐而不淫,哀而不伤。"

4) 3.26 子曰:"居上不宽,为礼不敬,临丧不哀,吾何以观之哉?"

5) 4.14 子曰:"不患无位,患所以立。不患莫己知,求为可知也。"

6) 5.11 子贡曰:"我不欲人之加诸我也,吾亦欲无加诸人。"子曰:"赐也,非尔所及也。"

7) 6.18 子曰:"知之者不如好之者,好之者不如乐之者。"

8) 7.28 互乡难与言。童子见,门人惑。子曰:"与其进也,不与其退也,唯何甚? 人洁己以进,与其洁也,不保其往也。"

2. Think about the following questions and discuss them with your fellow students.

1) According to Youzi, filial piety and fraternal duty are the essence of benevolence. Based on the study of this unit, do you think this view would be shared by Confucius?

2) In your opinion, how should a truly filial son treat his parents?

Supplementary Reading: Arthur Waley as a Translator of Confucian Classics

文质彬彬的君子(gentleman)及君子之文
——亚瑟·韦利译《论语》

亚瑟·韦利(Arthur Waley, 1889—1966),英国现代著名汉学家。除了熟练掌握多种西文外,他还精通汉文、满文、梵文、蒙古文、日文等东方语言。韦利专门研究中国思想史、中国绘画史、中国文学和日本文学,成绩斐然,共著书40种,翻译中日文化著作46种。他对中日古典诗词的翻译尤其值得称道。他的代表性译作有《诗经》和《源氏物语》。他还翻译过《道德经》和《论语》,质量上乘,广受称誉。韦利的《论语》译本在众多译本中脱颖而出,被选入《大中华文库》。本书的《论语》即以其译本为底本。

韦利是继理雅各之后最重要的英国汉学家。韦利其人其文可以用文质彬彬去形容。"文质彬彬"出自《论语·雍也》。子曰:"质胜文则野;文胜质则史,文质彬彬,然后君子。""文质彬彬"是夫子用来描述君子的理想人格的。后来"文质"成为文艺学的重要理论范畴,还成为中国传统翻译学的核心范畴之一。对译文的生成和评价,讲求和突出文体辨析是中国译学的重要特色和传统。而从文体角度去探讨《论语》暨中国思想典籍的外译,同样是适用的。从《论语》翻译史文质的演变,可以清晰地发现韦利在文体上的作为和成就。如前所述,理雅各在翻译文体中不标奇立异。他的译文朴讷平淡,厚重少文,也就是说质胜于文。对此,辜鸿铭十分不满意。他认为理雅各的文学训练很不足,完全缺乏文体判断能力和文学感知力。作为反拨,辜氏的翻译特别重视文学的感知力。事实上,他以中国文人的身份从事翻译的。因此,他的译文过于流畅,反显油滑;过于精巧,反显虚浮。走到了文体的另一端——文胜于质。韦利对于文体风格有着明确的追求。他较好地协调了中英文各自的特点,他较好地协调了《论语》编撰者和译者自身的文风。在译文文体中,他还较好地协调了文和质这两个文体要素。一方面,在句子内部和句群,他刻意经营节奏、韵律、意像。连原文细微的语气都用各种各样的方式成功地再现出来。这是韦利译文"文"的一面。另一方面,在措辞上,无论是普通词汇还是核心术语,他似乎并不讲究,常常径直拿来最常见最常用的词。例如,"仁"译作 Goodness,"士"译作 knight,君子译作 gentleman。"刚、毅、木、讷"的"木"居然译作 tree-like。措辞简洁平实,体现了韦利"质"的文体追求。"文质"的分子用高妙的手段调和起来,成就了文质彬彬的译文上品。韦利也因此被马理斯(Morris)称为"天才的文体家(stylist)""当代最好的文体家"。

从原初意义上,"文质彬彬"是夫子用来描述君子的人格理想的。而文质彬彬的韦利译文源于其人的文质彬彬。走进韦利最好的方式,或许是探究其专业和职业的复合身份。韦利既是以实证求真见长的学者,又是天马行空、激情四溢的诗人。前者讲究质朴,后者讲究"言之无文,行而不远"。韦利早年在剑桥大学国王学院接受过系统而严格的西方古典文学,包括梵文经典训练,后长期在大英博物馆从事研究工作。在学术上,他还受到清代朴学,尤其顾颉刚疑古的历史研究思想的影响。韦利的《论语》翻译从微观到宏观都体现了训练有素的跨文化学者的眼光和手段。在微观的字词层面,他采用了"由词通道"的语言诠释策略。由字的知识考古,求得《论语》集撰时的原初意义。在宏观的篇章层面,韦利大胆推测存在两部《论语》。第三至第九篇,思想连贯,结构谨严,浑然一体。这是可信的原初《论语》。第一第二两篇以及第十至第二十篇,内容和性质极为驳杂,思想与文体多有扞格之处。这是后人假托或伪造的《论语》。韦利的《论语》疑古后来被白牧之、白妙之夫妇系统提升为层累的《论语》文本说。韦利和白氏夫妇的《论语》疑古在学术上或可讨论,但背后的求真精神却无可疑议。韦利的另一个职业和专业身份是诗人和诗歌翻译家。他对东西方语言和文学有一种天生的文学感知力,使他能够很好地把捉《论语》的情感逻辑,并在译文中以近于散文诗的语言表现出来。关于韦利诗人翻译家的身份,学术界已经有了很深入的探讨,在此不赘。学者的职业和专业塑造了韦利质朴厚重的人格,而诗人翻译家的身份又塑造了他才气纵横的文人型人格。从中国文化角度来说,韦利是一个"文质彬彬"的君子;而从英国文化角度来说,他则是一个当之无愧的英伦绅士。

《论语》中的君子有着很丰富的内涵,很难用外语翻译。而英语的 gentleman 也有着很丰富的内涵,不仅仅是举止优雅得体而已。有趣而发人深省的是,韦利用 gentleman 去对应君子。他强调找不到更好的英文词去翻译中国的君子。我们认为这是绝佳的翻译。

综上所述,韦利其人是文质彬彬的君子(gentleman),其文是文质彬彬的君子之文。

Unit Seven
Confucius on "Being a Gentleman"—Selected Readings of *The Analects of Confucius* (3)

"gentlemen"(君子) and "sages"(圣人) are two types of morally and intellectually exalted people that Confucius often discussed. It is generally believed that it is easier for people to become a gentleman than a sage. Confucius said, "I have no hopes of meeting a sage. I would be content if I met someone who is a gentleman." In *The Analects of Confucius*, there are a large number of sayings dealing with such topics as what a gentleman is, how a gentleman's virtues are manifested, and how people could become a gentleman. This shows that the gentleman is one of the ideal personalities that Confucius and his disciples admired and promoted. Since there are many sayings about being a gentleman, this unit does not contain all the relevant sayings, but only some representative ones.

Selected Readings of *The Analects of Confucius(3)* and Notes

1.5 The Master said, A country of a thousand war-chariots cannot be administered unless the ruler attends strictly to business①, punctually observes his promises, is economical in expenditure, shows affection towards his subjects in general, and uses the labour of the peasantry only at the proper times of year.

① "敬事",韦利译作 attends strictly to business(专注于事务)。理雅各译作 reverent attention to business(恭谨地专注于事务)。辜鸿铭译作 be serious in attention to business(严肃认真地处理事务)。安乐哲译作 carry out your official duties respectfully(恭谨地执行公务)。林戊荪译作 devote himself whole-heartedly to state affairs(全身心地致力于国家事务)。

1.5 子曰:"道①千乘之国②,敬事③而信,节用④而爱人,使民⑤以时⑥。"
① 道:通"导",治理。
② 千乘之国:指诸侯国,因诸侯可出兵车千乘,故有此称谓。
③ 敬事:职责上负责认真地做事。

④ 节用：节制使用财物。
⑤ 使民：役使民众。
⑥ 以时：以，凭借、根据；时，本意为时间，此处代指恰当的时间，通常指农闲时节。

2.12　The Master said, A gentleman is not an implement①.

① "器"，韦利译作 implement（器皿）。理雅各和林戊荪译作 utensil（工具）。辜鸿铭译作 a mere machine fit only to do one kind of work（一个只合适做一种工作的可怜的机器）。安乐哲译作 vessels（容器）。【编者按语】辜鸿铭将一个名词扩展为一个短语名词，属于释译。优点是意义充分，缺点是不够简练。

2.12　子曰："君子不器①。"

① 不器：器，器具。具有一定的使用功能，无功能则成废物，故不器。指君子不以有用有利为目标，而是在修养一种内在价值，不以外在的利用衡量其价值。

2.13　Tzu-kung asked about the true gentleman①. The Master said, He does not preach what he practices till he has practised what he preaches.

① "君子"，韦利译作 the true gentleman（真正的绅士）。理雅各译作 the superior man（卓越的人士；位高权重的人）。辜鸿铭译作 a wise and good man（智慧良善的人）。安乐哲译作 exemplary person（模范）。林戊荪译作 the man of honor（讲求尊严的人）。

2.13　子贡问君子。子曰："先行其言①，而后从之。"

① 先行其言：先做其所说的事。

2.14　The Master said, A gentleman can see a question from all sides without bias①. The small man is biased and can see a question only from one side.

① "周而不比"，韦利译作 see a question from all sides without bias（不带偏见地从各方面看问题）。理雅各译作 catholic and no partisan（心胸开阔而无偏私）。辜鸿铭译作 impartial, not neutral（公正但不中立）。安乐哲译作（Exemplary persons）associating openly with others are not partisan（与其他人坦荡交往的君子不会结党营私）。林戊荪译作（A man of honor）associate with many but does not form a clique（君子与许多人交往但不结成帮派）。

2.14　子曰："君子周而不比，小人比而不周。"

3.7　The Master said, Gentlemen never compete①. You will say that in archery they do so. But even then they bow and make way for one another when they are going up to the archery-ground, when they are coming down and at the subsequent drinking-bout. Thus even when competing, they still remain gentlemen.

① "争",韦利译作 compete(竞争)。理雅各译作 contentions(争执)。辜鸿铭译作 compete in anything he does(做什么都争先恐后)。安乐哲译作 be competitive(有好胜心的)。林戊荪译作 contention(竞争;争执)。

3.7 子曰:"君子无所争。必也射①乎!揖让②而升③,下而饮④。其争也君子。"

① 射:此处指古代的射礼,一种比赛射箭的竞赛活动。
② 揖让:揖,作揖;让,谦让。
③ 升:指登上射箭的场地。
④ 下而饮:退下射箭场地饮酒。

4.8 The Master said, In the morning, hear the Way①; in the evening, die content!

① "道",韦利和林戊荪译作 the Way(道)。理雅各译作 the right way(正确的路)。辜鸿铭译作 wisdom(智慧)。安乐哲译作 the way(道路)。

4.8 子曰:"朝闻道,夕死可矣!"

4.11 The Master said, Where gentlemen set their hearts upon moral force (tê), the commoners set theirs upon the soil①. Where gentlemen think only of punishments②, the commoners think only of exemptions.

① "土",韦利译作 the soil(土壤)。理雅各译作 comfort(舒适)。辜鸿铭译作 position(地位)。安乐哲和林戊荪译作 land(土地)。
② "刑",韦利译作 punishments(惩罚)。理雅各和林戊荪译作 the sanctions of law(法律的制裁)。辜鸿铭译作 justice(正义)。安乐哲译作 fairness(公平)。

4.11 子曰:"君子怀①德②,小人怀土③;君子怀刑④,小人怀惠⑤。"

① 怀:思念。
② 德:德性。
③ 土:家乡、居所。
④ 刑:惩罚。
⑤ 惠:好处。

4.12 The Master said, Those whose measures are dictated by mere expediency[①] will arouse continual discontent.

①"利",韦利译作 expediency(权宜之计)。理雅各和辜鸿铭译作 advantage(好处;有利)。安乐哲译作 personal profit(个人的利益)。林戊荪译作 self-interest(自私自利)。
【编者按语】韦利将本句的主语理解为 the rulers and upper classes in general(统治者或上层阶级)。其他译者多理解为一般人。

4.12　子曰:"放[①]于利而行,多怨[②]。"
① 放:通"仿",效法。
② 怨:仇恨。

4.16　The Master said, A gentleman takes as much trouble to discover[①] what is right as lesser men take to discover what will pay.

①"喻",韦利译作 take as much trouble to discover(努力去发现)。理雅各译作 the mind of the superior man is conversant with(君子关注或聚焦)。辜鸿铭译作 see... in a question(在一个问题上看到)。安乐哲译作 understand(理解)。林戊荪译作 think in terms of(从……角度考虑)。

4.16　子曰:"君子喻于义,小人喻于利。"

4.24　The Master said, A gentleman covets the reputation[①] of being slow in word but prompt in deed.

①"欲",韦利译作 covets the reputation(希望得到好名声)。理雅各译作 wishes(希望)。辜鸿铭和安乐哲译作 want(想要)。林戊荪译作 prefer(更喜欢)。

4.24　子曰:"君子欲[①]讷於言,而敏于行。"
① 欲:此处为希望、期望。

5.15　Of Tzu-ch'an the Master said that in him were to be found four of the virtues that belong to the Way of the true gentleman. In his private conduct he was courteous, in serving his master he was punctilious[①], in providing for the needs of the people he gave them even more than their due; in exacting service from the people, he was just.

①"敬",韦利译作 punctilious(谨守规则的;一丝不苟的)。理雅各和林戊荪译作 respectful(恭敬的)。辜鸿铭译作 serious(严肃的)。安乐哲译作 deferential(恭敬的)。

5.15　子谓子产[①],"有君子之道四焉:其行己也恭,其事上也敬,其养民也惠,其使民也义。"

① 子产:春秋时期郑国政治家,致力于国家政治改革,成效显著。

6.16 The Master said, When natural substance prevails over ornamentation, you get the boorishness of the rustic①. When ornamentation prevails over natural substance, you get the pedantry of the scribe②. Only when ornament and substance are duly blended do you get the true gentleman.

① "野",韦利译作 the boorishness of the rustic(乡下人的粗陋)。理雅各译作 rusticity(粗陋)。辜鸿铭译作 rude men(粗鲁的人)。安乐哲译作 boorish(粗陋的,乡气的)。林戊荪译作 uncouth(粗鲁的)。

② "史",韦利译作 the pedantry of the scribe(书记员的迂腐)。理雅各译作 the manners of a clerk(书记员的做派)。辜鸿铭译作 literati(文人)。安乐哲译作 an officious scribe(爱管闲事的书记员)。林戊荪译作 pedantic(迂腐的)。

6.16 子曰:"质①胜文②则野③,文胜质则史④。文质彬彬⑤,然后君子。"
① 质:朴质,未经修饰的。
② 文:文采。
③ 野:郊外之地,表示粗鄙,而朱熹将其解释为野人(乡野之人)。
④ 史:文采繁复。
⑤ 彬彬:朱熹认为,"彬彬,犹班班,物相杂而适均之貌"。

8.7 Master Tsêng said, The true Knight of the Way① must perforce be both broad-shouldered and stout of heart②; his burden is heavy and he has far to go. For Goodness is the burden he has taken upon himself; and must we not grant that it is a heavy one to bear? Only with death does his journey end; then must we not grant that he has far to go?

① "士",韦利译作 the true Knight of the Way(护道的真正骑士)。理雅各和林戊荪译作 the scholar(学者)。辜鸿铭译作 an educated gentleman(受过教育的绅士)。安乐哲译作 scholar-apprentices(学者-学徒)。【编者按语】韦利的译法最特异。

② "弘毅",韦利译作 broad-shouldered and stout of heart(肩膀宽阔,心理强大)。理雅各译作 breadth of mind and rigorous endurance(心胸开阔,精力充沛,富有耐力)。辜鸿铭译作 strength and resoluteness of character(强健有力,性格坚毅)。安乐哲译作 strong and resolved(强健而坚定)。林戊荪译作 strong and steadfast(强健而坚毅)。

8.7 曾子曰:"士①,不可以不弘毅②,任重③而道远。仁以为己任,不亦重乎,死而后已,不亦远乎。"

① 士:此处指德才兼备的男子。
② 毅:刚强坚韧。
③ 任重:责任重大。

12.4 Ssu-ma Niu asked about the meaning of the term Gentleman. The Master said, The Gentleman neither grieves nor fears. Ssu-ma Niu said, So that is what is meant by being a gentleman—neither to grieve nor to fear? The Master said, On looking within himself he finds no taint①; so why should he either grieve or fear?

① "不疚",韦利译作 he finds no taint(他没有发现自己的污点)。理雅各译作 he discovers nothing wrong(他没有发现自己做错了事)。辜鸿铭译作 finds no cause for self-reproach(没有发现自我谴责的理由)。安乐哲译作 there is nothing to be ashamed of(没有做需要羞愧的事)。林戊荪译作 one has a clear conscience(自己良心清白)。

12.4 司马牛①问"君子"。子曰:"君子不忧不惧。"曰:"不忧不惧,斯谓之君子矣乎?"子曰:"内省不疚②,夫何忧何惧?"

① 司马牛:名耕或说名犁,字子牛,为孔子重要弟子之一。
② 疚:愧对他人而良心不安。

12.16 The Master said, The gentleman calls attention to the good points in others①; he does not call attention to their defects. The small man does just the reverse of this.

① "成人之美",韦利译作 call attention to the good points in others(宣扬他人的优点)。理雅各译作 seek to perfect the admirable qualities of man(尽力完善他人的优点)。辜鸿铭译作 encourage men to develop the good qualities in their nature(鼓励人们去发展本性中的好品质)。安乐哲译作 help to bring out the best in others(帮助他人显露他们的最佳品质)。林戊荪译作 help others to realize their best aims(帮助他人实现他们的最佳目标)。

12.16 子曰:"君子成①人之美②,不成人之恶③;小人反是。"

① 成:助成。
② 美:美好品质。
③ 恶:恶劣品质。

13.23 The Master said, The true gentleman is conciliatory① but not accommodating②. Common people are accommodating but not conciliatory.

① "和",韦利译作 conciliatory(和解的)。理雅各译作 affable(和蔼可亲的)。辜鸿铭译作 sociable(友善随和的)。安乐哲和林戊荪译作 harmony(和谐)。

② "同",韦利译作 accommodating(讨好的)。安乐哲译作 adulatory(谄媚的)。辜鸿铭译作 familiar(亲昵的)。安乐哲译作 sameness(相同)。林戊荪译作 identity of views(观点一致)。

13.23 子曰:"君子和①而不同②;小人同而不和。"

① 和:本意为和谐,此处指使人际关系融洽。
② 同:相同,聚合。

13.26 The Master said, The gentleman is dignified①, but never haughty; common people are haughty, but never dignified.

① "泰",韦利和辜鸿铭译作 dignified(庄严的;端庄的)。理雅各译作 dignified ease(端庄安闲;从容静娴)。安乐哲译作 distinguished(尊贵的;卓越的)。林戊荪译作 composed(镇定的;端庄的)。

13.26 子曰:"君子泰①而不骄②;小人骄而不泰。"

① 泰:心态安定,不骄不躁。
② 骄:自大自矜。

14.7 The Master said, It is possible to be a true gentleman and yet lack Goodness①. But there has never yet existed a Good man who was not a gentleman.

① "不仁",韦利译作 lack Goodness(缺少仁德)。理雅各译作 not always virtuous(不总是仁德的)。辜鸿铭译作 who are not moral characters(不是有道德的人)。安乐哲译作 There have been occasions (on which an exemplary person) fails to act in an authoritative manner(君子未行仁道,时而有之)。林戊荪译作(We have seen) cases of a man of honour not being humane(我们见过君子不行仁道的情况)。【编者按语】这句话有两解。一是"不行仁道"。韦利和辜鸿铭据此理解翻译。二是"不总是行仁道",理雅各,安乐哲和林戊荪均作此解。

14.7 子曰:"君子而不仁者有矣夫?未有小人而仁者也!"

14.24 The Master said, The gentleman can influence those who are above him①; the small man can only influence those who are below him.

① "君子上达",韦利译作 The gentleman can influence those who are above him(君子

能够影响他的上级）。理雅各译作 The progress of the superior man is upwards; the progress of the mean man is downwards（君子向上进步；小人向下沉沦）。辜鸿铭译作 A wise and good man looks upward in his aspirations; a fool looks downwards（智慧而良善的人志存高远；傻瓜志向卑下）。安乐哲译作 The exemplary person takes the high road, while the petty person takes the low（君子走上高尚的路，小人走着卑下的路）。林戊荪译作 The man of honour reaches for higher things. The petty-minded man reaches for lower things（讲求尊严的人追求高尚，心胸狭窄的人追求卑下）。【编者按语】本句古今学人各有解释，译文各异。

14.24 子曰："君子上达[①]；小人下达[②]。"
① 上达：向上行，一般指通达于道或仁义。
② 下达：向下行，指通达于利益。

14.30 The Master said, The Ways of the true gentleman are three. I myself have met with success in none of them. For he that is really Good is never unhappy, he that is really wise is never perplexed, he that is really brave is never afraid. Tzu-kung said, That, Master, is your own Way[①]!

① "君子自道也"，韦利译作 That, Master, is your own Way!（夫子呀，那正是您自己的道!）。理雅各译作 Master, that is what you yourself say!（夫子呀，您自己正说明了这一点!）。辜鸿铭译作 That is what you say of yourself, Sir（先生，这说的正是您自己呀!）。安乐哲译作 That is the path that you yourself walk, Sir（先生，这正是您自己走的路!）。林戊荪译作 That is just a modest way by which the Master describes himself（那正是夫子描述自己的谦逊的说法）。

14.30 子曰："君子道者三，我无能[①]焉：仁者不忧；知者不惑；勇者不惧。"子贡曰："夫子自道[②]也!"
① 无能：无法做到。
② 自道：称述自己。

15.19 The Master said, A gentleman has reason to be distressed if he ends his days without making a reputation for himself.[①]

① "没世"，韦利译作 he ends his day（人去世时）。理雅各译作 after his death（人死后）。辜鸿铭译作 die（死亡）。安乐哲译作 end their days（人去世时）。林戊荪译作 disappear from this world（从这个世界消失）。【编者按语】"没世"有两种理解。一是死后，即当求身后名。理雅各据此译。二是死时，即当求身前名。其他译者据此译。

15.19　子曰:"君子疾①没世②而名不称③焉。"
① 疾:忧虑。
② 没世:去世。
③ 名不称:美名不被称颂。

15.20　The Master said, 'The demands that a gentleman makes are upon himself; those that a small man makes are upon others.'

15.20　子曰:"君子求①诸己;小人求诸人。"
① 求:责备。

15.22　The Master said, A gentleman does not Accept① men because of what they say. Nor reject sayings, because the speaker is what he is.
① "举",韦利译作 accept(接受)。理雅各和安乐哲译作 promote(提拔)。辜鸿铭译作 uphold(支持)。林戊荪译作 approve of(赞成)。

15.22　子曰:"君子不以言举①人;不以人废言。"
① 举:推荐,此处特指举荐做官。

15.31　The Master said, A gentleman, in his plans, thinks of the Way; he does not think how he is going to make a living. Even farming sometimes entails times of shortage; and even learning may incidentally lead to high pay①. But a gentleman's anxieties concern the progress of the Way; he has no anxiety concerning poverty.
① "禄",韦利译作 high pay(高薪水)。理雅各译作 emolument(报酬)。辜鸿铭译作 the rewards of official life(公职的报酬)。安乐哲译作 an official salary(官职的薪水)。林戊荪译作 being an official with earnings(成为一个带薪的官员)。【编者按语】韦利在译文中增加了两个副词 sometimes(有时候)和 incidentally(偶然地,侥幸地)。他似乎在淡化做官求禄的追求。其实,孔子在劝学劝禄。

15.31　子曰:"君子谋①道不谋食;耕也,馁②在其中矣;学也,禄在其中矣。君子忧道不忧贫。"
① 谋:谋求,意为为获得某事而计划筹算。
② 馁:饥饿。

16.8　Master K'ung said, There are three things that a gentleman fears: he fears the will of Heaven①, he fears great men, he fears the words of the Divine Sages. The small man does not know the will of Heaven and so does not fear it. He treats great men with contempt, and scoffs at the words of the Divine Sages.

①"天命",韦利译作 the will of Heaven(上天的意志)。理雅各译作 the ordinances of Heaven(上天的指令)。辜鸿铭译作 the Laws of God(上帝的法则)。安乐哲译作 the propensities of tian(天的习性)。林戊荪译作 the mandate of Heaven(上天的诏令)。【编者按语】安乐哲的译法属于异化,刻意回避西方的语汇(即 Heaven 和 God)。其他几种属于归化,径直采用了西方宗教常用的语汇。

16.8　孔子曰:"君子有三畏①:畏天命,畏大人,畏圣人之言。小人不知天命而不畏也,狎②大人,侮圣人之言。"

① 畏:敬畏。
② 狎:关系亲近而态度不庄重。

16.10　Master K'ung said, The gentleman has nine cares①. In seeing he is careful to see clearly, in hearing he is careful to hear distinctly, in his looks he is careful to be kindly; in his manner to be respectful, in his words to be loyal, in his work to be diligent. When in doubt he is careful to ask for information; when angry he has a care for the consequences②, and when he sees a chance of gain, he thinks carefully whether the pursuit of it would be consonant with the Right.

①"思",韦利译作 care(关注点)。理雅各译作 things which are subjects with him of thoughtful consideration(他深思熟虑的事情)。辜鸿铭译作 objects which a wise man aims at(智者视之为目标的事情)。安乐哲译作 things in mind(心目中的事情)。林戊荪译作 occasions which calls for careful consideration(需要仔细思考的场合或时机)。

②"难",韦利和辜鸿铭译作 consequences(后果)。理雅各译作 the difficulties(困难)。安乐哲译作 regret(后悔;悔恨)。林戊荪译作 possible consequences(可能的后果)。

16.10　孔子曰:"君子有九思①:视思明,听思聪,色思温,貌思恭,言思忠,事思敬,疑思问,忿思难②,见得思义。"

① 思:欲求、考虑到。
② 忿思难:遇到不顺意而引发怨恨之事时,应该考虑到后患。

Exercises

1. Put the following sentences into English.

1) 1.4 曾子曰:"吾日三省吾身:为人谋而不忠乎?与朋友交而不信乎?传不习乎?"

2) 1.14 子曰:"君子食无求饱,居无求安,敏于事而慎于言,就有道而正焉,可谓好学也已。"

3) 4.9 子曰:"士志于道,而耻恶衣恶食者,未足与议也!"

4) 7.38 子温而厉,威而不猛,恭而安。

5) 7.37 子曰:"君子坦荡荡,小人长戚戚。"

6) 8.13 子曰:"笃信好学,守死善道。危邦不入,乱邦不居,天下有道则见,无道则隐。邦有道,贫且贱焉,耻也;邦无道,富且贵焉,耻也。"

7) 16.7 孔子曰:"君子有三戒;少之时,血气未定,戒之在色;及其壮也,血气方刚,戒之在斗;及其老也,血气既衰,戒之在得。"

8) 17.24 子贡曰:"君子亦有恶乎?"子曰:"有恶。恶称人之恶者,恶居下流而讪上者,恶勇而无礼者,恶果敢而窒者。"曰:"赐也,亦有恶乎?""恶徼以为知者,恶不孙以为勇者,恶讦以为直者。"

2. Pick one of the following questions and write an essay about 200 words.

1) Based on the content of this unit, what are the key qualities of a gentleman as described by Confucius?

2) Make a comparison of the concept of "gentleman" in China and the United Kingdom.

Supplementary Reading: Roger T. Ames as a Translator of Confucian Classics

《论语》暨中国古代思想典籍新译的模式·范式·体式
——安乐哲译《论语》《中庸》

安乐哲(Roger T. Ames, 1947—),国际知名汉学家、美国夏威夷大学教授、北京大学人文讲座教授。主编《东西方哲学》。安乐哲著述甚丰,代表译作有《论语》《孙子兵法》《道德经》《孝经》。本书以其《论语》《中庸》英译本作为参照文本。

《论语》暨《四书》的英译已经整整两个世纪,积淀相当深厚,光是《论语》就有60多个译本。从传统译学角度,这些经典的翻译近乎完美。然而,经典之所以是经典,正在于经典常读常新,常译常新。当下,《论语》外译如何进一步开拓诠释空间,取得新的突破,是

"中华文化走出去"的重要课题。一些海外汉学家已经做了有益的探索,安乐哲是其中杰出的代表。在中国古代思想典籍外译的运作模式、新诠新译的范式和语言及文体的体式上,他都作了有益的尝试,为未来的经典新铨新译提供了重要启示。

第一,专家合译模式的运作。安乐哲本有汉学家加哲学家的复合身份,但是他在从事中国古代思想典籍英译时,有意识地引入了合作翻译的模式,邀约了美国著名哲学家郝大维(David L. Hall)、罗思文(Henry Rosemont, Jr.),参与了《论语》《中庸》《孝经》等经典的翻译。这两位合作者不只在汉学领域造诣精深,他们在美国新实用主义哲学、怀海特哲学、古希腊哲学等领域都有学术专长。这是翻译主体由个人到团体的改变,其意义不容小觑。专家合译的好处显而易见。各个译者可以在翻译的各个层面和阶段各展所长,各补所短。这对于经典翻译尤其必要和重要。事实上,安乐哲的合译模式使他们的经典翻译研究性和艺术性大大增强,学术含量大大提高。这些译本本身有成为经典的可能。从历史角度来看,经典翻译(尤其是宗教经典)专家合译模式曾经是主流的翻译模式。《圣经》的《七十子希腊文本》《圣经》汉译的和合本是《圣经》翻译合译模式的典型例子。唐宋佛典翻译的译场是合译模式的制度性安排。毫不夸张地说,佛典翻译和《圣经》翻译的高度成就,都是凝聚了集体智慧合译的结果。近代以来,林纾的合译产生了中国近代文学的经典。而49年之后,马恩列斯的经典文献的汉译和中国领袖著作的外译都是围绕着专家团体合译模式运作的。在当代《论语》暨中国古代思想典籍的翻译中,白牧之、白妙之夫妻的《论语》合译也奉献出别具一格的译作。

第二,新诠新译范式的建立。"新诠新译"语出安乐哲、郝大维合译的《中庸》书名——《切中伦常——〈中庸〉的新诠与新译》。这里"新诠"是指译者对于经典的新的系统性的和有学术深度的理论研究。"新诠新译"不仅仅指翻译的时间次序,更意味着只有新诠才能新译,新译必须基于新诠。这是安乐哲的刻意追求和文本建构实践。儒学典籍的英译从一开始就是英国汉学研究的一个部分。英语典籍翻译的特点是研译并重,以译促研,以研助译。历时来看,儒学典籍的英译经历了以译为主、以研为辅,研译并重到以研为主、以译为辅的三个历史阶段。如果说理雅各代表了第一个阶段,韦利、刘殿爵代表了第二个阶段,安乐哲和他的合译者代表了第三个阶段。他们提供了当代儒学经典翻译的范式。以研带译、以研为主显在的表征是安乐哲译本的研究性副文本的篇幅大大增加,大大超过了译文正文本。《中庸》译文正文只有37页,而副文本达181页。《论语》译文正文只有111页,而副文本达213页。研究压倒翻译的局面清晰可见。事实上,新译必须基于新诠,已经成为欧美汉学界的共识。经典复译的意义和必要性大概正在于此。具体就安乐哲和他的合作者的新诠而言,他们不满足于个别字句的新的注解,而是建构了系统的新诠新译范式。这个范式主要包括当代学术视角、基于新发现材料的诠释、新的比较文化视域和面向当代及现实的导向。首先,安乐哲的新诠体现在翻译中贯穿统一的当代哲学视角。《论语》的译者采用了西方哲学的视角去进行诠释,由来已久。安乐哲团队的新诠体现在哲学视角的当代化和精细化。他们将《论语》《中庸》翻译统一于新实用主义和怀海特哲学,将它们置于"情境化艺术"的哲学语境进行诠释。用西方当代哲学去系统深入诠释和翻译《论语》和《中庸》,这是开拓性的尝试。其次,《定州论语》提供的新材料提供了新的诠释的空间。学术创新除了凭借理论创新外,还依赖新发现的材料。安乐哲团队用1973年出土的《论语》汉简与《论语》传世本作了详尽的校勘比照,对一些章句做了新诠新译。再次,新诠新译还包括新的比较文化视域和面向当代及现实的导向。安乐哲团队在新诠新译中突出了比较文化视域。《论语》译本书名的副标题即为"比较哲学的视域"。《中庸》译本的第二章即为"比较视域下的《中庸》新诠:哲学和宗教性的取径"。该书附录二是中西哲学比较的专文《儒学与杜威的实用主义:一种对话》。与以往面向文本和历史的经典翻译导向不同,他们进行文化比较的目的是提供与西方哲学不同的东方思维方式,从而丰富和改造西方的文化资源,以便更好地认识自身和世界。

第三,中西语言体式的深入研究和译文独特体式的追求。读一读安乐哲团队的《论语》《中庸》译文,不难发现它们具有高度的辨识度,文体风格精悍硬峭,自成一体,不同于理雅各的厚重少文、辜鸿铭的繁缛雕琢、韦利的文质彬彬、刘殿爵的平易畅白。这种独特文体的建构源于译者的哲学语言观和对汉语文言的深入研究。站在形而上学的高度,他们比较了西语和先秦文言的特征。相对于西语的"实在性""本质性",中国文言文则是一种"事件性"的语言。为了突出这一特征,译者普遍而刻意地使用动名词,以动制静。他们还较多地使用简单句、短句和并列句,而不是复合句、长句,来表达"一个连续的、片段的事件世界"。译者对"事件性"的强调和具体的落实方法有助于构成了精悍硬峭的风格。

20世纪90年代以来,中国本土《论语》暨中国古代思想典籍的外译勃兴,在译本数量上压倒了同期海外汉学界。然而,新译虽多,新的翻译运作模式和新诠新译的思考和实践却不多。结果是高质量的译本寥寥无几。安乐哲及其合作者的开拓性尝试给了我们宝贵的启示,有助于弥补国内典籍翻译的短板。

Unit Eight
Confucius on "Governance"—Selected Readings of *The Analects of Confucius* (4)

Confucius made a rather systematic and profound discussion of governance(为政). His discussion on governance can be divided into two fields: the aims of governance and the mechanism of governance. In Confucius' view, the primary aim of governance is to establish a good social order, in which different people have their own places and are given their own shares of benefits, e.g., "Let the ruler be a ruler, the subject a subject, the father a father, the son a son". The ideal governance was later called the benevolent government by Mencius. Confucius went on to claim that the key to good governance is for the ruler to cultivate his own character, so that he can inspire his subjects to follow his example, thus naturally achieving a good political order. The content of this unit is mainly related to these two aspects of governance.

Selected Readings of *The Analects of Confucius*(4) and Notes

1.10 Tzu-Ch'in said to Tzu-kung, When our Master arrives in a fresh country he always manages to find out about its policy. Does he do this by asking questions or do people tell him of their own accord? Tzu-kung said, Our Master gets things by being cordial, frank, courteous, temperate, deferential[①]. That is our Master's way of enquiring—a very different matter, certainly, from the way in which enquiries are generally made.

① "温、良、恭、俭、让",韦利译作 being cordial, frank, courteous, temperate, deferential(热诚的、坦率的、有礼的、温和的、恭敬的)。理雅各译作 be benign, upright, courteous, temperate, and complaisant(和善的、正直的、有礼的、温和的、谦恭的)。辜鸿铭译作 be gracious, simple, earnest, modest and courteous(和蔼的、纯朴的、真诚的、谦逊的、有礼的)。安乐哲译作 be cordial, proper, deferential, frugal, and unassuming(热诚的、守规矩的、恭敬的、节俭的、不做作的)。林戊荪译作 be temperate, kind, courteous, restrained and magnanimous(温和的、良善的、有礼的、克制的、宽容的)。

1.10 子禽①问于子贡曰:"夫子至于是邦也,必闻其政,求之与,抑与之与?"子贡曰:"夫子温、良、恭、俭、让以得之。夫子之求之也,其诸异乎人之求之与?"

① 子禽:姓陈名亢,字子禽。可能是孔子的弟子。

2.1 The Master said, He who rules by moral force (*tê*)①is like the pole-star, which remains in its place while all the lesser stars do homage to② it.

① "德",韦利译作 moral force(道德力量)。理雅各和林戊荪译作 virtue(美德)。辜鸿铭译作 moral sentiment(道德情感)。安乐哲译作 excellence(卓越)。

② "共",韦利译作 do homage to(向……致敬)。理雅各译作 turn toward it(朝向……而运行)。辜鸿铭和林戊荪译作 revolve round it(围绕着……转)。安乐哲译作 pay it tribute(向……致敬)。

2.1 子曰:"为政以德,譬如北辰①居其所而众星共②之。"

① 北辰:北极星。
② 共:通"拱",围绕。

2.3 The Master said, Govern the people by regulations, keep order among them by chastisements, and they will flee① from you and lose all self-respect. Govern them by moral fore, keep order among them by ritual and they will keep their self-respect and come to you of their own accord②.

① "免",韦利译作 flee(逃跑)。理雅各译作 avoid the punishment(避免惩罚)。辜鸿铭译作 keep away from wrong-doing(避免做坏事)。安乐哲译作 avoid punishments(避免惩罚)。林戊荪译作 know how to stay out of trouble(知道如何不惹麻烦)。【编者按语】"免"韦利译作 flee,与原意不符。但应是刻意为之,与下文的 come to you 呼应。

② "格",韦利译作 come to you of their own accord(自愿投奔你)。理雅各译作 become good(变得良善)。辜鸿铭译作 emulate what is good(效仿良善的行为)。安乐哲译作 order themselves(自律)。林戊荪译作 know the correct course to take(知道该走正道)。【编者按语】"格"的意义众多。韦利在此解作"来"。与前面的 flee 呼应,亦是妙解。

2.3 子曰:"道①之以政,齐之以刑,民免②而无耻;道之以德,齐之以礼,有耻且格③。"

① 道:通"导",引导。
② 免:避免、逃避。

③ 格:停止或匡正。

2.19 Duke Ai asked, What can I do in order to get the support of the common people? Master K'ung replied, If you 'raise up the straight and set them on top of① the crooked', the commoners will support you. But if you raise the crooked and set them on top of the straight, the commoners will not support you.

① "错诸",韦利译作 set...on top of(把……放在上面)。理雅各译作 set aside(把……放在一边)。辜鸿铭译作 put down(放下;弃置)。安乐哲译作 place...over(把……放在上边)。林戊荪译作 promote...over(把……置于其上)。

2.19 哀公问曰:"何为则民服?"孔子对曰:"举直①错诸枉,则民服;举枉错诸直,则民不服。"

① 举直:举荐正直者做官。

3.19 Duke Ting (died 495 B.C.) asked for a precept concerning a ruler's use of his ministers and a minister's service to his ruler. Master K'ung replied, saying, A ruler in employing his ministers should be guided solely by the prescription of ritual①. Ministers in serving their ruler, solely by devotion to his cause.

① "礼",韦利译作 the prescriptions of ritual(礼规)。理雅各译作 the rules of propriety(行为规范)。辜鸿铭译作 (treat)...with honour(礼遇)。安乐哲译作 ritual propriety(礼仪规范)。林戊荪译作 the rituals(礼仪)。

3.19 定公①问:"君使臣,臣事君,如之何?"孔子对曰:"君使臣以礼,臣事君以忠。"

① 定公:鲁定公,鲁国国君。

12.11 Duke Ching of Ch'i asked Master K'ung about government. Master K'ung replied, saying, Let the prince be a prince, the minister a minister, the father a father and the son a son. The Duke said, How true! For indeed when the prince is not a prince, the minister not a minister, the father not a father, the son not a son, one may have a dish of millet① in front of one and yet not know if one will live to eat it.

① "粟",韦利译作 millet(粟,小米)。理雅各和辜鸿铭译作 rcvenue(收入)。林戊荪和安乐哲译作 grain(谷物)。

12.11　齐景公问政于孔子。孔子对曰:"君君①,臣臣,父父,子子。"公曰:"善哉! 信如君不君,臣不臣,父不父,子不子,虽有粟,吾得而食诸?"

① 君君:前一个"君"为名词,即君主;后一个"君"为动词,按照君的方式行动。"君君"一般被译为君主应该按照君主应有的方式行为。其他几个语词结构与此类似。

12.14　Tzu-chang asked about public business. The Master said, Ponder over it untiringly at home①; carry it out loyally when the time comes. (Literally, 'Home it untiringly, carry it out loyally'.)

① "居之无倦",韦利译作 ponder over it untiringly at home(在家里不知疲倦地仔细琢磨)。理雅各译作 The art of government is to keep its affairs before the mind without weariness(治理的艺术是把治理事务时时放在心上,不知疲倦)。辜鸿铭译作 Be patient in maturing your plans(耐心地酝酿完善你的计划)。安乐哲译作 Be unflagging in deliberating upon policy(在酝酿政策时,要不知疲倦)。林戊荪译作 Never slacken your efforts at your post(在职时,永不懈怠)。【编者按语】钱穆认为"居之,一说居住,一说居心"。韦利释为"居家"似误。

12.14　子张问"政"。子曰:"居①之无倦②;行之以忠。"

① 居:处于,特指处于某种政治职位。
② 无倦:没有懈怠、厌烦。

12.17　Chi K'ang-tzu asked Master K'ung about the art of ruling. Master K'ung said, Ruling (chêng) is straightening (chêng). If you lead along a straight way①, who will dare go by a crooked one?

① "子帅以正",韦利译作 If you lead along a straight way(如果你领导大家走正路)。理雅各译作 If you lead on the people with correctness(如果你带头端正)。辜鸿铭译作 If you yourself, sir, are in order(如果你自己行为正派)。安乐哲译作 If you, Sir, lead by doing what is proper(如果你带头做正确的事)。林戊荪译作 If you set an example by being upright(如果你行为端正,做出榜样)。

12.17　季康子问政于孔子,孔子对曰:"政者,正也,子帅①以正,孰敢不正?"

① 帅:本意为率领,引申为带头。

12.18　Chi K'ang-tzu was troubled by burglars. He asked Master K'ung what he should do. Master K'ung replied saying, If only you were free from desire①, they would not steal even if you paid them to.

① "欲",韦利译作 desire(欲望)。理雅各和林戊荪译作 covetous(贪图他人财物的)。辜鸿铭译作 wish for wealth(贪图财富)。安乐哲译作 greedy(贪婪的)。

12.18　季康子患盗,问于孔子。孔子对曰:"苟子之不欲,虽赏之不窃。"

12.19　Chi K'ang-tzu asked Master K'ung about government, saying, Suppose I were to slay those who have not the Way in order to help on those who have the Way①, what would you think of it? Master K'ung replied saying, You are there to rule, not to slay. If you desire what is good, the people will at once be good. The essence② of the gentleman is that of wind; the essence of small people is that of grass. And when a wind passes over the grass, it cannot choose but bend.

① "杀无道,以就有道",韦利译作 slay those who have not the Way in order to help on those who have the Way(杀死那些无道的人,以激励有道的人)。理雅各译作 killing the unprincipled for the good of the principled(杀死不守规则的人,以利守规则的人)。辜鸿铭译作 putting to do death the wicked in the interests of the good(为了好人的利益而把恶人处死)。安乐哲译作 kill those who have abandoned the Way (dao 道) to attract those who are on it(杀死那些背离了道的人,吸引守道之人)。林戊荪译作 killing those who do not follow the Way so as to move the people closer to those who follow the Way(杀死不走正道的人,以使人们靠拢走正道的人)。

② "德",韦利译作 essence(本质)。辜鸿铭译作 the moral power(道德力)。安乐哲译作 excellence(优秀;卓越)。林戊荪译作 morality(道德)。【编者按语】"君子之德风,小人之德草"理雅各译作 The relation between superiors and inferiors is like that between the wind and the grass(上下级的关系就像风和草的关系)。这一释译对于一贯主张实践字句忠实的理雅各来说,颇不寻常。

12.19　季康子问政于孔子曰:"如杀无道①,以就②有道③,何如?"孔子对曰:"子为政,焉用杀? 子欲善,而民善矣! 君子之德风;小人之德草;草上之风必偃④。"

① 无道:没有道的人。
② 就:成就。
③ 有道:具有道的人。
④ 偃:仰面倒下,此处为倒下。

13.1　Tzu-lu asked about government. The Master said, Lead them①;

encourage them②! Tzu-lu asked for a further maxim. The Master said, Untiringly.

① "先之",韦利译作 lead them(领导他们)。理雅各和辜鸿铭译作 go before the people with your example(用你的榜样,引领人民)。安乐哲和林戊荪译作 set an example yourself(让你自己身先垂范)。

② "劳之",韦利译作 encourage them(鼓励他们)。理雅各译作 be laborious in their affairs(他们做事不遗余力)。辜鸿铭译作 show them your exertion(向他们展示你倾尽全力)。安乐哲译作 urge the people on(鼓励人们前行)。林戊荪译作 the people will work hard(人民会努力劳作)。【编者按语】"劳之"理解的关键在于"谁劳"。一说,统治者"劳",理雅各和辜鸿铭从此说。二说,人民"劳",韦利、安乐哲和林戊荪采用此说。从"先之劳之"的排比结构看,统治者鼓励或督促人民辛苦劳作,此解似更合原意。

13.1　子路问"政"。子曰:"先之,劳①之。"请益。曰:"无倦。"

① 劳:本意为劳动,引申为慰劳。

13.2　Jan Yung, having become steward of the Chi Family, asked about government. The Master said, Get as much as possible done first by your subordinates①. Parden small offences. Promote men of superior capacity. Jan Yung said, How does one know a man of superior capacity, in order to promote him? The Master said, Promote those you know, and those whom you do not know other people will certainly not neglect.

① "先有司",韦利译作 Get as much as possible done first by your subordinates(先让你的下属竭尽全力)。理雅各译作 Employ first the services of your various officers(首要是让你的下属官员尽职尽责)。辜鸿铭译作 Leave the initiative in the details of government to the responsible heads of the department(把治理的细节委托给相关部门的首长,让他发挥主观能动性)。安乐哲译作 set an example yourself for those in office(你应该率先垂范,给属下官员作榜样)。林戊荪译作 set an example for your subordinates(为你的下属做榜样)。

13.2　仲弓为季氏宰,问"政"。子曰:"先有司,赦小过,举贤才。"曰:"焉知贤才而举之?"曰:"举尔所知。尔所不知,人其舍诸①!"

① 舍诸:舍,舍弃;诸,"之乎"合称,"之"代指人才,"乎"表疑问。

13.3　Tzu-lu said, If the prince of Wei were waiting for you to come and administer his country for him, what would be your first measure? The Master said, It would certainly be to correct language①. Tzn-lu said, Can I have heard you aright? Surely what you say has nothing to do with the matter②. Why should language be corrected? The Master said, Yu! How boorish you are! A gentleman, when things he does not understand are mentioned, should maintain an attitude of reserve. If language is incorrect, then what is said does not concord with what was meant; and if what is said does not concord with what was meant, what is to be done cannot be effected. If what is to be done cannot be effected, then rites and music will not flourish. If rites and music do not flourish, then mutilations and lesser punishments will go astray. And if mutilations and lesser punishments go astray, then the people have nowhere to put hand or foot. Therefore the gentleman uses only such language as is proper for speech, and only speaks of what it would be proper to carry into effect. The gentleman, in what he says, leaves nothing to mere chance.

① "正名",韦利译作 correct language(修正语言)。理雅各译作 rectify names(修正名称)。辜鸿铭译作 defining the names of things(定义事物的名称)。安乐哲译作 insure that names properly(正确使用名称)。【编者按语】钱穆和杨伯峻都认为孔子要纠正的是古代礼制、名分上的用词不当,而不是一般的用词不当。

② "迂",韦利译作 Surely what you say has nothing to do with the matter(你的话与说的事八竿子打不着)。理雅各译作 wide of the mark(不着调;不正确)。辜鸿铭译作 too impractical(太不切实际)。安乐哲译作 impractical(不切实际)。林戊荪译作 pedantic(迂腐的)。【编者按语】韦利认为本章的"连锁论证"(chain argument)缺少逻辑意义,只有文学和修辞上的意义。从西方逻辑学角度,各命题之间没有因果关联。这种"连锁论证"的方式在儒家后来的著作中多有存在。韦利因此认为本章是后期掺入。

13.3　子路曰:"卫君①待子为政,子将奚②先?"子曰:"必也正名③乎!"子路曰:"有是哉,子之迂④也!奚其正?"子曰:"野⑤哉,由也!君子于其所不知,盖阙⑥如也。名不正则言不顺,言不顺则事不成,事不成则礼乐不兴,礼乐不兴则刑罚不中⑦,刑罚不中,则民无所措手足。故君子名之必可言也,言之必可行也。君子于其言,无所苟⑧而已矣。"

① 卫君:卫出公,名辄,他的父亲曾被其祖父驱逐出卫国,祖父去世后,其父想要夺回王位,遭到卫出公的反对。此处,子路问的正是此事。

② 奚:什么,哪个。

③ 正名:端正名分。

④ 迂:本意为偏远,此处指绕的太远。子路觉得正名距离政治治理关系太远,故有此说。

⑤ 野:粗鲁。

⑥ 阙：空缺。此处指君子对自己不知道的事情，不加评论。
⑦ 中：不偏不倚，表示刑罚公正。
⑧ 苟：马虎、随意。

13.5　The Master said, A man may be able to recite the three hundred *Songs*; but, if when given a post in the government, he cannot turn his merits to account, or when sent on a mission to far parts he cannot answer particular questions①, however extensive his knowledge may be, of what use is it to him?

① "专对"，韦利译作 he cannot answer particular questions（他不能回答特定的问题）。理雅各译作 he cannot give his replies unassisted（无人一旁协助，他无法正确应答）。辜鸿铭译作 who...has nothing to say for himself（无话为自己辩护）。安乐哲译作 be unable to act on his own initiative（不能发挥主观能动性地工作）。林戊荪译作 incapable of using his own initiative（不能发挥主观能动性地工作）。

13.5　子曰："诵诗三百，授之以政，不达；使于四方，不能专对；虽多，亦奚以为？"

13.11　The Master said, 'Only if the right sort of people had charge of a country for a hundred years would it become really possible to stop cruelty and do away with slaughter①.' How true this saying is!

① "胜残去杀"，韦利译作 stop cruelty and do away with slaughter（停止残忍，废除杀戮）。理雅各译作 transform the violently bad, and dispense with capital punishment（改造好暴烈的坏人，废除死刑）。辜鸿铭译作 they could make deeds of violence impossible and could thus dispense with capital punishment（他们可以使暴力的行为变得不可能，因此可以废除死刑）。安乐哲译作 overcome violence and dispense with killing altogether（克服暴力，完全废除杀戮）。林戊荪译作 cruelty will have been banished and killings will have disappeared（残忍将被去除，杀戮将要消失）。

13.11　子曰："'善人为邦百年，亦可以胜残去杀矣。'诚哉是言也！"

13.12　The Master said, If a Kingly Man were to arise, within a single generation Goodness would prevail.

13.12　子曰："如有王者，必世而后仁。"

13.13　The Master said, Once a man has contrived to put himself aright, he will find no difficulty at all in filling any government post. But if he cannot put himself aright, how can he hope to succeed in putting others right?

13.13 子曰:"苟正其身矣,于从政乎何有? 不能正其身,如正人何?"

13.16 The 'Duke' of Shê asked about government. The Master said, When the near approve and the distant approach.

【编者按语】approve, approach 压头韵。

13.16 叶公问政。子曰:"近者说,远者来。"

13.17 When Tzu-hsia was Warden of Chü-fu, he asked for advice about government. The Master said, Do not try to hurry things. Ignore minor considerations. If you hurry things, your personality will not come into play①. If you let yourself be distracted by minor considerations, nothing important will ever get finished.

① "欲速,则不达",韦利译作 if you hurry things, your personality will not come into play(如果你匆匆忙忙做事,你的能力就不能发挥)。理雅各译作 Desire to have things done quickly prevents their being done thoroughly(快速做完事的意愿会妨碍做事的彻底)。辜鸿铭译作 If you are in a hurry to get things done, things will not be done thoroughly and well(如果你匆匆忙忙做事,事情就不会做得彻底和完美)。安乐哲译作 If you try to rush things, you won't achieve your ends(你如果匆忙做事,就不会达到目标)。林戊荪译作 Haste makes waste(匆忙会导致浪费)。

13.17 子夏为莒父宰。问政。子曰:"无欲速,无见小利。欲速,则不达;见小利,则大事不成。"

Exercises

1. Put the following sentences into English.

1) 5.25 颜渊、季路侍。子曰:"盍各言尔志?"子路曰:"愿车马,衣轻裘,与朋友共,敝之而无憾。"颜渊曰:"愿无伐善,无施劳。"子路曰:"愿闻子之志。"子曰:"老者安之,朋友信之,少者怀之"。

2) 9.12 子贡曰:"有美玉于斯,韫椟而藏诸? 求善贾而沽诸?"子曰:"沽之哉,沽之哉! 我待贾者也"。

3) 15.1 卫灵公问陈于孔子。孔子对曰:"俎豆之事,则尝闻之矣;军旅之事,未之学也。"明日遂行。在陈绝粮,从者病,莫能兴。子路愠见,曰:"君子亦有穷乎?"曰:"君子固穷,小人穷斯滥矣"。

4) 17.1 阳货欲见孔子,孔子不见,归孔子豚。孔子时其亡也,而往拜之,遇诸涂。谓孔子曰:"来!予与而言。"曰:"怀其宝而迷其邦,可谓仁乎?"曰"不可。""好从事而亟失时,可谓智乎?"曰"不可。""日月逝矣,岁不我与。"孔子曰:"诺,吾将仕矣。"

2. Use these statements as topics and debate with your fellow students.

1) Confucius paid much attention to the virtues of a monarch, claiming that it is of prime importance in politics. Do you agree with him?

2) Some people think that the political philosophy of Confucianism has modern relevance. Do you agree to this statement?

Supplementary Reading: Ku Hung-ming as a Translator of Confucian Classics

特出的缺点和隐秘的优点
——辜鸿铭译《论语》《中庸》《大学》

辜鸿铭(1857—1928),名汤生,字鸿鸣,祖籍福建省惠安市,生于南洋英属马来西亚槟榔屿,曾留学英法德,归国后长期为张之洞的幕僚,晚年任教北京大学。辜氏学贯中西,著有英文《中国的牛津运动》(中文名《清流传》)和《中国人的精神》(中文名《春秋大义》)。他的代表性译作有《论语》《中庸》《大学》。其译文均作为本书的参照译文。

辜鸿铭翻译了《四书》中的三部,均在西方出版并产生了较大影响。他的译作引起了两极的评价。褒奖者以林语堂为代表。他在《〈论语〉译英文序》中说:"辜鸿铭先生向以英文译《中庸》,已为众所崇仰。而有《〈论语〉译英文》一书,业已绝版,我留意搜求数年,始由美国国会图书馆借得传抄,知其为精心结构之作,不禁狂喜……英文文字超越出众,200年来未见其右。造词用字皆属上乘"。这不是一般意义上的酬酢谀词。林语堂编译的《孔子的智慧》收录了辜译《中庸》,并作了说明:"下列的所有翻译都是我自己的,只有关于《中庸》的那一章例外。辜鸿铭对该章的翻译是如此的聪明绝妙,同时又是如此的正确和明了"。换言之,辜译简直尽善尽美。贬低者,除了胡适以外,王国维对辜鸿铭的翻译作了声色俱厉的苛评。他认为,辜译有大弊两条。一是"求经义贯穿统一";二是以西释东——"以西洋哲学解释《中庸》。"此外还有小弊若干。王国维对于辜译《中庸》的批评同样适用于后者《论语》和《大学》的翻译,因为辜鸿铭译经之法一以贯之。

按照现代翻译的标准,辜鸿铭英译的缺点特出而刺目。王国维指出的大弊和小弊,言之凿凿,条条有理。事实上,我们再挑出几条大弊小疵也非难事。而辜氏翻译的优点长处却并非如林语堂所言"显而易见",褒奖他的"任何理由都是多余的"。我们认为王国维批评辜译的大弊却正是辜鸿铭翻译的特色甚至优点。现择其大端,缕述如下:

第一,辜鸿铭首开国人外译中国经典以及"以西释东"的先河。在中华国运衰微,中国文化颓势毕现的存亡绝续之际,辜鸿铭将中国文化的核心典籍译成英文,致力于在域外弘扬中国文化,具有重要的历史意义。在辜鸿铭之前,中国经典的外译都是由西方传教士、汉学家承担,在"拿去主义"中,不乏有意无意的误读甚至歪曲贬低。而国人主动"送去主义"自辜鸿铭始。时至今日,中国典籍的"送去主义"浩然成为潮流。辜鸿铭开风气之先,理应铭记。在中国典籍核心术语的翻译中,辜鸿铭"以西洋哲学解释《中庸》",用蕴含西方哲学的 substance, reality, positive, negative 等词去对译。这是当时中国典籍外译的主流做法,辜鸿铭固不能免。但是在随文评点中,辜鸿铭采用了"以西释东"的方式做了平衡。他大量引用了西方哲人,如歌德、阿诺德、康德等人的言论,论证中国经典思想的合理性和权威性。这种另类"格义"也是前无古人的。在中西文化交流中,辜鸿铭虽然尚未明确建立"中西文化互释互证"意识,但在中国文化处于弱势地位的情况下,他的独辟蹊径亦是智勇之举。

第二,辜鸿铭典籍翻译"求经义贯穿统一"是十分有益的对外传播的尝试。借此,他努力呈现中国某部经典暨中国经典整体系统性的思想和理论面貌。众所周知,先秦的中国典籍常常呈现片段零碎的文本面目,对于中国经典在西方的接受和传播十分不利。西方读者习惯了文本中心论点单一突出,论证严密系统的思想内容呈现方式。辜鸿铭学贯中西,洞察了中西文化和思想的这一重要差异,在翻译实践中进行了贯穿统一的诠释尝试。基于其道德本体或本位观,他用伦理学,即以 morality(道德)的词族为核心术语去贯穿统一《论语》《中庸》《大学》的翻译。例如,"和"译为 moral order;"仁"译为 moral sense;"德"为 moral law,等等。从翻译的忠实来看,辜氏的统一的做法,似乎穿凿附会,削足适履,但是从中外文化交流和传播学的角度,我们不能不承认这是十分有益而且成功的尝试。在中国典籍英译的早期代表理雅各的译文中,虽然不乏以基督教神学诠释中国经典的例子,但很难说他是以基督教神学贯穿统一他的中国经典翻译。辜鸿铭或许是最早有意识用某一思想——儒学伦理学——贯穿统一中国经典翻译的人。后来,出现了以历史学、哲学、人类学、文学等贯穿统一中国典籍外译的种种诠释路径。关于中国典籍外译的贯穿统一,我们还会在下面的专题中探讨。

第三,辜鸿鸣有意识地采用了释译的翻译方法。鉴于理雅各翻译文体的厚重少文,辜鸿铭充分发挥了译者的主体性,以"六经注我"的方式对原文进行了大胆的诠释性的翻译,即释译。这体现了在他译文的各个层次——从普通语词、专有名词、核心术语、段落、篇章以及全书篇章的重组。与理雅各释译的浅度相比,辜氏的释译属于深度释译。毋庸讳言,在某些方面和地方,辜鸿铭越过了翻译的边界,对于原文作了过度阐释。辜氏对于中国典籍释译的经验和教训需要进一步深入探讨和记取。关于中国典籍的释译,我们会在下面的专题中探讨。

第四，辜鸿鸣的中国经典翻译是较早以大众读者为目标读者的。辜氏之前的几部《论语》译本都是以传教士、西方来华从业人员、旅行者为目标读者的，其读者人群相当小众。辜鸿铭的目标读者群为"受过教育的英国人""普通英国人""一般英国人"(《英译〈论语〉序》)。西方汉学家普遍有意识为大众读者翻译《论语》暨中国思想典籍，这要等到20世纪中后叶。辜鸿铭大众读者导向的超前意识，难能可贵。

第五，辜鸿铭的中国经典翻译以现实为导向。具体而言，是为西方现实服务的。一般认为，中国思想典籍的外译主要有两个导向：一是面向文本和历史；二是面向理论与现实。而前者是主流。因为典籍是历史的产物，求真常常是这一类翻译的追求。在面向理论和现实导向中，面向现实又属于支流旁门。现实导向意味着翻译是为现实服务的，是为了揭示和解决西方社会和文化的现实难题。辜译中国经典的目的十分明确：以中国传统道德为药方，为现代西方诊病疗伤，为困境中的西方寻求出路。近几十年来，新儒家、西方汉学家和一些哲学家研究译介《论语》暨中国思想经典，揭示和倡扬它们对于当代世界的价值。辜鸿铭早在19、20世纪转换之际，就有此先见之明，也是开风气之先的。

按照今天"忠实""对等"的翻译标准，辜鸿铭《论语》《中庸》《大学》的翻译明显是不达标的。他几乎在翻译的所有层次和方面都不循常理，不守常态——他对于字句忠实的漠视，阐释的过度，等等。他似乎总是在刻意求奇求怪。总而言之，辜鸿铭作为翻译家的缺点是特出的。而其优点长处却一点都不突出，是潜隐于其译文的字里行间和篇章深处的。辜鸿铭又不是一个乐于和善于翻译理论建构的人。对于自己翻译中国经典的做法，他说得很少。对于王国维严苛的翻译批评，他未做只言片语的自我辩护。但是，如果我们能够耐下心来，由其皮求其骨，由其奇求其正，由其文求其理，由其术求其道，则不难从这个晚清怪杰的译文中发现其优点长处，从中汲取中国经典外译和中译外理论的启示。而辜鸿铭译文的优点和启示似乎并不限于本文已经揭示的几条。

Unit Nine
Confucius on "Rites and Music"—Selected Readings of *The Analects of Confucius* (5)

Although it is generally believed that benevolence and righteousness(仁义) are the core ideas of Confucius, it is the civilization of rites and music(礼乐) that Confucius envisioned. This is because, in Confucius' political philosophy, rites and music are thought to be the inevitable path to benevolent government. Rites and music were originally meant to correct the names; i.e. through the practice of rites and music, it is possible to cultivate the love of the superior and the filial piety and fraternity of the inferior, so that the good political order could be maintained. Confucius was considered to be an ardent advocate of restoring rites and music of the Zhou Dynasty, which were lost in his time. Moreover, he was a persistent practitioner of rites and music. Confucius' attitude toward rites and music influenced Confucian attitudes toward rites and music in latter generations. Heated debates arose over conservatism and innovation of rites and music of the Zhou Dynasty in the Chinese history.

Selected Readings of *The Analects of Confucius* (5) and Notes

2.5   Mêng I Tzu asked about the treatment of parents. The Master said, Never disobey①! When Fan Ch'ih was driving his carriage for him, the Master said, Mêng asked me about the treatment of parents and I said, Never disobey! Fan Ch'ih said, In what sense did you mean it? The Master said, While they are alive, serve them according to ritual. When they die, bury them according to ritual and sacrifice them according to ritual.

① "无违",韦利译作 Never disobey!（永远不要违背!）。理雅各译作 It is not being disobedient(孝在于不违命)。辜鸿铭译作 Do not fail in what is required of you(要求你做的,必须做好)。安乐哲译作 Do not act contrary(不做相反的事)。林戊荪译作 Do not go against the rules(不违反规则)。【编者按语】韦利注释说"无违"指 disobey the rituals(不违反礼),而不是"不违反父母之命",与朱熹的注释"不背于理"有相通之处。理雅各与辜

鸿铭的表述都很含糊。

2.5 孟懿子①问孝。子曰:"无违。"樊迟御②,子告之曰:"孟孙问孝于我,我对曰,'无违。'"

樊迟曰:"何谓也?"子曰:"生,事之以礼;死,葬之以礼,祭之以礼。"

① 孟懿子:鲁国人,与孔子同时代,姓仲孙,也称孟孙,名何忌,世称仲孙何忌。"懿"为其谥号。

② 御:驾车。

3.9 The Master said, How can we talk about the ritual of the Hsia? The State of Ch'i supplies no adequate evidence. How can we talk about the ritual of Yin? The State of Sung supplies no adequate evidence. For there is a lack both of documents and of learned men①. But for this lack we should be able to obtain evidence from these two States.

① "文献",韦利译作 documents and learned men(文件和有学问的人)。理雅各译作 records and wise men(档案和智者)。辜鸿铭译作 the literary monuments(不朽的文学作品)。Ames 译作 documentation and men of letters(文献和文人)。林戊荪译作 documentation(文献)。【编者按语】韦利对"夏礼吾能言之"和"殷礼吾能言之"均用问号标点,即"我们无法讨论夏礼殷礼",因为夏殷的后世无法提供足够的文献。而传世本及各注疏均用句号。韦利的诠释独具一格。

3.9 子曰:"夏礼,吾能言之,杞①不足征②也;殷礼吾能言之,宋③不足征也。文献不足故也,足则吾能征之矣。"

① 杞:杞国,在今河南杞县,为夏代后裔所居住的地方。

② 征:证实。

③ 宋:宋国,在今河南商丘,为商代后裔所居住的地方。

3.12 Of the saying, 'The word "sacrifice" is like the word "present"①'; one should sacrifice to a spirit as though that spirit was present' the Master said, If I am not present at the sacrifice, it is as though there were no sacrifice.

① "祭如在",韦利译作 The word "sacrifice" is like the word "present"("祭祀"恰如"在场")。理雅各译作 He sacrificed to the dead, as if they were present(他祭祀死者,就像他们在场一样)。辜鸿铭译作 Confucius worshipped the dead as if he actually felt the presence of the departed ones(孔子敬拜死者,似乎他真的感觉到死者的存在)。安乐哲译作 the expression "sacrifice as though present"("祭如在"这个词语)。林戊荪译作

When the Master offered sacrifice to the dead, he did so as if they were present(当孔夫子向死者致祭时,他当作死者在场)。【编者按语】"祭如在。祭神如神在"有两说。一说,此两句为古语,下文子曰云云是孔子对古语的感慨。韦利和安乐哲从此说。二说,此两句是说孔子临祭时的动作神情。理雅各、辜鸿铭和林戊荪从此说。

3.12 祭如在,祭神如神在。子曰:"吾不与①祭,如不祭。"
① 与:参与。

3.14 The Master said, Chou could survey① the two preceding dynasties. How great a wealth of culture!② And we follow upon Chou.

① "监",韦利译作 survey(全面考察,审议)。理雅各译作 view(考察;探视)。辜鸿铭译作 be founded on(建立在……基础上)。安乐哲译作 look back to(回望)。林戊荪译作 learn from(向……学习)。

② "郁郁乎文哉",韦利译作 How great a wealth of culture!(周文化多么丰富呀!)。理雅各译作 How complete and elegant are its regulations!(周的规则多么健全而典雅呀!)。辜鸿铭译作 How splendidly rich it is in all the arts!(周的文明多么丰富而辉煌呀!)。安乐哲译作 Such a wealth of culture!(周文化是如此之丰富呀!)。林戊荪译作 And how rich its culture!(周的文化多么丰富呀!)

3.14 子曰:"周监①于二代②,郁郁③乎文哉! 吾从周。"
① 监:通"鉴",借鉴。
② 二代:指夏和商两代。
③ 郁郁:文采很盛之貌。

3.15 When the Master entered the Grand Temple he asked questions about everything there. Someone said, Do not tell me that this son of a villager from Tsou is expert in matters of ritual. When he went to the Grand Temple, he had to ask about everything. The Master hearing of this said, Just so! Such is the ritual①.

① "是礼也",韦利译作 Just so! Such is the ritual(恰恰如此! 这才是礼!)。理雅各译作 This is a rule of propriety(这是礼仪规则)。辜鸿铭译作 That is the correct form(那才是正确的做法)。安乐哲译作 to do so is itself observing ritual propriety(这样做本身就是在遵守礼仪)。林戊荪译作 It accords with the rituals to ask questions(提出种种问题就是在遵守礼仪)。

3.15 子入太庙①,每事问。或曰:"孰谓鄹②人之子知礼乎? 入太庙,每事问。"子闻之,曰:"是礼也。"

① 太庙:此处指鲁国国君的祖庙,即供奉周公旦的庙。
② 鄹:孔子出生之地,在今山东曲阜南,又写作"陬"。

3.17　Tzu-kung wanted to do away with the presentation of a sacrificial sheep at the Announcement of each New Moon. The Mater said, Ssu! You grudge① sheep, but I grudge ritual.

① "爱",韦利和安乐哲译作 grudge(爱惜;不情愿给)。理雅各译作 love(爱)。辜鸿铭译作 save(保留;节省)。林戊荪译作 care for, hold dear(关心;珍惜)。

3.17　子贡欲去①告朔②之饩羊③,子曰:"赐也！尔爱④其羊,我爱其礼。"
① 去:废除。
② 告朔:朔,本意指农历每月初一。此处指古代历法,其中包含一年十二个月的主要政治事务。春秋时代,天子在每年冬季颁朔给诸侯,诸侯将其藏之祖庙,至每月的朔日,朝于庙,告而受行之。此处"告朔"就指的是诸侯在庙中告而受行的仪式。
③ 饩羊:作为祭祀的羊。
④ 爱:怜爱。

3.23　When talking to the Grand Master of Lu about music, the Master said, Their music in so far as one can find out about it began with a strict unison①. Soon the musicians were given more liberty; but the tone remained harmonious, brilliant, consistent, right on till the close.

① "翕如也",韦利译作 a strict unison(严格的协奏)。理雅各译作 all the parts should sound together(乐曲的每个部分都应当协奏和声)。辜鸿铭译作 the full volume of sound in the piece should be heard(必须让人听到乐曲的最大音量)。安乐哲译作 playing in unison(同调演奏)。林戊荪译作 the different instruments all join in(不同的乐器协奏)。

3.23　子语①鲁大师②乐,曰:"乐其可知也:始作,翕③如也;从④之,纯⑤如也,皦⑥如也,绎⑦如也,以成。"
① 语:此处作动词,意为告诉。
② 大师:"大"通"太",大师为周代的乐官名称。
③ 翕:合,聚。
④ 从:"从"通"纵",展开,扩展。
⑤ 纯:本意为蚕丝,表示单一丝织品,无杂,此处引申为善好。
⑥ 皦:音节清晰。
⑦ 绎:连续不断。

3.25　The Master spoke of the Succession Dance① as being perfect beauty and at the same time perfect goodness; but of the War Dance as being perfect beauty, but not perfect goodness.

①《韶》,韦利译作 the Succession Dance(禅让乐舞)。理雅各译作 the Shao(韶乐)。辜鸿铭译作 a famous piece of music (the most ancient then known in China) 著名的乐曲(已知中国最古老的乐曲)。安乐哲译作 the Shao music(韶乐)。林戊荪译作 the music Shao(韶乐)。【编者按语】古代文献中专有名词有译音和译意或释意两种方法。理雅各、安乐哲和林戊荪采用了第一种方法。韦利和辜鸿铭采用了第二种方法。韦利注云,韶乐是舜承尧禅让时的乐舞。辜鸿铭用普通名词替代专有名词。

3.25　子谓《韶》①:"尽美矣,又尽善也。"谓《武》②:"尽美矣,未尽善也。"
①《韶》:歌颂舜的一种乐舞。
②《武》:歌颂周武王的一种乐舞。

6.25　The Master said, A gentleman who is widely versed in letters and at the same time knows how to submit his learning to the restraints of ritual is not likely, I think, to go far wrong①.

①"弗畔",韦利译为 is not likely to go far wrong(不太会错得太远)。理雅各译作 not overstep what is right(不逾越正确的规则)。辜鸿铭译作 is not likely to get into wrong track(不太可能误入歧途)。安乐哲译作 remain on course without straying from it(走在正道上,而不偏离)。林戊荪译作 will not go astray(不会误入歧途)。

6.25　子曰:"君子博学于文,约之以礼,亦可以弗畔①矣夫!"
① 畔:通"叛",指背叛。不过此处的背叛非背叛某人,而是指偏离了仁,即所谓的离经叛道。

8.2　The Master said, Courtesy not bounded by the prescriptions of ritual① becomes tiresome②. Caution not bounded by the prescriptions of ritual becomes timidity, daring becomes turbulence, inflexibility becomes harshness. The Master said, When gentlemen deal generously with their own kin, the common people are incited to Goodness. When old dependents are not discarded, the common people will not be fickle.

①"礼",韦利译作 the prescriptions of ritual(礼仪的规定)。理雅各译作 the rules of propriety(礼仪的规则)。辜鸿铭译作 judgement(判断力)。安乐哲译作 observing ritual propriety(遵守礼仪)。林戊荪译作 observing the rituals(遵守礼仪)。

② "劳",韦利译作 tiresome(令人困倦的)。理雅各译作 laborious bustle(累人的忙乱)。辜鸿铭译作 pedantry(迂腐)。安乐哲译作 lethargy(疲倦)。林戊荪译作 tiresome labor(令人疲惫的苦力)。

8.2 子曰:"恭而无礼则劳①;慎而无礼则葸②;勇而无礼则乱③;直而无礼则绞④。君子笃于亲,则民兴于仁。故旧⑤不遗,则民不偷⑥。"

① 劳:费力。
② 葸:恐惧害怕的样子。
③ 乱:危害、混乱。
④ 绞:说话尖刻伤人。
⑤ 故旧:代表老朋友。
⑥ 偷:苟且。

9.3 The Master said, The hemp-thread crown is prescribed by ritual. Nowadays people wear black silk, which is economical; and I follow the general practice①. Obeisance below the daïs is prescribed by ritual. Nowadays people make obeisance after mounting the daïs. This is presumptuous, and though to do so is contrary to the general practice, I make a point of bowing while still down below.

① "从众",韦利和辜鸿铭译作 follow the general practice(遵从普遍的做法)。理雅各译作 follow the common practice(按常规的做法做)。安乐哲译作 follow accepted practice(遵从常规做法)。林戊荪译作 follow the former practice(我遵从过去的做法或旧习)。【编者按语】林戊荪译的"前一种"做法,指戴"麻冕",而不是"纯冕"。据杨伯峻说:"绩麻做礼帽,依照规定,要用二千四百缕经线。麻质较粗,必须织得非常细密,这很费工。若用丝,丝质细,容易织成,因而省俭些。"林认为丝麻贵,故有此误。

9.3 子曰:"麻冕①,礼也;今也纯②,俭;吾从众。拜下③,礼也;今拜乎上,泰④也。虽违众,吾从下。"

① 麻冕:用缁布制作的礼冠。
② 纯:丝。
③ 拜下:指堂下而拜。
④ 泰:傲慢。

12.1 Yen Hui asked about Goodness. The Master said, 'He who can himself submit to ritual① is Good. If (a ruler) could for one day'' himself submit to ritual', everyone under Heaven would respond to his Goodness. For Goodness is something that must have its source in the ruler himself; it cannot be got from others.

Yen Hui said, I beg to ask for the more detailed items[②] of this (submission to ritual). The Master said, To look at nothing in defiance of ritual, to listen to nothing in defiance of ritual, to speak of nothing in defiance of ritual, never to stir hand or foot[③] in defiance of ritual. Yen Hui said, I know that I am not clever; but this is a saying that, with your permission, I shall try to put into practice.

① "礼",韦利和林戊荪译作 ritual(礼仪)。理雅各译作 propriety(礼节;得体)。辜鸿铭译作 the ideal of decency and good sense(得体和常识的理想)。安乐哲译作 ritual propriety(*li* 礼)(礼仪)。【编者按语】"礼"还常译作 rite, ceremony, customs, etiquette, morals, worship, rules of proper behavior。辜鸿铭和安乐哲的译法属于释译。前者属于过度诠释。后者将两个常用译语综合。

② "目",韦利译作 the more detailed items(更详细的事项)。理雅各译作 the steps of that process(那个过程的步骤)。辜鸿铭译作 practical rules to be observed(应当遵循的实际规则)。安乐哲译作 what...entails.(使……成为必要)。林戊荪译作 the essentials(基本要素)。

③ "动"韦利译作 stir hand or foot(动手或动脚)。颇为形象。理雅各译作 make movement(移动)。辜鸿铭译作 act or move(行动或移动)。安乐哲和林戊荪译作 do anything(做任何事)。

12.1　颜渊问"仁"。子曰:"克己复礼[①],为仁。一日克己复礼,天下归仁焉。为仁由己,而由仁乎哉?"颜渊曰:"请问其目[②]?"子曰:"非礼勿视,非礼勿听,非礼勿言,非礼勿动。"颜渊曰:"回虽不敏,请事[③]斯语矣!"

① 克己复礼:克制自己的私人意志和欲求,力图回到礼之中。
② 目:大的项目中分出的小项目。
③ 事:实践,从事。

15.17　The Master said, The gentleman who takes the right as his material to work upon[①] and ritual as the guide in putting what is right into practice, who is modest in setting out his projects and faithful in carrying them to their conclusion, he indeed is a true gentleman.

① "质",韦利译作 material to work upon(做工的质料)。理雅各译作 consider...to be essential(认为……至关重要)。辜鸿铭译作 the substance of his being(他存在的实质)。安乐哲译作 one's basic disposition(人的基本性情)。林戊荪译作 his basic principle(他的基本原理)。

15.17　子曰:"君子义以为质①,礼以行之,孙②以出③之,信以成之;君子哉!"

① 质:本质、基础、根本。
② 孙:通"逊",谦逊。
③ 出:说出。

15.32　The Master said, He whose wisdom brings him into power①, needs Goodness to secure that power. Else, though he get it, he will certainly lose it. He whose wisdom brings him into power and who has Goodness whereby to secure that power, if he has not dignity wherewith to approach the common people, they will not respect him. He whose wisdom has brought him into power, who has Goodness whereby to secure that power and dignity wherewith to approach the common people, if he handles them contrary to the prescriptions of ritual, is still a bad ruler.

① "知及之",韦利译作 He whose wisdom brings him into power(靠智慧获得权位的人)。理雅各译作 When a man's knowledge is sufficient to attain(当人的知识足够使他获得权位)。辜鸿铭译作 There are men who attain knowledge by their understanding(有一些人通过理解力获得知识)。安乐哲译作 When persons come to a realization(当人们意识到)。林戊荪译作 When a man has enough knowledge to attain office(当一个人有足够的知识去做官)。

15.32　子曰:"知及之,仁不能守之;虽得之,必失之。知及之,仁能守之,不庄①以涖②之;则民不敬。知及之,仁能守之,庄以涖之,动之不以礼;未善也。"

① 庄:恭敬。
② 涖:来、到。

20.3　The Master said, He who does not understand the will of Heaven① cannot be regarded as a gentleman. He who does not know the rites cannot take his stand. He who does not understand words, cannot understand people.

① "命",韦利译作 the will of Heaven(上天的意志)。理雅各译作 the ordinances of

Heaven(上天的训令)。辜鸿铭译作 religion(宗教)。安乐哲译作 the propensity of circumstances(大环境;大趋势)。林戊荪译作 destiny(命运)。【编者按语】韦利、理雅各和辜鸿铭均对"命"均做了宗教性解读。安乐哲作了哲学性解读。而林戊荪从杨伯峻的理解,属于人文主义阐释。

20.3 子曰:"不知命①,无以为君子也。不知礼,无以立也。不知言,无以知人也。"

① 命:天命。

Exercises

1. Put the following passage into Chinese.

However, judging on the basis of the *Analects* alone, we find that Confucius exerted great influence on Chinese philosophical development in that, first of all, he determined its outstanding characteristic, namely humanism.

As pointed out in the previous chapter, the humanistic tendency had been in evidence long before his time. But it was Confucius who turned it into the strongest driving force in Chinese philosophy. He did not care to talk about spiritual beings or even about life after death. Instead, believing that "man can make the Way(*Tao*) great", and not that "the Way can make man great", he concentrated on man. His primary concern was a good society based on good government and harmonious human relations. To this end he advocated a good government that rules by virtue and moral example rather than by punishment or force. His criterion for goodness was righteousness as opposed to profit. For the family, he particularly stressed filial piety and for society in general, proper conduct or *li* (propriety, rites).

More specifically, he believed in the perfectibility of all men, and in this connection he radically modified a traditional concept, that of the *chun-tzu*, or superior man. Literally "son of the ruler", it came to acquire the meaning of "superior man", on the theory that nobility was a quality determined by status, more particularly a hereditary position. The term appears 107 times in the *Analects*. In some cases it refers to the ruler. In most cases, however, Confucius used it to denote a morally superior man. In other words, to him nobility was no longer a matter of blood but of character—a concept that amounted to social revolution. Perhaps, it is more correct to say that it was an evolution, but certainly it was Confucius who firmly established the new concept. His repeated mention of Yao and Shun and Duke Chou as models seems to suggest that he was looking back to the past. Be that as it may, he was looking to ideal men rather than to a supernatural being for inspiration.

2. Prepare a 8-minute speech on the social functions of rites and music in Confucianism or the relationship between rites and music and benevolence.

Supplementary Reading: On the Unity Strategy of Translating Chinese Classics

简论中国古代思想典籍外译的"统一"策略
——以《论语》英译为例

中国古代思想典籍的外译有宏观和微观两个重要问题需要把握。微观问题就是我们论述和引述的字句层面话语转换的"释译"。另一个是宏观层面的"统一"问题。这个问题比较隐性,常不为人注意。中国古代思想典籍的统一是指在外译中用一种路径、范式、策略、方法等将源语文本表面上的杂乱无章、漫无头绪统一起来,成为一个较为严整的体系。如是统一,是将中国古代思想典籍的内在体系显示出来,同时又因为体系的完备,便于中国古代思想典籍的域外接受。粗略地说,统一的方式可以分为学术和思想路径的统一、翻译策略和方法的统一、言语类型的统一以及文体风格的统一和传播及目的读者设定的统一。但不限于此。对于中国古代思想典籍的外译,统一至关重要。从某种意义上来说,译本只有可以辨识出某种形式的统一,这样的译作才有学术和思想价值。换言之,中国古代思想典籍外译的译者如果没有统一的意识,没有将之落实到翻译实践。这样的译者无可称述,不会在中国古代思想典籍外译史上留下印迹。因为篇幅的限制,本文仅就中国古代思想典籍外译的学术和思想路径的统一略做阐释。我们以《论语》英译作为例子。

中国古代思想典籍英译旨在英语世界暨域外的传播,以域外读者为目的读者群。因此不能不考虑域外思想暨文本的呈现形态和读者的思维定式和阅读习惯。就英美人的思维方式、话语表达惯例、学术规范而言,一个思想类文本必须有内在及外在的统一性(unity),有一个或多个核心概念或范畴"贯串"其中,构成一个逻辑严密自洽、意义自足的体系(system)。不仅宏大的学派、思想要统一,即使一本书一篇文章,甚至一段话都要统一于一个核心思想或命题。从文本呈现形式来说,作为儒学最高经典的《论语》恰恰缺乏统一性(unity)和体系(system)。《论语》主要由孔子与弟子的对话组成,属于片段式的语录体。以黑格尔为代表的西人对于《论语》以及孔子的偏见,与其文本呈现方式不无关系。

在过去两百年《论语》英译史中,如何将《论语》内在的体系显化,外在的片段性整合统一起来,中西方译者进行过有益的尝试。各派译师,各显神通:柯大卫的神学路径,理雅各的语文学路径,辜鸿铭的道德哲学路径,林语堂和庞德的文学路径,韦利的史学和诗学路径、陈荣捷的中国经学路径,安乐哲、罗斯文的后现代哲学路径,白牧之、白妙之的现代史学路径等等。他们的译本之所以能够成为经典,或者成为《论语》的重要译作,原因是多方面的。我们认为,根本的原因就在于它们鲜明地体现了某一种统一的学术和思想路径。凭借这种统一的体系,这些译作不仅赢得了西方暨域外读者的欢迎,还赢得了西方学术界的认可,更提升了《论语》暨儒学的整体研究水平。

中国思想典籍外译用什么具体的方法和手段实现学术和思想的统一呢? 从《论语》的译史来看,主要有以下几种。一、最极端的方法是拆散原作的篇章,另立主题去统领章句。这样便于整体上把握孔子的思想。较早进行这样大胆尝试的是林语堂。在《孔子的智慧》第五章,他"根据思想性质予以重编"。分立的主题有夫子自述、旁人描写、孔子的感情与艺术生活、谈话的风格、霸气、急智与智慧、人道精神与仁、以人度人、中庸为理想、论为政、论教育、礼与诗。这样的重编凸显了林语堂以孔子其人为中心的文学路径。丁往道的《论语》节译本也采用了主题重编的方法。本书编选《论语》时,也用主题统领章句。二、稍许温和的方法是在副文本中采用主题索引。这样既不破坏原作的文本结构,又用主题为线索予以整合。陈荣捷在《中国哲学原典》中用礼乐、孔子、仁、道、德、正名、人文主义等十九个主题制作了主题索引。他的重编显然有别于林语堂。他用人文主义为核心范畴去统领《论语》和整个中国哲学。近年在中国影响较大的李零的《丧家狗——我读论语》亦可为佐证。除了本书,他专门编写了一个索引的附录。其中最重要的是主题摘录,他列出了天命、人性、人品等十三个主题,以之重编《论语》。《论语》英译副文本的其他诸如人名、地名索引等等,事实上也是统一的方法,构成颇有价值的"小体系"。三、更为常见的方法是通过译文副文本的建构,尤其是长篇学术性导言的撰写,梳理《论语》的思想和理论体系,或建构自己的诠释体系。《论语》英译史中有特色、有成就的译者无不如此——理雅各、韦利、辜鸿铭、林语堂、安乐哲、庞德、罗思文、白氏夫妻。四、还有一种常见的统一方法:《论语》关键词暨核心术语的详释详解以及在译文中的统一贯穿。思想文本的关键词的定义和辨识本身,是学术体系化首要的一步。某些核心术语在译文文本中不断重现,事实上勾连贯穿了某些核心思想,有助于构成体系化的思想和文本。《论语》译本对"仁""礼""义""孝""道""天"等核心术语进行专门阐释已经构成了现代《论语》英译的定规和传统。在此基础上,进行全文统一贯穿是一些译者深思熟虑的选择。辜鸿铭在《论语》暨《大学》《中庸》译文用 morality 的词族构成的核心术语统一贯穿全书,为其道德哲学奠定了最坚实的基础。安乐哲、罗思文综合了核心术语的多种呈现方式。译文中,术语以译语、拼音、汉字全面呈现[如 ritual propriety(li 礼)],并以此方式贯穿全书。虽然有些冗余,但避免了一词多译带来的意义的混乱。他们用 authoritative 词族去翻译"仁",并贯穿统一全文,是其建构《论语》学术体系的重要组成部分,也是其《论语》译本最有特色和辨识度、同时也是最有争议的地方。

对《四书》暨中国古代思想典籍的贯穿统一暨体系化不独外译如此。为了《大学》思想的贯通,理学体系的完整,朱熹增补了部分段落,并调整了《大学》篇章次序。也不独《论语》英译如此。在《大学》英译中,辜鸿铭根据己意重新调整了章句次序,建构了自己的诠释体系。它既不同于古本也不同于今本。在篇章句次序素无争议的《中庸》,他也大胆作出了篇章次序的调整。这也出于辜鸿铭对于译本学术与思想的统一的考量。《四书》暨中国古代思想典籍的贯穿统一暨体系化是外译的重要课题,深入研究有待未来。

Unit Ten
Confucius as a Man—Selected Readings of *The Analects of Confucius* (6)

The reason why Confucianism has been handed down for thousands of years is not simply that *Analects of Confucius* contains a lot of moral lessons, but that Confucius himself was an example of such lessons. In *Analects of Confucius*, there are many insightful sayings that qualify him as "a Teacher for All Ages". The greatness of Confucius' personality lies not only in the fact that he was a gentleman who strictly observed the moral code he promoted, but in the fact that he was always implementing the doctrine of the mean in his conduct, instead of going to extremes. Furthermore, Confucius had all the basic emotions of a human being, but he sublimated them with a Way that allowed him to maintain a calm state of mind in any time of distress, and this is what makes Confucius different from ordinary people. In *Analects of Confucius*, Confucius as a man is not only seen in Confucius' own words, but also in the comments of his disciples and others, both of which can be detected in this unit.

Selected Readings of *The Analects of Confucius* (6) and Notes

2.4　The Master said, At fifteen, I set my heart upon learning. At thirty, I had planted my feet firm upon the ground①. At forty, I no longer suffered from perplexities. At fifty, I knew what were the biddings of Heaven. At sixty, I heard them with docile ear②. At seventy, I could follow the dictates of my own heart; for what I desired no longer overstepped the boundaries of right.

①"而立",韦利译作 I had planted my feet firm upon the ground(我稳稳地立足于地上)。理雅各译作 I stood firm(我稳稳地站着)。辜鸿铭译作 I had formed my opinions and judgment(我已经形成了自己的观点和判断力)。安乐哲译作 I took my stance(我立稳脚跟)。林戊荪译作 I could stand on my own(我能够独立站立或行事)。

②"耳顺",韦利译作 I heard them(the biddings of Heaven) with docile ear(我用顺服的耳朵倾听上天的律令)。理雅各译作 my ear was an obedient organ for the reception of truth(我的耳朵是个驯良的器官,能够接受真理)。辜鸿铭译作 I could understand whatever I heard without exertion(我能够毫无费力地理解我听到的一切)。安乐哲译作 my ear was attuned(我的耳朵已经调节好,准备倾听)。林戊荪译作 I was able to distinguish right from wrong in what other people told me(我能够判断他人所述的是非对错)。

2.4　子曰:"吾十有五而志于学,三十而立①,四十而不惑,五十而知天命,六十而耳顺②,七十而从心所欲不逾矩③。"

① 立:本意是站立,此处应该作为能够独立参与社会生活理解。根据孔子所说:"立于礼。"(《论语·泰伯》),又说:"不知礼,无以立也。"(《论语·尧曰》)可知,礼是培养一个人独立参与社会活动的重要条件。在古代,一个人懂得礼,并且能够合宜地行礼,正标志着一个人可以正式独立参与社会生活,也是一个人成熟的标志。

② 耳顺:古代学者对此词有不同理解,郑玄为代表的一派解释是,能够听到别人语言中的微言大义。另一派以清代焦循为代表,认为顺就是不违,即能够接受与自己不同的意见或一些詈骂之声,无碍于心。

③ 不逾矩:逾,穿过、越过;矩,画直角的工具,引申为法度、准则。

7.2　The Master said, I have listened in silence and noted what was said①, I have never grown tired of learning nor wearied of teaching others what I have learnt. These at least are merits which I can confidently claim②.

① "默而识之",韦利译作 I have listened in silence and noted what was said(我默默地倾听,记住听到的话)。理雅各译作 the silent treasuring up of knowledge(默默地储存知识)。辜鸿铭译作 to mediate in silence(在静默中沉思)。安乐哲译作 to quietly persevere in storing up what is learned(积累学养,默默坚持)。林戊荪译作 to remember what I have learned(记住我学到的知识)。

② "何有于我哉",韦利译作 These at least are merits which I can confidently claim(至少这些是我可以自豪地宣称拥有的优点)。理雅各译作 Which one of these things belongs to me?(上述几点我究竟拥有哪一点呢?)。辜鸿铭译作 Which one of these things can I say that I have done?(上述几件事,我究竟做到了哪一件呢?)。安乐哲译作 Is it not me?(这不就是我吗?)。林戊荪译作 Which of these goals are beyond me?(这些目标哪一个我没有达到呢?)。【编者按语】韦利、安乐哲和林戊荪从孔子"自信、自豪"角度理解,而理雅各和辜鸿铭则从孔子"自谦、自逊"角度理解。

7.2　子曰:"默而识①之,学而不厌②,诲人不倦,何有于我哉?"

① 识:记住。

② 厌:满足。

7.3 The Master said, The thought that 'I have left my moral power(*tê*) untended, my learning unperfected, that I have heard of righteous men, but been unable to go to them①; have heard of evil men, but been unable to reform them'—it is these thoughts that disquiet me.

① "徙",韦利译作 go to them[追随(义人)]。理雅各译作 move towards(趋向)。辜鸿铭译作 act up(积极地做)。安乐哲译作 attend to(忙着去做)。林戊荪译作 practice(实践)。

7.3 子曰:"德之不修,学之不讲,闻义不能徙①,不善不能改,是吾忧也。"

① 徙:迁移,引申为跟从、实践。

7.4 In his leisure hours① the Master's manner was very free-and-easy, and his expression alert and cheerful②.

① "燕居",韦利译作 in his leisure hours(在他的闲暇时分)。理雅各译作 When the Master was unoccupied with business(当夫子不忙于事务时)。辜鸿铭译作 in his disengaged hours(在他空闲的时间里)。安乐哲译作 When relaxing at home(夫子在家放松的时候)。林戊荪译作 During his moments of leisure at home(在他在家空闲的时刻)。【编者按语】"燕居"的英译体现了英语结构表达的丰富性。韦利、辜鸿铭和林戊荪使用了介词短语,而理雅各和安乐哲运用了时间状语从句和其变体(When [he was] relaxing at home)。

② "夭夭如也"韦利译作 his expression alert and cheerful(他的表情警觉而愉悦)。理雅各译作 he looked pleased(他看上去很高兴)。辜鸿铭译作 was always cheerful(总是很愉悦)。安乐哲译作 was good-natured and agreeable(性情温和、令人愉快)。林戊荪译作 appeared cheerful(看上去很愉快)。

7.4 子之燕居①,申申②如也,夭夭③如也。

① 燕居:没有政务的安居状态。
② 申申:申,有延缓,舒张之意,此处指伸腰。
③ 夭夭:放松闲散的状态。

7.5 The Master said, How utterly have things gone to the bad with me!① It is long now indeed since I dreamed that I saw the Duke of Chou.

① "甚矣吾衰也",韦利译作 How utterly have things gone to the bad with me(我的情况变得多么糟糕呀)。理雅各译作 Extreme is my decay(我衰老极了)。辜鸿铭译作 How my mental powers have decayed(我的脑力衰退得多么厉害呀)。安乐哲译作 My how I have regressed(天哪,我衰退到这种程度了)。林戊荪译作 How I have aged(我垂垂老矣)

7.5 子曰:"甚矣,吾衰也! 久矣,吾不复梦见周公①。"

① 周公:姬姓,名旦,周武王的弟弟,为周朝开国功臣。在周武王去世后,由于成王年幼,代为摄政。后平定叛乱,制礼作乐,为周朝的稳固作出了巨大的贡献。后世儒家经常以周公和孔子并称为圣人。

7.6 The Master said, Set your heart upon the Way, support yourself by its power①, lean upon Goodness, seek distractions in the arts.

① "据于德",韦利译作 support yourself by its power[用它(即道)的力量支持自己]。理雅各译作 Let every attainment in what is good be firmly grasped(让每一善的成就都能巩固)。辜鸿铭以为 hold fast to godliness(坚持对神的虔诚之心)。安乐哲译作 sustain yourself with excellence (*de* 德)(用德去强化自己)。林戊荪译作 persist in virtue(坚守德性)。

7.6 子曰:"志于道,据①于德,依②于仁,游于艺③。"
① 据:凭借、占据之意。
② 依:服从、按照之意。
③ 艺:六艺,指礼、乐、射、御、书、数。

7.15 The Master said, He who seeks only coarse food to eat, water to drink and bent arm for pillow, will without looking for it find happiness to boot. Any thought of accepting wealth and rank by means that I know to be wrong① is as remote from me as the clouds that float above.

① "不义",韦利译作 by means that I know to be wrong(用我认为是错误的方式)。理雅各译作 by unrighteousness(通过不义的方式)。辜鸿铭译作 through the sacrifice of what is right(通过牺牲正义的方式)。安乐哲译作 through inappropriate means(通过不合宜的方式)。林戊荪译作 immorally(不道德地)。

7.15 子曰:"饭①疏食②饮水,曲肱③而枕之,乐亦在其中矣。不义而富且贵,於我如浮云。"
① 饭:动词,吃或食用。
② 疏食:疏,粗略、稀疏,此处一般解释为粗粝的食物。
③ 肱:泛指胳膊。

7.18 The 'Duke of Shê' asked Tzu-lu about Master K'ung (Confucius).

Tzu-lu did not reply. The Master said, Why did you not say 'This is the character of the man: so intent upon enlightening the eager that he forgets his hunger, and so happy in doing so, that he forgets the bitterness of his lot① and does not realize that old age is at hand. That is what he is.'

① "忧",韦利译作 the bitterness of his lot(他命运的苦痛)。理雅各译作 his sorrow(他的悲伤)。辜鸿铭译作 his sorrows of life(他生活中忧伤的事)。安乐哲译作 worry(担忧)。林戊荪译作 his worries(他忧心的事)。

7.18 叶公①问孔子于子路,子路不对。子曰:"女奚不曰,其为人也,发愤忘食,乐以忘忧,不知老之将至云尔②。"

① 叶公:沈氏,名诸梁,字子高,为春秋时期著名的政治家。因为后封于叶邑,后人称为叶公。

② 云尔:语气助词,表示如此罢了。

7.20 The Master never talked of prodigies①, feats of strength, disorders or spirits.

① "怪",韦利译作 prodigies(古怪;异象)。理雅各译作 extraordinary things(异常的事物)。辜鸿铭译作 supernatural phenomena(超自然的现象)。安乐哲译作 strange happenings(发生的怪异的事)。林戊荪译作 miracles(奇迹;神迹)。【编者按语】miracles(奇迹;神迹)是基督教常用的语汇。

7.20 子不语怪①,力②,乱③,神④。

① 怪:指怪异之事。
② 力:指武力和权势。
③ 乱:政治上的叛乱。
④ 神:指灵验之事。

7.21 The Master said, Even when walking in a party of no more than three I can always be certain of learning from those I am with. There will be good qualities that I can select for imitation and bad ones that will teach me what requires correction in myself.

7.21 子曰:"三①人行,必有我师焉:择②其善者而从之,其不善者而改之。"

① 三:代表多,非确指。

② 择:挑选。

7.23　The Master said, My friends, I know you think that there is something I am keeping from① you. There is nothing at all that I keep from you. It take no steps about which I do not consult you, my friends. Were it otherwise, I should not be Ch'iu.

①"隐",韦利译作 keep from(隐瞒)。理雅各译作 have any concealment(有所隐瞒)。辜鸿铭译作 have some mysterious powers(有神秘的力量)。安乐哲译作 have something hidden away(有隐而不昭的东西)。林戊荪译作 keep something from you(对你们有所隐瞒)。

7.23　子曰:"二三子①以我为隐②乎?吾无隐乎尔。吾无行而不与二三子者,是丘也。"

① 二三子:子,为古代对男子的尊称。故该词相当于现代所说的诸君。
② 隐:隐藏。

7.24　The Master took four subjects for his teaching: culture, conduct of affairs, loyalty to superiors and the keeping of promises.

7.24　子以四教:文①,行②,忠③,信④。

① 文:此处作为教学方法来说,可理解为一切言教,特别指孔子所说的内容。
② 行:也指孔子的行为。
③ 忠:竭尽全力为学生的学习着想的状态。
④ 信:本意是言语真实,引申为诚实、不欺骗、确证、可靠等。

7.27　The Master said, There may well be those who can do without knowledge; but I for my part am certainly not one of them. To hear much, pick out what is good and follow it, to see much and take due note of it, is the lower of the two kinds of knowledge①.

①"知之次也",韦利译作 is the lower of the two kinds of knowledge(【多闻,多识】是两种知识中较低级的那种)。理雅各译作 this is the second style of knowledge(这是第二种类型的知识)。辜鸿铭译作 that is, perhaps, next to having a great understanding(或许这仅次于拥有杰出的理解力吧)。安乐哲译作 This is a lower level of wisdom(这是较低层次的智慧)。林戊荪译作 Knowledge attained this way is the second best(用这种方式获取的知识是次优的)。【编者按语】"生而知之"是最优,"多闻,多见"属于"学而知之"。故有"次"之说。

7.27 子曰:"盖有不知而作①之者,我无是也。多闻,择其善者而从之,多见而识之,知之次也。"

① 作:指创作,此处特指无凭无据而任意编造。

7.32 The Master said, As far as taking trouble goes, I do not think I compare badly with other people①. But as regards carrying out the duties of a gentleman in actual life, I have never yet had a chance to show what I could do.

① "文莫,吾犹人也",韦利译作 As far as taking trouble goes, I do not think I compare badly with other people(至于不厌其烦,我认为比得上其他人)。理雅各译作 In letters I am perhaps equal to other men(在文艺方面,我或许可以和其他人相比)。辜鸿铭译作 In the knowledge of letters and arts, I may perhaps compare myself with other men(在文艺的知识方面,我或许可以比得上其他人)。安乐哲译作 In the niceties of culture(*wen* 文), I am perhaps like other people(在文化精微的把握上,我也许与他人没有区别)。林戊荪译作 In classics, I am no worse than anyone else(在经典方面,我不比任何人差)。【编者按语】还有另一种断句的方式:文莫,吾犹人也。"文莫"连排,意为"努力"。分而断之,则意为"文化""文化传统""文学"。

7.32 子曰:"文,莫①吾犹人也。躬行君子,则吾未之有得。"

① 莫:朱熹将其解释为疑问词,杨伯峻认为其指"约莫"。不过,莫也有勉强之意,此处若将莫理解为勉强,则同样表达一种谦虚之意。

7.33 The Master said, As to being a Divine Sage or even a Good Man, far be it from me to make any such claim①. As for unwearying effort to learn and unflagging patience in teaching others, those are merits that I do not hesitate to claim. Kung-hsi Hua said, The trouble is that we disciples cannot learn!

① "则吾岂敢",韦利译作 far be it from me to make any such claim(我远远没有权利做如此宣示)。理雅各译作 how dare I *rank myself with them*(我怎么敢与他们相提并论呢?)。辜鸿铭译作 how should I dare to pretend to that(我怎么敢这样自诩呢)。安乐哲和林戊荪译作 How would I dare to consider myself(我怎么敢斗胆认为自己)。

7.33 子曰:"若圣与仁,则吾岂敢!抑为之不厌,诲人不倦,则可谓云尔已矣。"公西华曰:"正唯弟子不能学也。"

8.14 The Master said, He who holds no rank in a State① does not discuss its policies.

① "不在其位",韦利译作 He who holds no rank in a State(在国家机关没有职位的人)。理雅各译作 He who is not in any particular office(没有特定官职的人)。辜鸿铭译作 A man who is not in office in the government of a country(在国家政府中不担任职务的人)。安乐哲译作 an office you do not hold(你没有担任的职位)。林戊荪译作 while not in office(当你不在职的时候)。【编者按语】理雅各和韦利将"不在其位"转换为定语从句,林译为状语从句的变体(相当于 while you are not in office)。安乐哲将"不在其位,不谋其政"译为"Do not plan the policies of an office you do not hold",将"不在其位"译成了修饰性的定语成分。可见,英语表达的丰富性和灵活性。

8.14 子曰:"不在其位,不谋其政。"

9.4　There were four things that the Master wholly eschewed: he took nothing for granted①, he was never over-positive, never obstinate, never egotistic.

① "意",韦利译作 he took nothing for granted(他从不想当然)。理雅各译作 He had no foregone conclusions(他没有先定的结论)。辜鸿铭译作 He was free from self-interest(他杜绝利己)。安乐哲译作 he would not speculate(他不会妄测)。林戊荪译作 He never made groundless speculation(他不会作无依据的推想)。【编者按语】对于古汉语的单字英译,有多种方法。不仅可以用单个英语词对应,还可以译为短语或句子。

9.4　子绝四,毋①意②,毋必③,毋固④,毋我⑤。
① 毋:本意为禁止,此处通"无"。
② 意:猜测或幻想。
③ 必:本意为一定,此处朱熹解释为"期必",指期待一定有所收获。
④ 固:听不进别人的建议和劝导。
⑤ 我:自我。

9.6　The Grand Minister (of Wu?) asked Tzu-kung saying, Is your Master a Divine Sage? If so, how comes it that he has many practical accomplishments? Tzu-kung said, Heaven① certainly intended him to become a Sage; it is also true that he has many accomplishments. When the Master heard of it he said, The Grand Minister is quite right about me. When I was young I was in humble circumstances; that is why I have many practical accomplishments in regard to simple, everyday accomplishments? No, he is in no need of them at all.

① "天",韦利、理雅各和林戊荪均译作 Heaven(天)。辜鸿铭译作 God(上帝)。安乐

哲译作 *tian*(天)。【编者按语】安乐哲认为"天"译作 Heaven 和 God 完全是西方式的理解,去除了中国文化的独特性。所以选择了异化的策略,译音加汉字。

9.6　太宰①问于子贡曰:"夫子圣者与! 何其多能也?"子贡曰:"固②天纵之将圣,又多能也。"子闻之曰:"太宰知我乎? 吾少也贱③,故多能鄙事④。君子多乎哉? 不多也!"

　　① 太宰:周代的官名,主要负责各类典籍、辅佐王治。
　　② 固:本来。
　　③ 贱:指社会身份低贱。
　　④ 鄙事:乡野之人所做的那些事情,泛指卑贱的事务。

10.1　At home in his native village his manner is simple and unassuming①, as though he did not trust himself to speak. But in the ancestral temple and at Court he speaks readily②, though always choosing his words with care.

　　① "恂恂",韦利译作 simple and unassuming(淳朴而自然)。理雅各译作 simple and sincere(简朴而真诚)。辜鸿铭译作 shy and diffident(羞怯)。安乐哲译作 most deferential(极为恭谨)。林戊荪译作 very respectful(很恭谨)。
　　② "便便言"韦利译作 he speaks readily(他自如地说话)。理雅各译作 he spoke minutely on every point(他每一点都详尽地说到)。辜鸿铭译作 he speaks readily(他自如地说话)。安乐哲和林戊荪译作 he spoke articulately(他讲得头头是道)。

10.1　孔子于乡党,恂恂如①也,似不能言者。其在宗庙朝廷,便便②言,唯谨尔。

　　① 恂恂如:温顺恭敬之貌。
　　② 便便:善于言辞之貌。

11.9　When Yen Hui died the Master wailed without restraint①. His followers said, Master, you are wailing without restraint! He said, Am I doing so? Well, if any man's death could justify abandoned wailing, it would surely be this man's!

　　① "哭之恸",韦利译作 wail without restraint(放声痛哭)。理雅各译作 bewail him exceedingly(为他恸哭)。辜鸿铭译作 he cried out in an outburst of grief(他因为巨大的悲痛而放声大哭)。安乐哲译作 grieve for him with sheer abandon(无节制地痛悼)。林戊荪译作 weep bitterly(伤心地痛哭)。

11.9　颜渊死,子哭之恸。从者曰:"子恸①矣!"曰:"有恸乎? 非夫人之为恸而谁为!"

① 恸:大哭,表示极为悲痛。

14.45   Tzu-lu asked about the qualities of a true gentleman. The Master said, He cultivates in himself the capacity to be diligent in his tasks[①]. Tzu-lu said, Can he not go further than that? The Master said, He cultivates in himself the capacity to ease the lot of other people[②]. Tzu-lu said, Can he not go further than that? The Master said, He cultivates in himself the capacity to ease the lot of the whole populace. If he can do that, could even Yao or Shun find cause to criticize him?

① "敬",韦利译作 be diligent in his tasks(忠于职守)。理雅各译作 reverential carefulness(恭谨于事)。辜鸿铭译作 order his conversation aright(言辞谨慎)。安乐哲译作 being respectful(保持恭谨的态度)。林戊荪译作 become respectable(变得令人敬重)。【编者按语】"敬"有两解。一是尊敬,恭敬,敬重。Ames 与林作此理解。二是忠于职守。韦利作此解。理雅各巧妙地用 reverential carefulness 融汇了两种意义。辜鸿铭的翻译属于过度阐释。

② "安人",韦利译作 ease the lot of other people(让其他人时运顺达)。理雅各译作 give rest to others(让其他人休息)。辜鸿铭译作 for the happiness of others(为了他人的幸福)。安乐哲译作 bringing accord to their peers(给同僚带来和谐)。林戊荪译作 bring peace and security to his fellowmen(给自己的同伴带来和平和安全)。【编者按语】"安人"之"人",指政府百官(钱穆),区别于下文的"百姓"。安乐哲的译法最分明。韦利加注"other gentlemen(其他君子)"。理雅各和辜鸿铭的译法不够清晰。林戊荪生造了 fellowmen 以达意。

14.45   子路问君子,子曰:"修己以敬。"曰:"如斯而已乎?"曰:"修己以安人。"曰:"如斯而已乎?"曰:"修己以安百姓。修己以安百姓,尧、舜其犹病[①]诸!"

① 病:困难。

18.5   Chieh Yü, the madman of Ch'u, came past Master K'ung, singing as he went:

Oh phoenix, phoenix

How dwindled is your power!

As to the past, reproof is idle,[①]

But the future may yet be remedied.

Desist, desist!

Great in these days is the peril of those who fill office.

Master K'ung got down, desiring to speak with him; but the madman hastened his step and got away, so that Master K'ung did not succeed in speaking to him.

① "往者不可谏",韦利译作 As to the past, reproof is idle(至于过去,责难是没有效果的)。理雅各译作 As to the past, reproof is useless(至于过去,责难没有用)。辜鸿铭译作 The past, it is useless now to change(过去呀,现在已经无从改变)。安乐哲译作 No use rebuking what has already passed(责难已经过去的事,毫无用处)。林戊荪译作 The past is beyond retrieve(过去已经无法追索)。

18.5 楚狂接舆①歌而过孔子曰:"凤兮!凤兮!何德之衰?往者不可谏,来者犹可追。已而!已而!今之从政者殆②而!"孔子下③,欲与之言。趋而辟之,不得与之言。

① 接舆:陆通,字接舆,春秋时楚国隐士。楚昭王曾重金聘请而不就,后隐居峨眉山。
② 殆:陷入困境。
③ 下:此处指下车。

Exercises

1. Put the following passage into English.

孔子论学习

其一,在学习的态度上,孔子认为追求学问首先在于爱学、乐学。只有好学、乐学,才能真正学好。其次,要有踏踏实实的精神,默默地记住学到的知识,努力学习而永不满足。再次,要专心致志,知难而进。追求学问是一个艰难的过程,读书人要立志于追求道义和真理,要敢于知难而进。再次,要虚心求教,不耻下问,应随时随地注意向他人学习,取人之长,补己之短。

其二,在学习的方法上,孔子主张边学习边将学习的东西用于实践中去检验,在温习旧知识的同时学习新的知识。与此同时,孔子还特强调学思结合,应该把学习积累和钻研思考相结合,二者不能偏废。另外,孔子还非常重视学习上的精益求精,反对一知半解、浅尝辄止。

其三,在学习的内容上,孔子主张在学习专精的基础上要博、要广。他提出要用四种东西作为学习纲要,那就是文化知识、德行修养、忠诚笃厚和坚守信约,这四项内容对于自己和别人都具有重要意义。

其四,对于学习的目的,孔子认为重点在于"学以致用",要注重理论与实践的紧密结合。

2. Prepare a presentation on one of the following topics.

1. Confucius as a man gives people some important inspirations so that they could live a better and more meaningful life.

2. As "a Teacher for All Ages", what distinguishes Confucius from common teachers?

Supplementary Reading: Lin Wusun as a Translator of *The Analects of Confucius*

《论语》英译的"国家标准"与超越"国际标准"的愿景
——林戊荪译《论语》

林戊荪(1928—2021)曾任中国外文局局长、中国翻译工作者协会常务副会长、《北京周报》副总编辑和负责人、《中国翻译》杂志主编,2002年1月被中国译协表彰为"资深翻译家"。代表译作有《孙子兵法》《论语》。林氏被誉为我国当代翻译以及中外文化交流事业的杰出代表。

20世纪90年代之后,《论语》在中国经典外译中是热点中的热点,已出版了20多个英译本,而且每隔一两年都有新的译本问世。找出其中代表性的译作并不容易。在许渊冲和林戊荪的权衡中,几经考虑,我们还是选择了后者的译本。林译是本书《论语》英译的参照文本。

选择林戊荪,不仅仅是因为他显赫的行政、文化、学术地位,还在于他的译本代表了当代中国《论语》英译的最高水平,更在于他的译作在当代中国《论语》的翻译中具有代表性。从某种意义上,林氏的译作是《论语》暨中国思想经典外译的国家标准。用它做标准,国内同期同类译作的是非得失和水平高低的估量,就有了相对客观的标准。与英美译者代表的国际水平相比,中国大陆一代译者的特点和优缺点都可以凸显出来。

首先,林氏确定了《论语》暨中国思想经典外译总体文本构架即体例的国家标准。林译正文本包括文言中英文对照,各篇概要和章句脚注。林译副文本包括双序(他序和自序)、长篇绪论、索引(包括历史人物、孔子弟子、术语)。绪论内容丰富,包括六项:一、孔子其人;二、《论语》及孔子的思想;三、孔子、苏格拉底和耶稣;四、孔子与其思想的重要影响;五、孔子的弟子;六、《论语》中的主要术语。与同时期许多中国译本相比,林氏的译文体例较为科学而完备。绪言还表明他有着清晰而强烈的跨文化传播意识和中西文化比较自觉。林氏确定了《论语》翻译体例的国家标准不是谁规定的，也不是其行政和学术地位使然，而是这一体例符合中外文化传播的规律和中国思想经典外译的规律，还与理雅各创设、久已确定和公认的中国思想经典外译的国际标准体例基本吻合。

其次，林氏的翻译方法、翻译文体体现了国家标准，具有很强的代表性。他的翻译方法可以概括为语文性翻译。也就是说，特别重视章句字面的翻译。他采用的是现代英语的标准书面语。他的翻译依据着标准的工具书和语法手册。语汇及术语的选择和句式的安排都体现了高度的标准性。简言之，在翻译的准确度、地道性、流畅性上，林译达到了国内30年来《论语》英译的最高水平。林氏贡献了一个标准译本，无愧于他当代中国翻译"国手"的身份。

再次，林氏对孔子、孔子思想和孔子影响的诠释体现了中国对外文化交流或对外宣传口径和尺度的标准性。他在绪论中强调孔子的"和为贵""和而不同""道并行而不悖"的思想，由此阐发了多元文化和平共处、和谐社会和和谐世界的文化理念。这是当代中国对外文化交流的主旋律。林氏一生从事中国官方的对外文化交流和政治宣传，其专业和职业身份在《论语》的诠释和翻译中留下明确的痕迹，这是十分自然的事。《论语》在英语国家的翻译主要是学术研究导向的。林氏的对外文化交流导向，是有其合法性和合理性的。在中国对外文化交流或对外宣传上，也是有必然性和必要性的。

林氏《论语》译文的标准同时意味着译者个人的隐身。他对《论语》思想的诠释和价值的确认，代表了中国主流社会和官方的口径，几乎看不到他个人对于孔子和《论语》的见解。另外，林译《论语》在学术性和文艺性上也存在着缺失。国际汉学界在20世纪90年代之后《论语》翻译的新一轮高潮中，学术性得到了极大的强化。孔子暨《论语》思想的诠释新的研究进路和新的见解不时出现，达到了相当高的学术水平，已经可以和中国学术界平等对话。而林译以及同期的大多数中国《论语》译本依然停留在推敲章句的语文翻译的层次，对孔子暨《论语》思想研究古今中外极为丰厚的积淀重视和利用不够。还有，林译虽然正确、流畅、地道，但缺少情感的渗透。《论语》表达了孔子及其弟子宁静、愤怒、哀伤、无奈、兴奋等各种情感和情绪，这些在林译和中国其他译本中没有能够充分而恰如其分地表现出来。《论语》的语气或从容舒缓或急促有力，而前者是《论语》语气的主流，需要细品慢嚼的夫子之言，林译常常以急促的语气表达出来，似乎夫子不能已于言。在文体文质方面，同样看不到精心的经营和精妙的调和。这不仅是林氏译文的不足，在许渊冲以及其他众多的中国译者中也是一个普遍的现象。

《论语》英译始自1809年马什曼的节译本，迄今已经有了两百多年的历史。20世纪90年代之前，《论语》的翻译主要由西方汉学家承担。虽有辜鸿铭、林语堂等中国译者参与其事，但只是配角。自20世纪90年代，中国以及英美同时展开了《论语》英译的新一轮高潮。英美译者贡献了十多个译本,而中国译者贡献几乎多了一倍,其中还有林戊荪的优秀译作,这是一件十分可喜的文化事件。《论语》暨中国思想经典外译终于从西方"拿去主义"变成了东方主动的"送去主义"。这体现了中国文化复兴的潮流和中国文化的自信。中国的诸多《论语》译本虽然存在着这样那样的缺点,然而,我们有信心,《论语》暨中国思想经典外译未来可以做得更好,超越"国际标准"的愿景一定能够早日实现。

Unit Eleven
The Great Learning (1)

As the first book of *Four Books*, *The Great Learning* (《大学》) was originally a chapter of *Book of Rites*. When Zhu Xi was compiling *Four Books and Annotations*, *The Great Learning* gained a status of its own and was officially listed as a primary Confucian classic alongside *The Analects of Confucius*, *Mencius* and *The Doctrine of the Mean*. Among *Four Books*, *The Great Learning* is considered an introduction to Confucianism. It is not due to its simplicity, but due to its advocation of "Three Programs and Eight Steps". It presents the phases and goals of learning Confucianism, being a guidebook for beginners. Zhu Xi said: "*The Great Learning* gives the full scale of self-cultivation and governance" and "It is a grand classic of bringing peace to the world and initiating the scheme of learning". In the Southern Song Dynasty, Confucian scholars paid even greater attention to *The Great Learning*. Zhu Xi was revising the annotations of *The Great Learning* in his last days. The Ming Confucian, Wang Yangming's thought of Extending Conscience("致良知") is said to come from *The Great Learning*.

The following text is based on the translation of Wing-Tsit Chan, coupled with reference translations by James Legge, Ku Hung-ming, Andrew Plaks and Lin Yutang.

The Great Learning (1) and Notes

Chu Hsi's Remark. Master Ch'eng I said, "*The Great Learning* is a surviving work of the Confucian school and is the gate through which the beginning student enters into virtue. It is only due to the preservation of this work that the order in which the ancients pursued their learning may be seen at this time. The *Analects* and the *Book of Mencius* are next to it. The student should by all means follow this work in his effort to learn, and then he will probably be free from mistakes."

子程子[①]曰:"《大学》,孔氏之遗书,而初学入德之门也。"于今可见古人为学次第者,独赖此篇之存,而《论》《孟》次之。学者必由是而学焉,则庶乎其不差矣。

The Text

The Way of learning to be great (or adult education) consists in manifesting the clear character[②], loving the people[③], and abiding (*chih*) in the highest good[④].

Only after knowing what to abide in can one be calm. Only after having been calm can one be tranquil. Only after having achieved tranquility[⑤] can one have peaceful repose[⑥]. Only after having peaceful repose can one begin to deliberate. Only after deliberation can the end be attained. Things have their roots and branches. Affairs have their beginnings and their ends. To know what is first and what is last will lead one near the Way.

① 《大学》,陈荣捷(Wing-Tsit Chan)、理雅各(James Legge)及他人多译作 The Great Learning(伟大的学问)。辜鸿铭译作 Higher Education(高等教育)。林语堂译作 Ethics and Politics(伦理学和政治学)。浦安迪(Andrew Plaks)译作 Ta Hsueh, The Highest Order of Cultivation(最高层次的修养)。

② "明德",陈荣捷译作 the clear character(清明的品格)。理雅各译作 illustrious virtues(杰出的德行)。辜鸿铭译作 intelligent(明)moral power(德)of our nature(人性颖悟的道德力)。林语堂译作 clear character(清明的德行)。浦安迪译作 the light of one's inner moral force(人的内在道德力之光)。【编者按语】辜鸿铭和浦安迪突出了天生的道德(moral)属性。

③ "亲民",陈荣捷译作 loving the people(爱人)。理雅各据程颐译作 renovate the people(新民)。辜鸿铭译作 make a new and better society(造就一个更好的社会)。林语堂译作 give new life to the people(赋予人民新的生命)。浦安迪译作 bringing the people to a state of renewal(使人处于更新的状态)。【编者按语】辜鸿铭作了创造性阐释。林语堂的翻译近于口语。

④ "止于至善",陈荣捷译作 abiding (*chih*) in the highest good(止于至善)。理雅各译作 rest in the highest excellence(止于最高的卓越)。辜鸿铭译作 abide in the highest excellence(安顿于最高的卓越)。林语堂译作 dwell(or rest)in perfecting, or the ultimate good(安定于完美或终极的善)。浦安迪译作 coming to rest in the fullest attainment of the good(在达到至善时才停顿下来休息)。

⑤ "静",陈荣捷和理雅各译作 tranquility(宁静)。辜鸿铭译作 peace and tranquility of mind(内心的平和安宁)。林语堂译作 calmness of mind(内心的平静)。浦安迪译作 an unruffled quietude(镇定自若)。

⑥"安",陈荣捷、理雅各和林语堂译作 peaceful repose(宁静;沉静;安详;从容)。辜鸿铭译作 peace and tranquility 或 serenity of soul(灵魂的平静和静穆)。浦安迪译作 an inner calm(内心的宁静)。【编者按语】"静"辜鸿铭译作 mind,"安"译作 soul,似神来之笔。

大学之道②,在明明德③,在亲民④,在止于至善⑤。知止而后有定,定而后能静,静而后能安,安而后能虑,虑而后能得。物有本末,事有终始。知所先后,则近道矣。

① 子程子:前一个"子"表示老师,后一个"子"是对于人的敬称。此处"程子"指的是北宋著名理学家程颐。

② 大学:此处特指成就大人之学。

③ 明明德:第一个"明"为动词,使……彰明,后一个"明"是形容词,鲜明的。整个句意为"使鲜明的德性得到彰显"。

④ 亲民:程颐认为,"亲"当作"新",使民众自我革新之意。

⑤ 至善:圆满的好。

The ancients who wished to manifest their clear character to the world would first bring order to their states. Those who wished to bring order to their states would first regulate their families①. Those who wished to regulate their families would first cultivate their personal lives. Those who wished to cultivate their personal lives would first rectify their minds②. Those who wished to rectify their minds would first make their wills sincere③. Those who wished to make their wills sincere would first extend their knowledge④. The extension of knowledge consists in the investigation of things. When things are investigated, knowledge is extended; when knowledge is extended, the will becomes sincere; when the will is sincere, the mind is rectified; when the mind is rectified, the personal life is cultivated; when the personal life is cultivated, the family will be regulated; when the family is regulated, the state will be in order; and when the state is in order, there will be peace throughout the world.

① "齐家",陈荣捷和理雅各译作 regulate their families(管理好家庭)。辜鸿铭译作 put their houses in order(使家庭井然有序)。林语堂译作 regulate their family life(管理好家庭生活)。浦安迪译作 put their royal houses into proper balance(使王室井然有序)。【编者按语】浦安迪认为《大学》的目标读者为王室成员,因有此译。

② "正心",陈荣捷译作 rectify their minds（正心）。理雅各译作 rectify their hearts（调整内心情绪）。辜鸿铭译作 put their minds in a proper and well-ordered condition（让心灵处于井然有序的状况）。林语堂译作 set their hearts right（正心）。浦安迪译作 set straight the seat of their emotive and cognitive faculties（调整好情感和认知功能）。【编者按语】mind 强调理智,heart 强调情感。"心"在其他场合还可以译作 soul（灵魂）或者 spirit（精神）。

③ "诚其意",陈荣捷和林语堂译作 make their wills sincere（诚其意志）。理雅各译作 be sincere in thoughts（思虑诚实）。辜鸿铭译作 have true ideas（有真正的主意）。浦安迪译作 achieve a state of integral wholeness in the inner depths of their consciousness（在意识的纵深处达到整合的境界）。【编者按语】will 强调意志,thought 强调思想, idea 强调具体的想法。

④ "致知",陈荣捷译作 extend their knowledge（扩展知识）。理雅各译作 extend to the outmost their knowledge（将知识扩展至极致）。辜鸿铭译作 acquire knowledge and understanding（获得知识和理解）。林语堂译作 acquire true knowledge（获得真正的知识）。浦安迪译作 expand to the utmost their range of comprehension（将理解力扩展至极致）。

古之欲明明德于天下者,先治其国。欲治其国者,先齐其家①。欲齐其家者,先修其身②。欲修其身者,先正其心。欲正其心者,先诚其意。欲诚其意者,先致其知③。致知在格物④。物格而后知至,知至而后意诚,意诚而后心正,心正而后身修,身修而后家齐,家齐而后国治,国治而后天下平。

① 齐其家:使得为父者尽父道,为子者尽子道,如此为齐于道。

② 修其身:对于身之本来的朴拙之状态加以修饰,使其具有文明之象。

③ 致其知:获得知识。

④ 格物:朱熹认为格物致格为动词,作推究理解。而物一般指世间一切可以把握的对象的泛称。由于《大学》中没有对此具体解释,不同注释家理解颇有分歧,此处亦不加详引。

From the Son of Heaven① down to the common people②, all must regard cultivation of the personal life as the root or foundation③. There is never a case when the root is in disorder and yet the branches④ are in order. There has never been a case when what is treated with great importance becomes a matter of slight importance or what is treated with slight importance becomes a matter of great importance.

Chu Hsi's Remark. The above is the text in one chapter. It is the words of Confucius, handed down by Tseng Tzu. The ten chapters of commentary which follow are the views of Tseng Tzu and were recorded by his pupils. In the traditional version there have been some mistakes in its arrangement. Now follows the new version fixed by Master Ch'eng I, and in addition, having examined the contents of the text, I(Chu Hsi) have rearranged it as follows:

① "天子",陈荣捷和浦安迪译作 the Son of Heaven(天子)。理雅各、辜鸿铭和林语堂译作 emperor(皇帝)。

② "庶人",陈荣捷译作 the common people(普通人)。理雅各译作 the mass of the people(百姓)。辜鸿铭译作 the lowest of the common people(百姓中最低位的人)。林语堂译作 the common men(普通人)。浦安迪译作 the simplest commoner(头脑最简单的普通人)。

③ "本",陈荣捷和林语堂译作 root or foundation(根或基础)。理雅各译作 root(根)。辜鸿铭译作 foundation(基础)。浦安迪译作 the 'roots' at its core(核心之根)。

④ "末",陈荣捷译作 the branches(树枝)。理雅各译作 what should spring from it(源于它的物)。辜鸿铭译作 That which is built on it(建基于它的物)。林语堂译作 upshoot or superstructure(结果或上层建筑)。浦安迪译作 the peripheral 'branches'(边缘的枝杈)。

【编者按语】"末"理雅各和辜鸿铭二人均使用了以一个名词性从句去对应。林语堂和浦安迪译为一个单词。还有一个选择,用名词性短语。

自天子以至于庶人,壹是皆以修身为本。其本乱而末治者否矣。其所厚者薄,而其所薄者厚,未之有也①!

*右②经③一章,盖孔子之言,而曾子④述之。其传十章,则曾子之意而门人记之也。旧本颇有错简,今因程子所定,而更考⑤经文,别为序次如左⑥:

① 厚薄:厚薄为反义词,厚有深、多、重等意,引申为重要的;而薄则具有浅、少、轻等意,引申为不重要的。

② 右:因古代书写习惯为上下直书,从右到左推进,故右,即指当前文字前面的内容。相应地,左指的是当前文字后面的内容。

③ 经:权威性典籍的称谓。

④ 曾子:字子舆,鲁国人,孔子的重要弟子之一。

⑤ 考:有多义,此处用作动词,指考察、检查。

⑥ 如左:等同于今日所谓的"如下文所示"。

*此句为朱熹所加,其后相同句式,皆为朱熹所增补,不再注解。

Chapters of Commentary

1. In the "Announcement of K'ang" it is said, "He was able to manifest his

clear character." In the "T'ai-chia" it is said, "He contemplated the clear Mandates of Heaven①". In the "Canon of Yao" it is said, "He was able to manifest his lofty character. These all show that the ancient kings manifested their own character."

Chu Hsi's Remark. The above first chapter of commentary explains manifesting the clear character.

① "明命",陈荣捷译作 the clear Mandates of Heaven(上天的明命)。理雅各译作 ordinance which lighted on it(照亮它的神谕)。辜鸿铭译作 the clear Ordinance of God(上帝之明命)。林语堂译作 clear mandates of Heaven(上天的明命)。浦安迪译作 the shining decree of Heaven(天的明亮的命令)。

《康诰》①曰:"克明德。"《大甲》②曰:"顾③諟④天之明命。"《帝典》⑤曰:"克明峻德⑥。"皆自明也。

＊右传⑦之首章,释明明德。

＊此段为朱熹所增补。后文所有标注＊的内容段落均为朱熹所增补内容,非《大学》原有内容。后文不再说明。

①《康诰》:《尚书·周书》中的一篇。
②《大甲》:即《太甲》,《尚书·商书》中的一篇。
③ 顾:顾念。
④ 諟(shì):此。
⑤《帝典》:《尧典》,是《尚书·虞书》中的一篇。
⑥ 克明峻德:《尧典》原句为"克明俊德"。"俊"与"峻"通,本意为峻峭之貌,引申为高大、尊崇之意。
⑦ 传:指对经文的解释文字,此为朱熹分章的结论,非《大学》原本之意。

2. The inscription on the bath-tub of King T'ang read, "If you can renovate yourself one day, then you can do so every day, and keep doing so day after day." In the "Announcement of K'ang", it is said, "Arouse people to become new①." The *Book of Odes*② says, "Although Chou is an ancient state, the mandate it has received from Heaven is new." Therefore, the superior man③ tries at all times to do his utmost [in renovating himself and others].

Chu Hsi's Remark. The above second chapter of commentary explains the renovating of the people.

3. The *Book of Odes* says, "The imperial domain of a thousand *li* is where

the people stay (*chih*)." The *Book of Odes* also says, "The twittering yellow bird rests (*chih*) on a thickly wooded mount." Confucius said, "When the bird rests. it knows where to rest. Should a human being be unequal to a bird?"

① "作新民",陈荣捷译作 arouse people to become new（唤醒人民做新人）。理雅各译作 to stir up the new people（让新的人民振作）。辜鸿铭译作 create a new society（创造一个新社会）。林语堂译作 become a new nation（成为新民族）。浦安迪译作 bring about the renewal of the people（带来人民的更新）。

② 《诗经》,陈荣捷译作 The Book of Odes（民谣集）。理雅各译作 The Book of Poetry（诗歌集）。辜鸿铭和林语堂译作 The Book of Songs（歌曲集）。浦安迪译作 the Songs（歌曲集）。

③ "君子",陈荣捷和理雅各译作 the superior man（上等人士）。辜鸿铭和林语堂译作 gentleman（绅士）。浦安迪译作 the man of noble character（品行高贵的人）。【编者按语】"君子"也有译作 the higher classes（上层人士）,prince（王子）,ruler（统治者）的。

汤①之《盘铭》②曰:"苟日新,日日新,又日新。"《康诰》③曰:"作新民。"《诗》④曰:"周虽旧邦,其命惟新。"是故,君子无所不用其极。⑤

* 右传之二章。释新民。

《诗》⑥云:"邦畿⑦千里,惟民所止。"《诗》⑧云:"缗蛮⑨黄鸟,止于丘隅。"子曰:"于止,知其所止,可以⑩人而不如鸟乎！"

① 汤:指商朝的开国君主汤。

② 盘铭:盘上所刻文字。

③ 《康诰》:《尚书·周书》中的一篇。

④ 《诗》:此指《诗经·大雅·文王》。

⑤ 无所不用其极:该词现多用于贬义,而此处指君子为了实现尽善尽美的事业,竭尽所能,各方面追求达到极致。

⑥ 《诗》:此指《诗经·商颂·玄鸟》。

⑦ 畿(jī):指王都所统辖的千里地域。

⑧ 《诗》:此指《诗经·小雅·缗蛮》。

⑨ 缗(mín)蛮:鸟叫声。

⑩ 可以:何以,表示为什么。

The *Book of Odes* says, "How profound was King Wen! How he maintained his brilliant virtue without interruption and regarded with reverence that which he abided (*chih*)." As a ruler, he abided in humanity①. As a minister, he abided in reverence. As a son, he abided in filial piety②. As a father, he abided in deep love. And in dealing with the people of the country, he abided in faithfulness.

The *Book of Odes* says, "Look at that curve in the Ch'i River. How luxuriant and green are the bamboo trees there! Here is our elegant and accomplished prince. [His personal life is cultivated] as a thing is cut and filed and as a thing is carved and polished. How grave and dignified! How majestic and distinguished! Here is our elegant and accomplished prince. We can never forget him!" "As a thing is cut and filed" refers to the pursuit of learning③. "As a thing is carved and polished" refers to self-cultivation④. "How grave and how dignified" indicates precaution⑤. "How majestic and distinguished" expresses awe-inspiring appearance. "Here is our elegant and accomplished prince. We can never forget him" means that the people cannot forget his eminent character and perfect virtue.

① "仁",陈荣捷译作 humanity(仁慈)。理雅各和林语堂译作 benevolence(仁慈)。辜鸿铭译作 love mankind(爱人类)。浦安迪译作 human kindness(仁慈)。

② "孝",陈荣捷、理雅各和林语堂译作 filial piety(孝道)。辜鸿铭译作 be a dutiful son(做一个尽责的儿子)。浦安迪译作 filial respect(孝敬)。

③ "学",陈荣捷译作 the pursuit of learning(学术追求)。理雅各译作 the work of learning(学习的劳作)。辜鸿铭译作 improve his knowledge(提升知识水平)。林语堂译作 polish his scholarship(提升学术水平)。浦安迪译作 the process of cultivation(修养的过程)。

④ "自修",陈荣捷译作 self-cultivation(自修)。理雅各译作 self-culture(自我修养)。辜鸿铭译作 make himself perfect(自我完美)。林语堂译作 cultivation of his character(品格的养育)。浦安迪译作 the perfection of the individual self(自我的完善)。

⑤ "恂栗",陈荣捷译作 precaution(预防;警惕)。理雅各译作 cautious reverence(敬畏)。辜鸿铭译作 seriousness of his mind(思维严肃)。林语堂译作 fear and caution(恐惧和谨慎)。浦安迪译作 fear and trembling(害怕和战栗)。

《诗》①云:"穆穆②文王,於③缉熙④敬止⑤!"为人君,止于仁;为人臣,止于敬;为人子,止于孝;为人父,止于慈;与国人⑥交,止于信。

《诗》⑦云:"瞻彼淇澳,菉竹猗猗。有斐⑧君子,如切如磋⑨,如琢如磨⑩。瑟⑪兮僩⑫兮,赫⑬兮喧⑭兮。有斐君子,终不可谖兮!"如切如磋者,道学也;如琢如磨者,自修也;瑟兮僩兮者,恂栗⑮也;赫兮喧兮者,威仪也;有斐君子,终不可谖⑯者,道盛德至善,民之不能忘也。

①《诗》:此指《诗经·大雅·文王》。

② 穆穆:"穆"通"睦",庄严之貌。

③ 於(wū):叹词。

④ 缉熙:逐渐地变得明亮,后引申为光明。

⑤ 止:助词,无意义。

⑥ 国人:指居住在国城之内的人,与郊人或野人相对。

⑦《诗》:此指《诗经·卫风·淇澳》。

⑧ 斐:有光采的,文雅的。

⑨ 切、磋:切,即切割,磋即磋光,此处指对象牙之类的骨进行切割磋光,加工成成品。

⑩ 琢、磨:琢,即雕琢,磨,即打磨,主要指对玉石进行加工,使其成为成品。

⑪ 瑟:矜庄貌。

⑫ 僩(xiàn):威严。

⑬ 赫:显明、盛大的样子。

⑭ 喧:威仪显赫。

⑮ 恂(xún)慄:矜严恭敬。

⑯ 谖(xuān):忘记。

The *Book of Odes* says, "Ah! the ancient kings[①] are not forgotten." [Future] rulers[②] deemed worthy what they deemed worth and loved what they loved, while the common people[③] enjoyed what they enjoyed and benefited from their beneficial arrangements. That was why they are not forgotten even after they passed away.

Chu Hsi's Remark. The above third chapter of commentary explains abiding in the highest good.

4. Confucius said, "In hearing litigations[④], I am as good as anyone. What is necessary is to enable people not to have litigations at all." Those who would not tell the truth will not dare to finish their words, and a great awe would be struck into people's minds[⑤]. This is called knowing the root.

Chu Hsi's Remark. The above fourth chapter of commentary explains the root and the branches.

① "前王",陈荣捷和林语堂译作 the ancient kings(古代的国王)。理雅各和辜鸿铭译作 the former kings(先前的王)。浦安迪译作 the Former Kings(先前的王)。

② "君子",陈荣捷译作[Future] rulers(未来的统治者)。理雅各和林语堂译作 future princes(未来的王)。辜鸿铭译作 the higher classes(上层阶级,上层人士)。浦安迪译作 the man of noble character(品行高贵的人)。

③"小人",陈荣捷、理雅各和林语堂译作 the common people(普通人)。辜鸿铭译作 the lower classes(下层阶级,下层人士)。浦安迪译作 the man of mean character(品行卑劣的人)。

④"听讼",陈荣捷、理雅各和浦安迪译作 hear litigations(审判官司)。辜鸿铭译作 decide lawsuits(决定诉讼)。林语堂译作 preside over lawsuits(主持诉讼)。

⑤"大畏民志",陈荣捷译作 a great awe would be struck into people's minds(让民众深怀敬畏)。理雅各译作 a great awe would be struck into men's mind(让民众深怀敬畏)。辜鸿铭译作 Watch therefore with fear and trembling over the hearts of the people.(因此要以敬畏和恂栗的态度看待民心)。林语堂译作 Thus the people are inspired with a great respect or fear(因此人们得以心存敬畏)。浦安迪译作 instil awe for justice in the hearts of the people(把对正义的敬畏灌输到人民心理)。【编者按语】多数译者的理解是"让民众敬畏"。只有辜鸿铭理解成"敬畏民众"。他的诠释符合现代政治"民主"的观念。

《诗》①云:"于戏(wūhū)②!前王③不忘!"君子贤其贤而亲其亲,小人乐其乐而利其利,此以没世不忘也。

* 右传之三章。释止于至善。

子曰:"听讼④,吾犹人也,必也使无讼乎!"无情者不得尽其辞。大畏民志,此谓知本。

* 右传之四章。释本末。

① 《诗》:此指《诗经·周颂·烈文》。
② 于戏(wūhū):感叹词。
③ 前王:指的是周文王和周武王。
④ 听讼:字面意为听取诉讼,即审理法律案件的活动。孔子曾任司空,即执掌司法事务,故有此说。

Exercises

1. Put the following passage into English.

《大学》之书,古之大学所以教人之法也。盖自天降生民,则既莫不与之以仁义礼智之性矣,然其气质之禀或不能齐,是不能皆有以知其性之所有而全之也。一有聪明睿智能尽其性者出于其间,则天必命之为亿兆之君师,使之治而教之,以复其性。此伏羲、神农、黄帝、尧舜所以继天立极,而司徒之职、典乐之官所由设也。

三代之隆,其法寖备,然后王宫、国都以及闾巷,莫不有学。人生八岁,则自王公以下,至于庶人之子弟,皆入小学,而教之以洒扫、应对、进退之节,礼乐、射御、书数之文;及其十有五年,则自天子之元子、众子,以至公、卿、大夫元士之适子,与凡民之俊秀,皆入大学,而教之以穷理、正心、修己、治人之道。此又学校之教、大小之节所以分也。

2. Discussion and composition.

1) Based on your study of this unit, please explain the relationship between "the Three Programs".

2) "Daxue" was translated into "The Great Learning", "Higher Education", "Ethics and Politics", "The Highest Order of Cultivation". Comment on these renditions.

Supplementary Reading: Wing-Tsit Chan: a Translator of Chinese Classics

身份视角下的华人的中国思想典籍英译
——陈荣捷编译《中国哲学文献选编》

陈荣捷(Wing-Tsit Chan,1901—1994),广东人。美籍华人学者、哲学史家、朱子学专家。1929年获哈佛大学哲学博士学位。前后任岭南大学、中山大学、夏威夷大学、达特茅斯学院、哥伦比亚大学教授。主编《东西方哲学》。代表性译作有《道德经》《近思录》《传习录》《六祖坛经》。编译有《中国哲学文献选编》(A Source Book in Chinese philosophy)。本书的《大学》以其英译为底本,以其《中庸》为参照文本。

身份理论已经被广泛应用于社会学、心理学、文学等各个领域,而用于翻译研究尚不多见。本文以身份理论为视角,论述陈荣捷的文化身份和专业职业身份对其中国古代思想典籍翻译的影响。而二者事实上又缠夹在一起,区分开来更多是为了讨论的方便。

第一,陈荣捷的中国文化身份决定了他对儒学暨中国哲学研究和翻译采取了护教弘教的立场。陈荣捷生长在中国,在中国完成了系统的中国传统文化训练。后来他留学美国,并加入了美国国籍。他的国籍身份虽然发生了变化,但是他的中国文化身份并未改变,甚至进一步凸显。陈荣捷的中国文化身份体现在他对于中国文化的高度认同和挚爱。这使得他的中国哲学的研究和翻译具有了独特的风貌,不同于西方汉学界的前辈和同辈。对于理雅各、韦利、安乐哲等西方汉学家来说,他们虽然一生致力于中国文化的翻译和研究。但是他们依然是西方文化本位的,把中国文化当作文化他者。他们的中国文化译介和研究主要是出于异质知识探寻,更多客观中立的学术立场。而陈荣捷、辜鸿铭、林语堂以及当代中国大陆的译者对于中国传统文化常常具有高度的认同和挚爱,把中国文化的域外传播和弘扬视为神圣的使命和不朽之盛业。陈荣捷1936年赴美工作生活。在将近60年的时间里,他将全部心血投入到美国的中国哲学的教学、研究和翻译。美国在二战前和战后初期,学术界都不重视儒学,尤其是理学。陈荣捷是北美大陆的儒学的拓荒者。

他最早在美国大学建立了中国哲学较为完备的教学体系。他最早在美国组织中国哲学的学术会议,他最早参与创办中国哲学的学术期刊《东西方比较哲学》。经过陈荣捷以及同好者的不懈努力,至1970年代,风气为之一变。以哥伦比亚大学和哈佛大学为中心,理学和新儒家的研究蔚为大观。1977年,陈荣捷先生海外教学40年纪念时,他曾作诗三首。兹录其二。

  海外教研四秩忙,攀缠墙外望升堂。
  写作唱传宁少睡,梦也周程朱陆王。
  廿载孤鸣沙漠中,而今理学忽然红。
  义国恩荣固可重,故乡苦乐恨难同。

  这首诗形象地概述了他在北美儒学沙漠中的筚路蓝缕和对于中国文化的魂牵梦萦。

  第二,陈荣捷的专业职业身份又直接影响了他译介的范围和方法。如果说文化身份隐性地影响他译介的话,他的专业职业身份直接影响着译介的每一个方面。陈荣捷的专业是中国哲学,具体而言是儒学,他尤其专长于宋明理学的研究。他的职业身份是大学哲学系的教授。他的专业训练和素养和职业职守为他的翻译的高水平提供了可靠的学术保障和各种便利。这具体体现在以下几个方面。首先,陈荣捷为儒学暨中国哲学正名。长期以来,中国古代思想是否属于哲学,西方一直有争议。在《中国哲学原典》的导言中,他旗帜鲜明地提出中国儒学属于哲学,其特色是以人文主义为本位;孔子为中国哲学确定了方向和特殊的述学方式;宋明理学是儒学暨中国哲学集大成的高峰。多亏陈荣捷及其同仁的努力,对儒学暨中国哲学的哲学学科身份的质疑越来越少。至20世纪80年代,中国哲学在西方可谓登堂入室。其次,他拓宽西方儒学暨中国哲学的广度和深度。一方面,他译介了中国哲学,尤其是宋明理学的专书《近思录》《传习录》。众所周知,英美汉学在很长一段时间,译介的重点以先秦典籍为主,陈荣捷的翻译大大拓展了研究的广度和深度。另一方面,他又耗费了巨大的心力编译了《中国哲学原典》。这部卷帙浩繁、体大虑周的著作为西方学术界提供了中国哲学历朝历代的代表性文献。如果说冯友兰编写的《中国哲学简史》(英文版)第一次用国际通用语言把中国哲学的历史演进细致地进行了梳理和符合西方学术规范的呈现,陈荣捷的这部著作为西方学界提供了丰富的第一手文献。二者在中国文化哲学儒学走向世界的历程中,堪称两个重要的里程碑。再次,陈荣捷的译介融汇中国传统学术和西方现代学术的方法和进路。他的译作一般都有长篇绪论、章节主旨、主题索引、译者按语。译作注释全面而详尽。《中国哲学原典》积译者十余年之功,全书共44章。所有的条目、名词、术语都有解释,所有引文皆有出处,注释多达三千余条。最后,陈荣捷的翻译确定了华人学者翻译的规范。他依仗华人对儒学暨中国古代思想典籍的深厚功底,对中国文献清仓查库,竭泽而渔。这种资料工夫是西方汉学家很难企及的。另外,他广泛参考借鉴前贤的翻译。以《四书》英译为例,他广泛地参考了理雅各、韦利、辜鸿铭、林语堂等人的翻译成果。他或择善而从或综合前贤的翻译,而不是刻意的求新求异。作为以求真为最高宗旨的学者,陈荣捷不追求译文风格的艺术性。他的厚重少文的风格,很接近理雅各。而在学术深度和专业性,则超过理雅各。他的中国哲学经典翻译成就令西人认可,国人折服。在论述《中国哲学原典》的翻译时,著名学者陈来认为"该书开创了很高的中文翻译标准,至今仍无人超越"。

在中国哲学走向世界的过程中,作为华人学者的陈荣捷在北美作出了开拓性的工作,学界赞誉他为"把东方哲学文化思想最为完备地介绍到西方的中国大儒"(陈来)。

Unit Twelve
The Great Learning (2)

The Great Learning has a special significance among *Four Books*. Because the other three books include a collection of sayings and conversations from Confucius and Mencius, there is no rigorous structure and no apparent ideological system. However, *The Great Learning* has a structure and a system, which present the overall body and learning order of Confucianism with the "Three Programs and Eight Steps" at the core. The Eight Steps are the basic conditions or elements for the realization of the Three Programs. In other words, the goal of the Eight Steps is to achieve the Three Programs. Therefore, they form a relationship of end and means.

The Great Learning (2) and Notes

5. This is called knowing the root①. This is called the perfecting of knowledge②.

   Chu Hsi's Remark. The above fifth chapter of commentary explains the meaning of the investigation of things and the extension of knowledge which is now lost. I have ventured to take the view of Master Ch'eng I and supplement it as follows: The meaning of the expression "The perfection of knowledge depends on the investigation of things (*ko-wu*)" is this: If we wish to extend our knowledge to the utmost, we must investigate the principles③ of all things we come into contact with, for the intelligent mind of man④ is certainly formed to know, and there is not a single thing in which its principles do not inhere. It is only because all principles are not investigated that man's knowledge is incomplete. For this reason, the first step in the education of the adult is to instruct the learner, in regard to all things in the world, to proceed from what knowledge he has of their principles, and investigate further until he reaches the limit. After exerting himself in this way for a long time, he will one day achieve a wide and far-reaching penetration⑤. Then the qualities of all things, whether internal or external, the refined or the coarse, will all be apprehended, and the mind, in its total substance and great functioning, will be perfectly intelligent. This is called the investigation of things. This is called the perfection of knowledge.

① "知本",陈荣捷和理雅各译作 knowing the root(知道根本)。辜鸿铭译作 That is the root of matter in knowledge(那就是知识的根本)。林语堂译作 know the root (or bottom) of things(知道事情的根本或底细)。浦安迪译作 understanding the fundamental core of moral cultivation(了解道德修养的根本)。

② "知之至也",陈荣捷译作 the perfecting of knowledge(知识的完善)。理雅各译作 the perfection of knowledge(知识的完善)。辜鸿铭译作 the highest knowledge(最高的知识)。林语堂译作 achieving true knowledge(or wisdom)(获得真正的知识或智慧)。浦安迪译作 the full attainment of understanding(透彻的理解)。

③ "理",陈荣捷和理雅各译作 principle(原理)。浦安迪译作 the intrinsic principles(内在原则)。

④ "人心之灵",陈荣捷和理雅各译作 the intelligent mind of man(人的灵心)。浦安迪译作 the innate intelligence of the human mind(人心内在的智慧)。

⑤ "豁然贯通",陈荣捷和理雅各译作 far-reaching penetration(深广的渗透)。浦安迪译作 a completely unobstructed flash of penetrating insight(灵光乍现,大彻大悟)。

此谓知本。此谓知之至也。

＊右传之五章,盖释格物、致知之义,而今亡矣。闲尝窃取程子之意以补之曰:"所谓致知在格物者,言欲致吾之知,在即物①而穷其理②也。盖人心之灵莫不有知,而天下之物莫不有理,惟于理有未穷,故其知有不尽也。是以大学始教,必使学者即凡天下之物,莫不因其已知之理而益穷之,以求至乎其极。至于用力之久,而一旦豁然贯通焉,则众物之表里精粗无不到,而吾心之全体大用无不明矣。此谓物格,此谓知之至也。"

＊此段为朱熹所增补。辜鸿铭和林语堂未采纳,未翻译。

① 即物:即,靠近、根据。该词表示根据事物。

② 穷其理:穷,穷尽;理,道理。

6. What is meant by "making the will sincere" is allowing no self-deception,

as when we hate a bad smell or love a beautiful color. This is called satisfying oneself①. Therefore the superior man will always be watchful over himself when alone. When the inferior man② is alone and leisurely, there is no limit to which he does not go in his evil deeds. Only when he sees a superior man does he then try to disguise himself, concealing the evil and showing off the good in him. But what is the use? For other people see him as if they see his very heart③. This is what is meant by saying that what is true in a man's heart will be shown in his outward appearance. Therefore the superior man will always be watchful over himself when alone. Tseng Tzu said, "What ten eyes are beholding and what ten hands are pointing to—isn't it frightening?" Wealth makes a house shining and virtue④ makes a person shining. When one's mind is broad and his heart generous, his body becomes big and is at ease. Therefore the superior man always makes his will sincere.

Chu Hsi's Remark. The above sixth chapter of commentary explains the sincerity of the will.

① "自谦",陈荣捷译作 satisfying oneself(自我满足)。理雅各译作 self-enjoyment(自我陶醉)。辜鸿铭译作 self-detachment(自我超脱)。林语堂译作 satisfy your own conscience(遵从自己的良知)。浦安迪译作 being at ease with oneself(自我安适)。

② "小人",陈荣捷译作 inferior man(地位低的人)。理雅各译作 the mean man(卑鄙的人)。辜鸿铭译作 immoral man(不道德的人)。林语堂译作 the common man(普通人)。浦安迪译作 the man of mean character(品行低下的人)。【编者按语】陈荣捷翻译的 inferior man 与上句 superior man 呼应,似更好。

③ "肺肝",陈荣捷译作 his very heart(心本身)。辜鸿铭和理雅各译作 his heart and veins(心和血管)。林语堂译作 heart(心)。浦安迪译作 his very lungs and liver(自身的肺肝)。

④ "德",陈荣捷与理雅各译作 virtue。辜鸿铭译作 moral quality(道德品质)。林语堂译作 character(品质)。浦安迪译作 inner moral force(内在的道德力)。

所谓诚其意者:毋自欺也,如恶恶臭,如好好色,此之谓自谦①,故君子必慎其独也! 小人闲居为不善,无所不至,见君子而后厌然②,掩其不善,而著其善。人之视己,如见其肺肝然,则何益矣。此谓诚于中,形于外③,故君子必慎其独也。曾子曰:"十目所视,十手所指,其严乎!"富润屋,德润身,心广体胖,故君子必诚其意。

* 右传之六章。释诚意。

① 自谦:谦,读为慊(qiè),通"惬",表示满足。朱熹认为,"谦,快也,足也"。"自谦"为自足。

② 厌然:此字多通"猒"(yàn),意为满足。引申为嫌恶、厌恶。

③ 诚于中,形于外:内心的真实想法表现为身体的相应行为。

7. What is meant by saying that cultivation of the personal life depends on the rectification of the mind is that when one is affected by wrath① to any extent, his mind will not be correct. When one is affected by fear to any extent, his mind will not be correct. When he is affected by fondness to any extent, his mind will not be correct. When he is affected by worries and anxieties, his mind will not be correct. When the mind is not present, we look but do not see, listen but do not hear, and eat but do not know the taste of the food. This is what is meant by saying that the cultivation of the personal life depends on the rectification of the mind.

Chu Hsi's Remark. The above seventh chapter of commentary explains the rectification of the mind in order to cultivate the personal life.

① "忿懥",陈荣捷译作 wrath(狂怒)。辜鸿铭和理雅各译作 passion(激情)。林语堂译作 anger(愤怒)。浦安迪译作 animosity and resentment(敌意和愤恨)。

所谓修身在正其心①者,身有所忿懥②,则不得其正;有所恐惧,则不得其正;有所好乐,则不得其正;有所忧患,则不得其正。心不在焉,视而不见,听而不闻,食而不知其味。此谓修身在正其心。

* 右传之七章。释正心修身。

① 正其心:使心得到端正。

② 忿懥:忿,意为悁、怒,即情绪急躁愤怒。懥,也表示怒气。

8. What is meant by saying that the regulation of the family depends on the cultivation of the personal life is this: Men are partial① toward those for whom they have affection and whom they love, partial toward those whom they despise and dislike, partial toward those whom they fear and revere②, partial toward those whom they pity and for whom they have compassion, and partial toward those whom they do not respect③. Therefore there are few people in the world who know what is bad in those whom they love and what is good in those whom they

dislike. Hence it is said, "People do not know the faults of their sons and do not know (are not satisfied with) the bigness④ of their seedlings." This is what is meant by saying that if the personal life is not cultivated, one cannot regulate his family.

Chu Hsi's Remark. The above eighth chapter of commentary explains the cultivation of the personal life in order to regulate the family.

① "辟",陈荣捷和理雅各译作 be partial towards(偏心)。辜鸿铭译作 be biased towards(偏见)。林语堂译作 lose their sense of judgement(失去判断力)。浦安迪译作 incline toward(偏向)。

② "畏敬",陈荣捷译作 fear and revere(畏敬)。理雅各译作 stand in awe and reverence(处于敬畏状态)。辜鸿铭译作 despise and dislike(蔑视和憎恶)。林语堂译作 fear(害怕)。浦安迪译作 hold in awe and respect(敬畏)。

③ "敖堕",陈荣捷译作 do not respect(不尊敬)。理雅各译作 they are arrogant and rude(他们傲慢粗鲁)。林语堂译作 pamper or are proud(宠溺或骄傲)。浦安迪译 arrogance or indifference(傲慢或漠视)。

④ "硕"陈荣捷译作 bigness(大)。理雅各和辜鸿铭译作 richness(丰富)。林语堂译作 the imperceptible growth(难以觉察的生长)。浦安迪译作 the eventual size(最终的尺寸)。

所谓齐其家在修其身者:人之其所亲爱而辟①焉,之其所贱恶而辟焉,之其所畏敬而辟焉,之其所哀矜②而辟焉,之其所敖惰③而辟焉。故好而知其恶,恶而知其美者,天下鲜矣!故谚有之曰:"人莫知其子之恶,莫知其苗之硕。"此谓身不修不可以齐其家。

* 右传之八章。释修身齐家。

① 辟(pì):摒除。
② 矜:爱惜、怜惜。
③ 惰:不敬、怠慢。

9. What is meant by saying that in order to govern the state it is necessary first to regulate the family is this: There is no one who cannot teach his own family and yet can teach others. Therefore the superior man (ruler) without going beyond his family, can bring education into completion in the whole state. Filial piety is that with which one serves his ruler. Brotherly respect① is that with which one serves his elders, and deep love② is that with which one treats the multitude.

The "Announcement of K'ang" says, "Act as if you were watching over an infant." If a mother sincerely and earnestly looks for what the infant wants, she may not hit the mark but she will not be far from it. A young woman has never had to learn about nursing a baby before she marries. When the individual families have become humane[3], then the whole country[4] will be aroused toward humanity. When the individual families have become compliant, then the whole country will be aroused toward compliance. When one man is greedy or avaricious, the whole country will be plunged into disorder. Such is the subtle, incipient activating force of things[5]. This is what is meant by saying that a single word may spoil an affair and a single man may put the country in order. (Sage emperors) Yao and Shun led the world with humanity and the people followed them. (Wicked kings) Chieh and Chou led the world with violence and the people followed them. The people did not follow their orders which were contrary to what they themselves liked. Therefore the superior man must have the good qualities in himself before he may require them in other people. He must not have the bad qualities in himself before he may require others not to have them. There has never been a man who does not cherish altruism (*shu*) in himself and yet can teach other people. Therefore the order of the state depends on the regulation of the family.

The Book of Odes says, "How young and pretty is that peach tree! How luxuriant is its foliage! This girl is going to her husband's house. She will rightly order her household." Only when one has rightly ordered his household can he teach the people of the country. *The Book of Odes* says, "They were correct and good to their elder brothers. They were correct and good to their younger brothers." Only when one is good and correct to one's elder and younger brothers can one teach the people of the country. *The Book of Odes* says, "His deportment[6] is all correct, and he rectifies all the people of the country." Because he served as a worthy example as a father, son, elder brother, and younger brother, therefore the people imitated him. This is what is meant by saying that the order of the state depends on the regulation of the family.

  Chu Hsi's Remark. The above ninth chapter of commentary explains regulating the family to bring order to the state.

  ① "弟",陈荣捷译作 brotherly respect(兄弟般的尊重)。理雅各译作 fraternal

submission(弟对兄的服从)。辜鸿铭译作 the duties of subordination in the family(家庭成员中服从的义务)。浦安迪译作 brotherly devotion(兄弟情深)。

②"慈",陈荣捷译作 deep love(深沉的爱)。理雅各和林语堂译作 kindness(仁爱)。辜鸿铭译作 the kindness of a father to his children(父亲对儿女的慈爱)。浦安迪译作 parental love(父母之爱)。

③"仁",陈荣捷译作 become humane(变得仁慈)。理雅各译作 the loving example(慈爱的榜样)。辜鸿铭译作 kindness and humanity(仁慈和人道)。林语堂译作 kindness(仁慈)。浦安迪译作 human kindness(人的仁慈)。

④"国",陈荣捷译作 the whole country(整个国家)。理雅各译作 state(国家)。辜鸿铭和林语堂译作 nation(国民)。浦安迪译作 the entire realm(全部领地)。

⑤"机"陈荣捷译作 the subtle, incipient activating force of things(万物精微的初始启动力)。理雅各译作 the nature of influence(影响的性质)。辜鸿铭译作 the power of influence(影响力)。林语堂译作 the law of things(万物的规则)。浦安迪译作 the hinge upon which all human affairs revolve(人类事务据之旋转的"铰链")。【编者按语】浦安迪的翻译与众不同。他将"机"字修辞化了。这是翻译的深化或美化。

⑥"仪",陈荣捷、理雅各、浦安迪及林语堂均译作 deportment(风度)。辜鸿铭译作 manners(仪态;举止)。

所谓治国必先齐其家者,其家不可教而能教人者,无之。故君子不出家而成教于国:孝者,所以事君也;弟者,所以事长也;慈者,所以使众也。《康诰》曰:"如保赤子",心诚求之,虽不中不远矣。未有学养子而后嫁者也!

一家仁,一国兴仁;一家让,一国兴让;一人贪戾①,一国作乱;其机如此。此谓一言偾②事,一人定国。尧舜帅天下以仁,而民从之;桀纣帅天下以暴,而民从之;其所令反其所好,而民不从。是故君子有诸己而后求诸人,无诸己而后非诸人。所藏乎身不恕,而能喻诸人者,未之有也。故治国在齐其家。

《诗》③云:"桃之夭夭④,其叶蓁蓁⑤;之子于归⑥,宜其家人。"宜其家人,而后可以教国人。《诗》云:"宜兄宜弟。"宜兄宜弟,而后可以教国人。《诗》云:"其仪不忒,正是四国。"其为父子兄弟足法,而后民法之也。此谓治国在齐其家。

* 右传之九章。释齐家治国。

① 贪戾:贪求无度、横征暴敛。
② 偾(fèn):破坏。
③《诗》:此指《诗经·周南·桃夭》。
④ 夭夭:植物生长茂盛艳丽之貌。

⑤ 蓁蓁(zhēn):浓密的样子。
⑥ 归:古代将妇女出嫁称为归。

10. What is meant by saying that peace of the world depends on the order of the state is this: When the ruler① treats the elders with respect, then the people will be aroused toward filial piety. When the ruler treats the aged with respect, then the people will be aroused toward brotherly respect. When the ruler treats compassionately the young and the helpless, then the common people will not follow the opposite course. Therefore the ruler has a principle with which, as with a measuring square②, he may regulate his conduct. What a man dislikes in his superiors, let him not show it in dealing with his inferiors③; what he dislikes in those in front of him, let him not show it in preceding those who are behind; what he dislikes in those behind him, let him not show it in following those in front of him; what he dislikes in those on the right, let him not apply it to those on the left; and what he dislikes in those on the left, let him not apply it to those on the right. This is the principle of the measuring square.

① "上",陈荣捷译作 ruler(统治者)。理雅各译作 sovereign(君主)。辜鸿铭和林语堂译作 those in authority(当权者)。浦安迪译作 those in superior positions(上级)。

② "絜矩",陈荣捷与理雅各译作 measuring square(量角器)。辜鸿铭和林语堂译作 self-measuring rule(自我衡量的准则)。浦安迪译作 the carpenter's square(木匠的三角尺)。

③ "下",陈荣捷、林语堂与理雅各译作 inferiors(下级)。辜鸿铭译作 those who are under him(地位比他低的人)。浦安迪译作 one's subordinates(inferiors)(下级)。

所谓平天下在治其国者:上老老①而民兴孝,上长长而民兴弟,上恤孤而民不倍②,是以君子有絜矩③之道也。所恶于上,毋以使下;所恶于下,毋以事上;所恶于前,毋以先后;所恶于后,毋以从前;所恶于右,毋以交于左;所恶于左,毋以交于右。此之谓絜矩之道。

① 老老:第一个"老"做动词,使……成为老,字面意思是使老人成为老人,即尊敬老人之意。其后,"长长"与此类似。
② 倍:通"背",有背离、背叛之意。
③ 絜矩:法度、规则。

The Book of Odes says, "How much the people rejoice in their prince①, a parent of the people!" He likes what the people like and dislikes what the people dislike. This is what is meant by being a parent of the people. *The Book of Odes* says, "Lofty is the Southern Mountain! How massive are the rocks! How majestic is the Grand Tutor Yin (of Chou)! The people all look up to you!" Thus rulers of states should never be careless. If they deviate from the correct path, they will be cast away by the world. *The Book of Odes* says, "Before the rulers of the Yin (Shang) dynasty lost the support of the people, they could have been counterparts of Heaven. Take warning from the Yin dynasty. It is not easy to keep the Mandate of Heaven"②. This shows that by having the support of the people, they have their countries, and by losing the support of the people, they lose their countries. Therefore the ruler will first be watchful over his own virtue. If he has virtue, he will have the people with him. If he has the people with him, he will have the territory. If he has the territory, he will have wealth. And if he has wealth, he will have its use. Virtue is the root, while wealth is the branch. If he regards the root as external (or secondary) and the branch as internal (or essential), he will compete with the people in robbing each other. Therefore when wealth is gathered in the rulers hand, the people will scatter away from him; and when wealth is scattered [among the people], they will gather round him. Therefore if the ruler's words are uttered in an evil way, the same words will be uttered back to him in an evil way; and if he acquires wealth in an evil way, it will be taken away from him in an evil way. In the "Announcement of K'ang" it is said, "The Mandate of Heaven is not fixed or unchangeable." The good ruler gets it and the bad ruler loses it. In *the Book of Ch'u* it is said, "The State of Ch'u does not consider anything as treasure; it considers only good [men] as treasure. Uncle Fan (maternal uncle to a prince of Chin in exile) said, 'Our exiled prince has no treasure; to be humane toward his parents is his only treasure.'"

① "乐只君子",陈荣捷译作 How much the people rejoice in their prince(人民多么热爱他们的王呀!)。理雅各译作 How much to be rejoiced in these princes(王多么受人民热爱呀!)。辜鸿铭译作 How the people love the prince(人民多么热爱王呀!)。林语堂译作 How the people are pleased with their ruler(人民多么喜欢他们的王呀!)。浦安迪译作 Joy be unto that prince among men(愿快乐降临到人民的王)。

② "峻命",陈荣捷与林语堂译作 the Mandate of Heaven(天命)。理雅各译作 the

great decree(伟大的命令)。辜鸿铭译作 the Great High Mission(至高至大的使命)。浦安迪译作 the great Mandate(伟大的命令)。

《诗》①云:"乐只②君子,民之父母。"民之所好好之,民之所恶恶之,此之谓民之父母。

《诗》③云:"节④彼南山,维⑤石岩岩⑥,赫赫⑦师尹⑧,民具尔瞻⑨。"有国者不可以不慎,辟则为天下僇矣。

《诗》⑩云:"殷之未丧师⑪,克配上帝;仪监于殷,峻⑫命不易。"道得众则得国,失众则失国。是故君子先慎乎德。有德此有人,有人此有土,有土此有财,有财此有用。德者本也,财者末也,外本内末,争民施夺。是故财聚则民散,财散则民聚。是故言悖而出者,亦悖而入;货悖而入者,亦悖而出。《康诰》曰:"惟命不于常!"道善则得之,不善则失之矣。《楚书》⑬曰:"楚国无以为宝,惟善以为宝。"舅犯⑭曰:"亡人⑮无以为宝,仁亲以为宝。"

① 《诗》:此指《诗经·小雅·南山有台》。
② 乐只:乐,愉悦;只,助词,无意义。
③ 《诗》:此指《诗经·小雅·节南山》。
④ 节:通"截",高耸之貌。
⑤ 维:发语词,无意义。
⑥ 岩岩:本意是山高,引申为险峻之貌。
⑦ 赫赫:赫,本意为火赤色,有显耀、光明之意,此处叠词为显著盛大。
⑧ 师尹:师,指太师,周代的三公(此根据《周礼》而来,以为太师、太傅、太保为三公。而据《礼记》等书,认为三公指司马、司徒、司空)之一;尹,尹氏,曾为太师。故后世用师尹代指三公。
⑨ 具尔瞻:具,通"俱";尔,你。瞻,瞻仰。
⑩ 《诗》:此指《诗经·大雅·文王》。
⑪ 师:本意为军队之编制,二千五百人为师。引申为众人。
⑫ 峻:崇高、伟大。
⑬ 《楚书》:楚昭王时编写的楚国史书。
⑭ 舅犯:晋文公重耳的舅舅,名狐偃,字子犯,简称为"舅犯"。
⑮ 亡人:特指重耳。

In the "Oath of Ch'in"① it is said, "Let me have but one minister, sincere and single-minded, not pretending to other abilities②, but broad and upright of mind, generous and tolerant toward others. When he sees that another person has a certain kind of ability, he is as happy as though he himself had it, and when he sees another man who is elegant and wise, he loves him in his heart as much as if he said so in so many words, thus showing that he can really tolerate others. Such a person can preserve my sons, and grandsons and the black-haired people (the common people)③. He may well be a great benefit to the country. But when a minister sees another person with a certain kind of ability, he is jealous and hates him, and when he sees another person who is elegant and wise, he blocks him so he cannot advance, thus showing that he really cannot tolerate others. Such a person cannot preserve my sons, grandsons, and the black-haired people. He is a danger to the country." It is only a man of humanity who can send away such a minister and banish him, driving him to live among the barbarian tribes and not allowing him to exist together with the rest of the people in the Middle Kingdom (China)④. This is what is meant by saying that it is only the man of humanity who can love or who can hate others. To see a worthy and not be able to raise him to office, or to be able to raise him but not to be the first one to do so—that is negligence⑤. To see bad men and not be able to remove them from office, or to be able to remove them but not to remove them as far away as possible—that is a mistake⑥. To love what the people hate and to hate what the people love—that is to act contrary to human nature, and disaster will come to such a person. Thus we see that the ruler has a great principle to follow. He must attain it through loyalty and faithfulness and will surely lose it through pride and indulgence.

① "秦誓",陈荣捷译作 the "Oath of Ch'in"(秦誓)。理雅各译作 The Declaration of the Prince of Qin(秦王的宣言)。辜鸿铭译作 In his speech from the Throne, the Duke of T'sin said(在他从王位作的讲演中,秦穆公说)。林语堂译作 The Oath of Mu of Chin(to his subjects)(秦穆公对他的臣民发出的誓言)。浦安迪译作 the "Oath of the Duke of Ch'in"(秦公的誓言)。

② "技"陈荣捷、理雅各和林语堂译作 ability(能力)。辜鸿铭译作 qualification(资格)。浦安迪译作 art or skill(技能)。

③ "黎民"陈荣捷译作 the black-haired people (the common people)(黑发的人民或普通民众)。理雅各、浦安迪、林语堂和辜鸿铭译作 the black-haired people(黑发的人民)。

④ "中国"陈荣捷译作 the Middle Kingdom (China)(中央王国或中国)。理雅各译作 the Middle Kingdom(中央王国)。辜鸿铭和林语堂译作 China(中国)。浦安迪译作 the lands of the Central States(中央王国的疆土)。

⑤ "命"陈荣捷译作 negligence(疏忽)。理雅各译作 disrespect(蔑视)。辜鸿铭译作 gross neglect of duty(玩忽职守)。林语堂译作 being disrespectful or negligent of one's duty toward his ruler(蔑视或对君主的事务玩忽职守)。浦安迪译作 sheer negligence(玩忽职守)。

⑥ "过"陈荣捷译作 mistake(错误)。理雅各、辜鸿铭、林语堂均译作 weakness(弱点)。浦安迪译作 grave error(严重错误)。

《秦誓》①曰:"若有一个臣,断断②兮无他技③,其心休休④焉,其如有容焉。人之有技,若己有之,人之彦圣,其心好之,不啻若自其口出,寔⑤能容之,以能保我子孙黎民,尚亦有利哉。人之有技,媢疾⑥以恶之,人之彦圣,而违之俾⑦不通,寔不能容,以不能保我子孙黎民,亦曰殆哉。"

唯仁人放流之,迸⑧诸四夷,不与同中国。此谓唯仁人为能爱人,能恶人。见贤而不能举,举而不能先,命也;见不善而不能退,退而不能远,过也。好人之所恶,恶人之所好,是谓拂人之性,菑⑨必逮⑩夫身。是故君子有大道,必忠信以得之,骄泰以失之。

① 《秦誓》:《尚书·周书》中的一篇。
② 断断:果敢、诚实的状态。
③ 技:技能或能力。
④ 休:歇息,此处之心中无事操劳之状态。
⑤ 寔:通"实",确实。
⑥ 媢疾:媢,指男子嫉妒妻妾。疾,即嫉,与"媢"的含义相似。
⑦ 俾:使、把。
⑧ 迸:驱逐四散。
⑨ 菑:通"灾",此处作灾。
⑩ 逮:到达、赶上之意。

There is a great principle for the production of wealth. If there are many producers and few consumers, and if people who produce wealth do so quickly and those who spend it do so slowly, then wealth will always be sufficient. A man of humanity develops his personality by means of his wealth, while the inhumane person develops wealth at the sacrifice of his personality①. There has never been a case of a ruler who loved humanity and whose people did not love righteousness②. There has never been a case where the people loved righteousness and yet the affairs of the state have not been carried to completion. And there has never been a case where in such a state the wealth collected in the national treasury did not continue in the possession of the ruler.

The officer Meng-hsien said, "He who keeps a horse [one who has just become an official] and a carriage does not look after poultry and pigs. [The higher officials] who use ice [in their sacrifices] do not keep cattle and sheep. And the nobles who can keep a hundred carriages do not keep rapacious tax-gathering ministers under them. It is better to have a minister who robs the state treasury than to have such a tax-gathering minister. This is what is meant by saying that in a state financial profit is not considered real profit whereas righteousness is considered to be the real profit. He who heads a state or a family and is devoted to wealth and its use must have been under the influence of an inferior man③. He may consider this man to be good, but when an inferior man is allowed to handle the country or family, disasters and injuries will come together. Though a good man may take his place, nothing can be done. This is what is meant by saying that in a state financial profit is not considered real profit whereas righteousness is considered the real profit.

Chu Hsi's Remark. The above tenth chapter of commentary explains ordering the state to bring peace to the world. There are altogether ten commentary chapters. The first four generally discuss the principal topics and the basic import. The last six chapters discuss in detail the items and the required effort involved. Chapter five deals with the essence of the understanding of goodness and chapter six deals with the foundation of making the personal life sincere. These two chapters, especially, represent the immediate task, particularly for the beginning student. The reader should not neglect them because of their simplicity.

① "仁者以财发身,不仁者以身发财",陈荣捷译作 A man of humanity develops his personality by means of his wealth, while the inhumane person develops wealth at the sacrifice of his personality(仁者凭借财富培养高贵的人格,不仁者靠牺牲人格敛财)。理雅各译作 The virtuous ruler, by means of his wealth, makes himself more distinguished. The vicious ruler accumulates wealth at the expense of life(有德行的统治者运用财富使自己出类拔萃,邪恶的统治者以自己的生命为代价聚敛财富)。辜鸿铭译作 Moral men make money to live. Immoral men live to make money(有德性的人为活着而挣钱。没有德性的人为挣钱而活着)。林语堂译作 The true man develops his personality by means of his wealth, and the unworthy man develops wealth at the expense of his personality(真人凭借财富培养高贵的人格,小人靠牺牲人格敛财)。浦安迪译作 A man motivated by human kindness uses his wealth to develop his person character, whereas a man who lacks human kindness will expend all his personal capacities in amassing wealth(仁者利用财富培养高贵的人格,不仁者靠牺牲人格敛财)。【编者按语】辜译有格言风格,但不够忠实。

② "义",陈荣捷、理雅各和林语堂译作 righteousness(正义)。辜鸿铭译作 honour and duty(荣誉和责任)。浦安迪译作 a sense of honour(尊严感)。

③ "小人",陈荣捷译作 inferior man(地位低的人)。理雅各译作 small, mean man(卑微的人)。辜鸿铭译作 base and ignoble person(低贱无德之人)。林语堂译作 petty officials(下层官员,小吏)。浦安迪译作 men of mean character(品行卑下的人)。

生财有大道,生之者众,食之者寡,为之者疾,用之者舒,则财恒足矣。仁者以财发①身,不仁者以身发财。未有上好仁而下不好义者也,未有好义其事不终者也,未有府库财非其财者也。

孟献子②曰:"畜马乘不察于鸡豚,伐冰之家不畜牛羊,百乘之家不畜聚敛之臣,与其有聚敛之臣,宁有盗臣。"此谓国不以利为利,以义为利也。长国家而务财用者,必自小人矣。彼为善之,小人之使为国家,菑害并至。虽有善者,亦无如之何矣! 此谓国不以利为利,以义为利也。

* 右传之十章。释治国平天下。凡传十章:前四章统论纲领指趣,后六章细论条目功夫。其第五章乃明善之要,第六章乃诚身之本,在初学尤为当务之急,读者不可以其近而忽之也。

【编者按语】此段为朱熹所加,意在总结全文。

① 发:发起、开启之意。
② 孟献子:孟孙氏,名蔑,谥号献,世称仲孙蔑。春秋时期鲁国外交家、政治家。

Exercises

1. Put the following passage into Chinese.

The importance of this little Classic is far greater than its small size would suggest. It gives the Confucian educational, moral, and political programs in a nutshell, neatly summed up in the so-called "three items": manifesting the clear character of man, loving the people, and abiding in the highest good; and in the "eight steps": the investigation of things, extension of knowledge, sincerity of the will, rectification of the mind, cultivation of the personal life, regulation of the family, national order, and world peace. Moreover, it is the central Confucian doctrine of humanity (*jen*) in application. Confucius said that there is a central thread running through his teachings, and that central principle is conscientiousness and altruism, which are two aspects of humanity. The eight steps are the blueprints for translating humanity into actual living, carefully maintaining the balance and harmony of the individual on the one side and society on the other. It is because of *the Great Learning* has ranked as a Confucian Classic and has exerted profound influence in the last eight hundred years.

2. Discussion and presentation.

1) After a critical reading of the full text of *The Great Learning*, please evaluate the overall ideological framework of Confucianism.

2) After reading the translations of *The Great Learning*, you must have noticed translators sometimes translate some words and clauses in the same way. What do you think of this phenomenon?

Supplementary Reading: Paraphrase as a Translation Method for Chinese Philosophical Classics(1)

简论释译(一)
——《论语》暨中国古代思想典籍的翻译方法

说到翻译方法,人们常常会想到直译和意译。事实上,这两个术语概念十分含糊。直译原本是"直接译"的缩略词,与"间接译"相对。二者都是翻译路径。意译的内涵和外延更不明晰。翻译原本主要就是译意(sense-for-sense),即翻译源语文本词意、句意、篇章的意义。而译音和译形都是次要的方法。相对中文直译与意译的含混,西方对应的 literal translation(逐词翻译)和 free translation(自由翻译)的二分法似乎要明晰一些。但是,后者的意思仍然不清不楚,因为我们不知道翻译中怎么自由、自由的度究竟在哪里。

一、释译(paraphrase)与以句子作为翻译单位

对于《论语》暨中国古代思想典籍的翻译,除了释译(paraphrase)我们找不到更好和可行的翻译方法。英国诗人兼翻译家约翰·德莱顿将翻译分为三类:一、Metaphrase(word-for-word,逐词翻译);二、Paraphrase(释译:译意不译词且有自由度的翻译);三、Imitation(拟作)。他认为第一、第三种翻译都是走极端,只有第二种才是中道。

以德莱顿的释译观为基础,我们可以建构现代意义的释译理论。传统译学把翻译过程分为译者的"理解"和"表达"和读者的"阅读"和"接受",而现代翻译诠释学认为二者都是"诠释"的过程。"理解"预设了原语文本意义的固定和清晰。而现代诠释学意义上的"诠释"预设了原语文本意义的漂移、含混、多元。对原语文本意义的把捉事实上是在多重意义中的选择。一方面,译者不得不在源语字词的几个、十几个意义上做出一种选择,在句子内部和句群之间的多个逻辑关系进行一种选择。在篇章和文本整体的数个主题思想之中做出一种选择。另一方面,译者应尽量呈现译文文本的多元性、复意性,提供一个开放性的文本。"理解"还预设了作者的显身和译者的隐身,即译者没有或没有充分的主体性。而"诠释"削减了作者的独断性,突出了译者的主体性,把诠释当作作者和译者的主体间的平等对话。源语文本的意义是作者与译者协商妥协(negotiate and compromise)的结果。而读者的"阅读"和"接受"也不是被动消极的,是译者和读者二元主体对于译语文本意义协商妥协的过程,是两个主体平等对话的过程。读者应发挥主体性,根据自己的视界对译文文本进行自主的诠释,达成视界融合。

释译不意味着随心所欲、天马行空的自主创作,而是基于原作意义的有节制的诠释。原作的意义可以适度地扩展或缩减(amplify or diminish),但不容改变。"原作者需时刻记在心上,译者便不会在意义上迷失。但是,译者译义不译词。原作的意义也可以扩展,但不容改变。翻译这么做就足够了:译者选择一些不削弱原文意义的表达方式。译者的话语链条可以拉伸到一个相当的程度。但是当他新造思想的话,我认为他就越界了。"(德莱顿)为了既保证诠释的自由度又不越"篡改"雷池一步,我们认为确定句子为翻译的基本单位至关重要。此相当于林语堂主张的句译。在翻译中,译者一句还作者一句,做到句子对等。在句子内部,单词、短语、分句,译者尽可以颠倒附益。但在句子以上的篇章单位,译者不能进行增删改的操作。这样做不同于边译边著的译述,也不同于打破原作文本篇章格局的编译。当然也不同于拟作。

二、《论语》释译的必要性和举例

《论语》暨中国古代思想典籍释译的必要性,源于先秦文言与西方近现代语言的巨大差异,源于东西古今文化的巨大差异,源于东西方思维方式和文本建构方式的巨大差异,同时源于原作(述)者和译者个体在文化素养、语言水平、专业素养、文学修养,乃至其个性、情绪的重大差异。简言之,《论语》暨中国古代思想典籍不释译,译者就无法翻译,不释译,译文就不可理解,无法接受。

为了说明释译的必要性,这里举一个《论语》章句作例子。子曰:"兴于诗,立于礼,成于乐。"(《泰伯篇》8.8)。较之《论语》中大量晦涩多义的章句,这个章句意义较为明晰。但即使如此,在英译中仍然有很多地方,需要译者发挥主动性进行自主诠释。首先,这是一个无主语的省略句。究竟是谁要或要谁"兴、立、成"呢?有几种可能性:一、"你们小子",即孔夫子门下弟子。这是主流的理解;二、孔夫子自我的形象描写或人格追求。"我就是这样的人",或"这是我的人格理想";三、对君子人格的描述及君子"为学""修身"的过程性主张,表述了"为学""修身"的先后次第。其次,"兴、立、成"几个谓语单字的意涵极为丰富,各有几种甚至十几种含义。因为汉语动词没有时态变化,译者必须确定这发生在过去、现在还是未来。再次,"兴、立、成"引导的三个分句是什么样的逻辑关系?是时间的先后关系还是共时关系?三者是递进、因果、假设还是条件的逻辑关系?因为有三个分句,三者的不同组合必然带来不同的解读。而这些逻辑关系都是开放性的,不确定的。还有,"诗、礼、乐"既可泛指,也可特指《诗》《礼》《乐》。最后,因为本章句缺少上下文和历史语境,这又留下巨大的诠释空间。我们甚至连这是孔子的话,还是这是古人的格言,孔子仅仅引用而已,都无法确认。

该章句的意义的多元性和不确定性由不同地域、不同时代、不同身份的译者以不同方式进行了诠释。上述的多元诠释在以下译文中以不同方式、不同程度,在不同层面体现出来,成就了百花齐放、各具风姿的文本面貌。

1. 理雅各:The Master said, It is by the Odes that the mind is aroused. It is by Rules of Propriety that the character is established. It is from Music that the finish is received.

2. 辜鸿铭:Confucius remarked, "In education sentiment is called out by the study of poetry; judgement is formed by the study of the arts; and education of the character is completed by the study of music."

3. 韦利:The Master said, Let a man be first incited by the *Songs*, then given a firm footing by the study of ritual, and finally perfected by music.

4. 安乐哲、罗思文:The Master said, "I find inspiration by intoning the songs, I learn where to stand from observing ritual propriety (*li* 礼), and I find fulfillment in playing music."

5. 林戊荪:The Master said, "In *the Book of Songs*, one finds inspiration; in ritual, the way to establishment; in music, self-perfection."

6. 刘殿爵:The Master said, Be stimulated by *the Odes*, take your stand on the rites and be perfected by music.

值得注意的是,该章句的诠释空间不止如此,空间几乎是无限大的。广而言之,未来因时代的不同、读者的不同、出版和赞助机制的不同,中外译者仍然会推出《论语》暨中国古代思想典籍的新诠释和新译本。经典之所以成为经典,大概就在于常释常新,常译常新。

Unit Thirteen
The Doctrine of the Mean（1）

Originally a chapter from *Book of Rites*, *The Doctrine of the Mean*(《中庸》) underwent the same journey as *The Great Learning* to become a Confucian classic. However, they mean differently for Confucian scholars. *The Great Learning* has a clear structure and system, outlining the scale and steps of Confucian learning. *The Doctrine of the Mean*, on the other hand, has a mixed and miscellaneous content. Although it is entitled *The Doctrine of the Mean*, its core ideas go beyond the idea of the mean. It covers such themes of sincerity(诚), harmony(和), the way of the gentleman(君子之道), and so on. *The Doctrine of the Mean* itself is so profound in meaning that Zhu Xi, in determining the order of *Four Books*, made it the last one. He believed that only after studying the three previous books could one understand the meaning of *The Doctrine of the Mean*.

The following text is based on the translation of James Legge(理雅各), coupled with the translations of Ku Hung-ming(辜鸿铭), Andrew Plaks(浦安迪), Roger T. Ames and David L. Hall(安乐哲、郝大维).

The Doctrine of the Mean(1) and Notes

[Chu Hsi's Remark]

My master, the philosopher Ch'ăng, says:—'Being without inclination to either side is called CHUNG; admitting of no change is called YUNG. By CHUNG is denoted the correct course to be pursued by all under heaven; by YUNG is denoted the fixed principle regulating all under heaven. This work contains the law of the mind, which was handed down from one to another, in the Confucian school, tiu Tsze-sze, fearing lest in the course of time errors should arise about it, committed it to writing, and delivered it to Mencius. The Book first speaks of one principle; it next spreads this out, and embraces all things; finally, it returns and gathers them all up under one principle. Unroll it, and it fills the universe; roll it up, it retires and lies hid in mysteriousness. The relish of it is inexhaustible. The whole of it is solid learning. When the skilful reader has explored it with delight till he has apprehended it, he may carry it into practice all his life, and will find that it cannot be exhausted.'

子程子曰:"不偏之谓中,不易之谓庸。中者,天下之正道,庸者,天下之定理。"此篇乃孔门传授心法,子思恐其久而差也,故笔之于书,以授孟子。其书始言一理,中散为万事,末复合为一理,"放之则弥六合,卷之则退藏于密",其味无穷,皆实学也。善读者玩索而有得焉,则终身用之,有不能尽者矣。

What Heaven[①] has conferred is called THE NATURE[②]; an accordance with this nature is called THE PATH *of duty* [③]; the regulation of this path is called INSTRUCTION[④]. The path may not be left for an instant. If it could be left, it would not be the path. On this account, the superior man does not wait till he sees things, to be cautious, nor till he hears things, to be apprehensive.

① "天",理雅各和浦安迪译作 Heaven(天)。辜鸿铭译作 God(上帝)。安乐哲译作 *tian* 天。【编者按语】"天"译作 God 或 Heaven,都有基督教的色彩。安乐哲径直移用汉字加音译,因为他觉得汉语"天"的意思太广漠,移用汉字加音译更好。他采用了异化的翻译策略,以保存原汁原味的汉语文化。

② "性",理雅各和浦安迪译作 nature(本性)。辜鸿铭译作 being(性)(存有)。安乐哲译作 natural tendencies(*xing* 性)(自然倾向)。【编者按语】理雅各的中国经典翻译常采用基督教神学常用词,而安乐哲常刻意避开。对于中国文化关键词,在译文中加注汉字,辜鸿铭是先行者之一。这样做既可以保留原字原意,也有助于关键字和核心概念的全篇贯穿统一。

③ "道",理雅各译作 path of duty(责任之道)。辜鸿铭译作 the moral law(道德律法)。安乐哲译作 the proper way(*dao* 道)(恰当的路)。浦安迪译作 the Way(大道)。【编者按语】对于中国文化关键词,安乐哲采用了综合法,即既有英译,也有拼音和汉字。

④ "教",理雅各译作 instruction(教学)。辜鸿铭译作 religion(教)(宗教)。安乐哲译作 education(*jiao* 教)(教育)。浦安迪译作 moral instruction(道德教育)。【编者按语】辜鸿铭和浦安迪翻译儒家经典有一个共同点,他们都强调儒家经典的道德属性,常用 moral 及其派生词作为核心词。

天命[①]之谓性[②],率性之谓道[③],修道之谓教[④]。道也者,不可须臾离也,可离非道也。是故君子戒慎乎其所不睹,恐惧乎其所不闻。

① 天命:天,儒家的最高价值实体或德性来源。命,本意与令相同,都是上级对下级下达指示。此处天命之意即天所降下的规则。

② 性:性的本意即生,此处为不变、必然、永恒之意,这也是儒家语境中性的基本

意涵。

③ 道:指的是事物发展的规律或行为的规范。按照本文的说法,完全顺从事物的本性就是道。

④ 教:朱熹认为,"若礼、乐、刑、政之属是也。"

There is nothing more visible than what is secret, and nothing more manifest than what is minute. Therefore the superior man is watchful over himself, when he is alone①. While there are no stirrings of pleasure, anger, sorrow, or joy, the mind may be said to be in the state of EQUILIBRIUM②. When those feelings have been stirred, and they act in their due degree, there ensues what may be called the state of HARMONY③. This EQUILIBRIUM is the great root *from which grow all the human actings* in the world④, and this HARMONY is the universal path *which they all should pursue*. Let the states of equilibrium and harmony exist in perfection, and a happy order will prevail throughout heaven and earth, and all things will be nourished and flourish.

In the first chapter which is given above, Tsze-sze states the views which had been handed down to him, as the basis of his discourse. First, it shows clearly how the path of duty is to be traced to its origin in Heaven, and is unchangeable, while the substance of it is provided in ourselves, and may not be departed from. Next, it speaks of the importance of preserving and nourishing this, and of exercising a watchful self-scrutiny with reference to it. Finally, it speaks of the meritorious achievements and transforming influence of sage and spiritual men in their highest extent. The wish of Tsze-sze was that hereby the learner should direct his thoughts inwards, and by searching in himself, there find these truths, so that he might put aside all outward temptations appealing to his selfishness, and fill up the measure of the goodness which is natural to him. This chapter is what the writer Yang called it, ——'The sum of the whole work.' In the ten chapters which follow, Tsze-sze quotes the words of the Master to complete the meaning of this.

① "慎其独也",理雅各译作 be watchful over himself when he is alone(独自一人时,对自己保持戒惧的态度)。辜鸿铭译作 watches diligently over his secret thoughts(不懈地监督自己隐秘的想法)。安乐哲译作 be ever concerned about their uniqueness(永远关注自己的独特性)。浦安迪译作 pays great heed to the core of his own individuality(极力关注自己个性的核心)。【编者按语】"独"字有两种解释。一是独处。二是独特性。

② "中",理雅各译作 equilibrium(宁静)。辜鸿铭译作 our true self or moral being(我们真正的自我或道德存在)。安乐哲译作 nascent equilibrium(萌生中的宁静)。浦安迪译

作 mean(中庸;平均值;中间)。

③ "和",理雅各、安乐哲、浦安迪均译作 harmony(和谐)。辜鸿铭译作 moral order(道德秩序)。

④ "天下",理雅各、辜鸿铭、安乐哲译作 world(世界)。浦安迪译作 the universe as a cosmic whole(和谐有序的宇宙)。

莫见乎隐,莫显乎微,故君子慎其独也。喜怒哀乐之未发,谓之中①;发而皆中节,谓之和②。中也者,天下之大本也;和也者,天下之达道也。致中和,天地位焉,万物育焉。

右第一章。子思述所传之意以立言:首明道之本原出于天而不可易,其实体备于己而不可离,次言存养省察之要,终言圣神功化之极。盖欲学者于此反求诸身而自得之,以去夫外诱之私,而充其本然之善,杨氏③所谓一篇之体要是也。其下十章,盖子思引夫子之言,以终此章之义。

① 中:情绪的未萌发状态被定义为中。
② 和:事物内部各个部分相互协调。
③ 杨氏:陈荣捷以为杨氏指的是杨时,朱熹曾多次引述了杨时的学说。

Chung-nî said, 'The superior man *embodies* the course of the Mean①; the mean man acts contrary to the course of the Mean. The superior man's embodying the course of the Mean is because he is a superior man, and so always maintains the Mean②. The mean man's acting contrary to the course of the Mean is because he is a mean man③, and has no caution.'

The above is the second chapter.

The Master said, 'Perfect is the virtue which is according to the Mean! Rare have they long been among the people, who could practice it!'

The above is the third chapter.

The Master said, 'I know how it is that the path of *the Mean* is not walked in: ——The knowing go beyond it, and the stupid do not come up to it. I know how it is that the path of the Mean is not understood: ——The men of talents and virtue go beyond it, and the worthless do not come up to it. There is nobody but eats and drinks. But they are few who can distinguish flavours.'

The above is the fourth chapter.

The Master said, 'Alas! How is the path of the Mean untrodden!'
The above is the fifth chapter.

① "中庸",理雅各译作 the course of the Mean(中庸之道)。辜鸿铭译作 universal moral order(普遍道德秩序)。安乐哲译作 focus on the affairs of the day(切中日用伦常)。浦安迪译作 the ideal of the mean in common practice(日用中庸的理想)。【编者按语】安乐哲将"中"理解为动词,"庸"为名词,构成动宾结构,强调过程性和事件性。

② "中",理雅各译作 maintain the Mean(合乎中道)。辜鸿铭译作 live his true self or moral being(活出真实的自我或道德主体)。安乐哲译作 abide in equilibrium(保持内心的宁静)。浦安迪译作 maintain a state of moral balance(保持道德平衡状态)。

③ "小人",理雅各译作 the mean man(卑贱的人)。辜鸿铭译作 the vulgar person(粗俗的人)。安乐哲译作 petty persons(低级的人)。浦安迪译作 men of base character(品行卑污的人)。

仲尼①曰:"君子中庸②,小人反中庸,君子之中庸也,君子而时中③;小人之中庸也,小人而无忌惮也④。"

＊右第二章。

① 仲尼:即孔子,名丘,字仲尼,鲁国陬邑(今山东曲阜市)人,儒学的开创者。
② 中庸:程颐认为,中,即不偏不倚;庸,即恒常不易。
③ 时中:时,时机;时中,指根据不同的情形作出合宜的行动。
④ 小人之中庸:是说小人总是根据时机作出放纵自己欲望的行为,这是他们恒常的表现。

子曰:"中庸其至矣乎！民鲜能久矣!"
＊右第三章。

子曰:"道之不行也,我知之矣:知者过之,愚者不及也。道之不明也,我知之矣:贤者过之,不肖者不及也。人莫不饮食也,鲜能知味也。"
＊右第四章。

子曰:"道其不行矣夫!"
＊右第五章。

The Master said, 'There was Shun:—He indeed was greatly wise! Shun loved to question *others*, and to study their words, though they might be shallow①. He concealed what was bad *in them*, and displayed what was good②. He took hold of the two extremes③, *determined* the Mean, and employed it in *his government of* the people. It was by this that he was Shun!'

The above is the sixth chapter.

The Master said, 'Men all say, "We are wise;" but being driven forward and taken in a net, a trap, or a pitfall, they know not how to escape. Men all say, "We are wise"; but happening to choose the course of the Mean④, they are not able to keep it for a round month.'

The above is the seventh chapter.

The Master said, 'This was the manner of Hûi;—he made choice of the Mean, and whenever he got hold of what was good, he clasped it firmly, as if wearing it on his breast, and did not lose it.'

The above is the eighth chapter.

The Master said, 'The kingdom, its State, and its families, may be perfectly ruled; dignities and emoluments may be declined; naked weapons may be trampled under the feet;—but the course of the Mean cannot be attained to.'

The above is the ninth chapter.

① "迩言"，理雅各译作 their words, though they might be shallow（他们虽然有些浅近的话）。辜鸿铭译作 near facts（相近事实）。安乐哲译作 familiar words（家常的话）。浦安迪译作 the deeper meaning of things in everyday speech（家常的话中的深刻意义）。

② "隐恶而扬善"，理雅各译作 He concealed what was bad in them, and displayed what was good（他遮掩他人的恶行，张扬他人的善行）。辜鸿铭译作 He looked upon evil merely as something negative; and he recognize only what was good as having a positive existence（他只是将恶视作消极的东西，而只是将善视作积极的存在）。安乐哲译作 passing over what was unhelpful to expand upon those ideas that had merit（忽略不利的因素以便扩张有利的思想）。浦安迪译作 He would keep men's evil deeds discreetly from view, while elevating the good for all to see（他会谨慎地遮掩他人的恶行，弘扬他人的善行）。

③ "执其两端"，理雅各译作 He took hold of their two extremes（他把捉住两个极端）。辜鸿铭译作 taking the two extremes of negative and positive（把握住消极和积极的两个极

端)。安乐哲译作 grasping these ideas at both ends(在两个终端把捉思想)。浦安迪译作 grasp both ends of moral spectrum(抓住道德"光谱"的两极)。

④"择乎中庸",理雅各译作 choose the course of the Mean(选择中道)。辜鸿铭译作 finding the true central clue and balance in their moral being(i.e. their normal, ordinary, true self) and following the line of conduct which is in accordance with it[在他们的道德中找到真正的中心线索和平衡点(即正常的、真正的自我)并遵从与之一致的行为规范]。安乐哲译作 having chosen to focus the familiar affairs of the day(zhongyong 中庸)(选择切中伦常之后)。浦安迪译作 they profess to choose the practice of the mean as their guiding principle(他们宣称要把中庸之道当作指导原则)。【编者按语】辜鸿铭和浦安迪均采用了释译的方法,似有些过度。

子曰:"舜①其大知也与!舜好问而好察迩言,隐恶而扬善,执其两端,用其中于民,其斯以为舜乎!"

＊右第六章。

① 舜:古代一位贤明的君主,其因为孝道而被尧推为君,受到儒家特别的推崇。

子曰:"人皆曰予知,驱而纳诸罟擭①陷阱之中,而莫之知辟②也。人皆曰予知,择乎中庸,而不能期月守也。"

＊右第七章。

子曰:"回之为人也,择乎中庸,得一善,则拳拳服膺而弗失之矣。"

＊右第八章。

子曰:"天下国家可均也,爵禄可辞也,白刃可蹈也,中庸不可能也。"

＊右第九章。

① 罟擭:捕捉禽兽之工具的代称。
② 辟:通"避",意为避开。

Tsze-lû asked about energy①. The Master said, 'Do you mean the energy of the South, the energy of the North, or the energy which you should cultivate yourself? To show forbearance and gentleness in teaching others; and not to revenge unreasonable conduct②: —this is the energy of Southern regions, and the good man makes it his study. To lie under arms; and meet death without regret: —this is the energy of Northern regions, and the forceful make it their study.

Therefore. the superior man cultivates a *friendly* harmony, without being weak[3].—How firm is he in his energy! He stands erect in the middle, without inclining to either side. —How firm is he in his energy! When good principles prevail in the government of his country, he does not change from what he was in retirement. —How firm is he in his energy! When bad principles prevail in the country, he maintains his course to death without changing. —How firm is he in his energy!'

The above is the tenth chapter.

The Master said, 'To live in obscurity, and yet practise wonders, in order to be mentioned with honour in future ages:—this is what I do not do. The good man tries to proceed according to the right path. But when he has gone halfway, he abandons it:—I am not able so to stop. The superior man accords with the course of the Mean. Though he may be all unknown, unregarded by the world, he feels no regret. —It is only the sage who is able for this.'

The above is the eleventh chapter.

① "强",理雅各译作 energy(能量)。辜鸿铭译作 force of character(品德的力量)。安乐哲译作 proper strength(合适的力)。浦安迪译作 power(力量)。

② "不报无道",理雅各译作 not to revenge unreasonable conduct(不去报复不理性的行为)。辜鸿铭译作 returning not evil for evil(不以恶报恶)。安乐哲译作 not retaliating against those who have lost the proper way(*dao* 道)(不对迷失了"正道"的人报复)。浦安迪译作 without exacting retribution for unjust treatment(不会因不公的待遇而寻求报复)。【编者按语】辜鸿铭译借用基督教的说法。

③ "和而不流",理雅各译作 cultivate a friendly harmony, without being weak(培植友好的和谐,同时又不怯懦)。辜鸿铭译作 be easy and accommodating and yet without weakness and indiscrimination(安闲随和,但强健有力,富于鉴别力)。安乐哲译作 bringing these different senses of 'strength' into harmony(*he* 和)and are not moved by the common flow(中和不同意义的"力",不为潮流所动)。浦安迪译作 be of an accommodating disposition, yet is not swept along by the current(性格随和,又不为潮流裹挟)。

子路问强,子曰:"南方之强与?北方之强与?抑而强与?宽柔以教,不报无道,南方之强也,君子居之。衽金革①,死而不厌,北方之强也,而强者居之。故君子和而不流②,强哉矫③!中立而不倚,强哉矫!国有道,不变塞焉,强哉矫!国无道,至死不变,强哉矫!"

* 右第十章。

① 衽金革:衽,卧席;金,兵器之类;革,甲胄之类。衽金革,即以兵器和甲胄为卧席,比喻时刻保持战斗的警觉。

② 和而不流:和,指保持整体的协调。流,指放任、放纵。

③ 矫:本意为直,朱熹认为,"矫,强貌。"

子曰:"素隐①行怪,后世有述焉,吾弗为之矣。君子遵道而行,半涂②而废,吾弗能已矣。君子依乎中庸,遁世③不见知而不悔,唯圣者能之。"

* 右第十一章。

① 素隐:素,据《汉书》作"索"。隐,即隐秘偏僻之意。素隐,意为探求隐秘偏僻之事物或提出冷僻的学说。

② 涂:通"途"。

③ 遁世:遁,本意为迁、避、逃。遁世,即远离世俗生活,处于隐退的状态。

The way which the superior man pursues, reaches wide and far, and yet is secret. Common men and women, however ignorant, may intermeddle with the knowledge of it; yet in its utmost reaches, there is that which even the sage[①] does not know. Common men and women, however much below the ordinary standard of character, can carry it into practice; yet in its utmost reaches, there is that which even the sage is not able to carry into practice. Great as heaven and earth are, men still find some things in them with which to be dissatisfied. Thus it is that, were the superior man to speak of his way in all its greatness, nothing in the world would be found able to embrace it, and were he to speak of it in its minuteness, nothing in the world would be found able to split[②] it. It is said in the Book of Poetry, 'The hawk flies up to heaven; the fishes leap in the deep.' This expresses how this *way* is seen above and below. The way of the superior man may be found, in its simple elements, in the intercourse of common men and women; but in its utmost reaches, it shines brightly through heaven and earth[③].

The twelfth chapter above contains the words of Tsze-sze, and is designed to illustrate what is said in the first chapter, that 'The path may not be left.' In the eight chapters which follow, he quotes, in a miscellaneous way, the words of Confucius to illustrate it.

① "圣人",理雅各译作 the sage(圣贤)。辜鸿铭译作 the wisest and holiest of men(最有智慧、最有神性的人)。安乐哲译作 sages(shengren 圣人)。浦安迪译作 the most perfectly cultivated of men(修养最高的人)。

② "破",理雅各和辜鸿铭译作 split(分割)。安乐哲译作 refine(精炼)。浦安迪译作 penetrate to its subtlest meaning(破解其最微妙的意义)。

③ "察乎天地",理雅各译作 it shines brightly through heaven and earth(光耀天地)。辜鸿铭译作 reigns supreme over heaven and earth(至高至上,支配天地)。安乐哲译作 sheds light upon the entire world(彻照世界)。浦安迪译作 it extends to the very edges of Heaven and Earth(它延伸至天地边缘)。

君子之道,费而隐①。夫妇之愚,可以与知焉,及其至也,虽圣人亦有所不知焉。夫妇之不肖,可以能行焉;及其至也,虽圣人亦有所不能焉。天地之大也,人犹有所憾。故君子语大,天下莫能载焉;语小,天下莫能破焉。《诗》云:"鸢②飞戾③天,鱼跃于渊。"言其上下察也。君子之道,造端乎夫妇,及其至也,察乎天地。

* 右第十二章。子思之言,盖以申明首章道不可离之意也。其下八章,杂引孔子之言以明之。

① 费而隐:朱熹认为,"费,用之广也。隐,体之微也。"然此处究竟如何理解"费而隐"的实际含义,尚难确定。

② 鸢:鸥一类的鸟。

③ 戾:到、至。

The Master said, 'The path is not far from man①. When men try to pursue a course, which is far from the common indications of consciousness, this course cannot be considered THE PATH. In the Book of Poetry, it is said, "In hewing an axe-handle, in hewing an axe-handle, the pattern is not far off." We grasp one axe-handle to hew the other; and yet, if we look askance from the one to the other, we may consider them as apart. Therefore, the moral man governs men, according to their nature, with what is proper to them②, and as soon as they change *what is wrong*, he stops. When one cultivates to the utmost the principles of his nature, and exercises them on the principle of reciprocity, he is not far from the path. What you do not like when done to yourself, do not do to others. In the way of the superior man there are four things, to not one of which have I as yet attained.—To serve my father, as I would require my son to serve me: to this I have not attained; to serve my prince, as I would require my minister to serve me: to this I have not attained; to serve my elder brother, as I would require my younger brother to serve me: to this I have not attained; to set the example in behaving to a friend, as I would require him to behave to me: to this I have not attained. Earnest in practising the ordinary virtues, and careful in speaking about them, if, in his practice, he has anything defective, the superior man dares not but exert himself; and if, in his words, he has any excess, he dares not allow himself such license. Thus his words have respect to his actions, and his actions have respect to his words; is it not just an entire sincerity which marks the superior man?'

The above is the thirteenth chapter.

① "道不远人",理雅各译作 The path is not far from man(道离人不远)。辜鸿铭译作 The moral law is not something away from the actuality of human life(道德法则不脱离人类生活的现实)。安乐哲译作 The proper way(dao 道) is not at all remote from people(正道离人一点不远)。浦安迪译作 The Way is not removed from man(道不远人)。

② "君子以人治人",理雅各译作 the moral man governs men, according to their nature, with what is proper to them(有德性的人依据人的本性,用合适他们的方式统治他们)。辜鸿铭译作 the moral man in dealing with people appeals to the common human nature(有德性的人在与人打交道前,诉诸共同的人性)。安乐哲译作 the exemplary person(junzi 君子) uses one person to mold others properly(君子用一个人作为典范去得当地塑造他人)。浦安迪译作 the man of noble character bases himself on his own human qualities when he comes to regulate those of other men(品德高尚的人在管理他人时,行事基于自己的人性)。

子曰:"道不远人,人之为道而远人,不可以为道。《诗》①云:'伐柯,伐柯②,其则不远。'执柯以伐柯,睨③而视之,犹以为远。故君子以人治人,改而止。忠恕违道不远,施诸己而不愿,亦勿施于人。君子之道四,丘未能一焉,所求乎子,以事父,未能也;所求乎臣,以事君,未能也;所求乎弟,以事兄,未能也;所求乎朋友,先施之,未能也。庸德之行,庸言之谨;有所不足,不敢不勉,有余,不敢尽;言顾行,行顾言,君子胡不慥慥尔④!"

* 右第十三章。

① 《诗》:指《诗·豳风·伐柯》。

② 伐柯:柯,斧柄。伐柯,即砍伐树木做斧柄。

③ 睨:斜视。

④ 慥慥:忠厚老实之貌。

The superior man does what is proper to the station in which he is①; he does not desire to go beyond this. In a position of wealth and honour, he does what is proper to a position of wealth and honour. In a poor and low position, he does what is proper to a poor and low position. Situated among barbarous tribes, he does what is proper to a situation among barbarous tribes. In a position of sorrow and difficulty, he does what is proper to a position of sorrow and difficulty. The superior man can find himself in no situation in which he is not himself. In a high situation, he does not treat with contempt his inferiors. In a low situation, he does not court the favour of his superiors②. He rectifies himself, and seeks for nothing from others, so that he has no dissatisfactions. He does not murmur against Heaven, nor grumble against men. Thus it is that the superior man is quiet and calm, waiting for the appointments *of Heaven*③, while the mean man walks in dangerous paths, looking for lucky occurrences. The Master said, 'In archery we have something like the way of the superior man. When the archer misses the centre of the target, he turns round and seeks for the cause of his failure in himself.'

The above is the fourteenth chapter.

① "素其位而行",理雅各译作 do what is proper to the station in which he is(根据自己的地位,做合适的事)。辜鸿铭译作 conform himself to his life circumstances(让自己适应自己的生活环境)。安乐哲译作 conduct themselves according to their station(根据自己的地位行事)。浦安迪译作 occupy his preordained station in life and act accordingly(居于命定的地位,并据此行事)。

② "援上",理雅各和辜鸿铭译作 court the favor of his superiors(谄媚上司)。安乐哲译作 cling to those above them(攀附居上位者)。浦安迪译作 clamber upward in an unseemingly way(难看地向上爬)。

③ "俟命",理雅各译作 wait for the appointments of the Heaven(等待上天的安排)。辜鸿铭译 wait for the appointment of God(等待上帝的安排)。安乐哲译作 stay on level ground in waiting what is to come(躺平,等待即将到来的事)。浦安迪译作 he awaits his destiny(他等待自己的命运)。【编者按语】关于中国文化术语如"命""天",较早的译者如理雅各和辜鸿铭有意无意采用了归化的译法。而较晚近的译者如安乐哲和浦安迪常刻意回避西方的文化术语。

君子素①其位而行,不愿乎其外。素富贵,行乎富贵;素贫贱,行乎贫贱;素夷狄,行乎夷狄;素患难,行乎患难,君子无入而不自得焉。在上位不陵下,在下位不援上,正己而不求于人,则无怨。上不怨天,下不尤人。故君子居易②以俟命③。小人行险以徼幸④。子曰:"射有似乎君子,失诸正鹄,反求诸其身。"

*右第十四章。

① 素:本来的、原有的。

② 居易:郑玄认为,"易,犹平安也。"

③ 俟命:等待命运的安排。

④ 徼幸:徼,通"侥";幸,幸运。

The way of the superior man may be compared to what takes place in travelling, when to go to a distance we must first traverse the space that is near, and in ascending a height, when we must begin from the lower ground. It is said in the Book of Poetry, 'Happy union with wife and children, is like the music of lutes and harps. When there is concord among brethren, the harmony is delightful, and enduring. *Thus* may you regulate your family, and enjoy the pleasure of your wife and children.' The Master said, 'In such a state of things, parents have entire complacence!'

The above is the fifteenth chapter.

君子之道,辟如行远必自迩,辟如登高必自卑。《诗》①曰:"妻子好合②,如鼓瑟琴。兄弟既翕③,和乐且耽④。宜尔室家,乐尔妻帑⑤。"子曰:"父母其顺矣乎!"

右第十五章。

① 《诗》:指《诗·小雅·常棣》。

② 好合:和睦。

③ 翕:本意为合拢,引申为一致、和顺。此处即取引申意。

④ 耽:《诗经》中原作"湛",意为安乐。

⑤ 帑:通"孥",本意为儿子,此处代指子女。

The Master said, 'How abundantly do spiritual beings① display the powers that belong to them! We look for them, but do not see them; we listen to them. but do not hear them; yet they enter into all things②, and there is nothing without them. They cause all the people in the kingdom to fast and purify themselves, and array themselves in their richest dresses, in order to attend at their sacrifices. Then, like overflowing water③, they seem to be over the heads, and on the right and left *of their worshippers*. It is said in the Book of Poetry, "The approaches of the spirits, you cannot surmise; — and can you treat them with indifference?" Such is the manifestness of what is minute! Such is the impossibility of repressing the outgoings of sincerity!'

The above is the sixteenth chapter.

① "鬼神",理雅各译作 spiritual beings(精神存在)。辜鸿铭译作 spiritual forces(精神之力)。安乐哲译作 gods and spirits(神和鬼)。浦安迪译作 ghosts and spirits(鬼和神)。

② "体物",理雅各译作 they enter into all things(他们进入所有事物)。辜鸿铭译作 it is inherent in all things(它内在于所有的事物)。安乐哲译作 they inform events(它们赋理[或质]于事物)。浦安迪译作 they inform the substance of all things(它们赋理[或质]于所有事物)。

③ "洋洋乎",理雅各译作 like overflowing water(像澎湃的水流)。辜鸿铭译作 like the rush of mighty waters(恰如汹涌的水流)。安乐哲译作 It is as through the air above our head is suffused with them(它们似乎弥漫在我们头上的空气中)。浦安迪译作 Their vital force billows like a great sea(他们的蓬勃的力像大海的波涛一样汹涌)。【编者按语】辜鸿铭、理雅各和浦安迪的翻译依据朱熹的注解。安乐哲的译法从郑玄注。

子曰:"鬼神之为德,其盛矣乎? 视之而弗见,听之而弗闻,体物①而不可遗,使天下之人齐明②盛服,以承祭祀。洋洋③乎如在其上,如在其左右。《诗》④曰:'神之格思⑤,不可度⑥思! 矧可射思!'夫微之显,诚之不可掩如此夫。"

右第十六章。

① 体物:郑玄注:"体,犹生也"。故体物即生育万物。
② 齐明:齐,通"斋",斋戒;明,整洁之貌。
③ 洋洋:郑玄认为,"洋洋,人想思其傍僾之貌。"
④《诗》:指《诗·大雅·抑》。
⑤ 格思:格,意思是至、到;思,语气助词。
⑥ 度:测度、揣测。

Exercises

1. Put the following passage into English.

大道之行也,天下为公。选贤与能,讲信修陆,故人不独亲其亲,不独子其子,使老有所终,壮有所用,幼有所长,鳏寡孤独废疾者,皆有所养。男有分,女有归。货恶其弃于地也,不必藏于己;力恶其不出于己身也,不必为己。是故,谋闭而不兴,盗窃乱贼而不作,故外户而不闭。是谓大同。

今大道既隐,天下为家,各亲其亲,各子其子,货力为己。大人世及以为礼,城郭沟池以为固,礼义以为纪;以正君臣,以笃父子,以睦兄弟,以和夫妇,以设制度,以立田里,以贤勇知,以功为己。故谋用是作,而兵由此起。禹、汤、文、武、成王、周公,由此其选也。此六君子者,未有不谨于礼者也。以著其义,以考其信,著有过,刑仁讲让,示民有常。如有不由此者,在执者去,众以为殃。是谓小康。

2. Discussion and composition.

Zhong Yong, the title of the book, has the largest number of English renditions among *Four Books*. Please try to collect as many as possible and try to explain why it is the case.

Supplementary Reading: Paraphrase as a Translating Method for Chinese Philosophical Classics(2)

简论释译(二)
《论语》暨中国古代思想典籍的翻译方法

三、释译的连续体

释译不是单一的翻译方法,而是一个翻译连续体(translational continuum)。在这个连续体的两端,分别是浅度释译和深度释译。而居中的是中度释译或适度释译。三者依据译者诠释的程度和译文的篇幅不同而不同,都是合译理、合法度的翻译方法。显而易见,适度释译是最理想的方法。在句式篇章和思想内容的各个层面,原作和译文铢两悉称,无不足与有余。这是翻译的理想,只能接近很难达到。浅度释译和深度释译虽然不合中道,但他们依然是有效而且常常是实际使用的翻译方法。其偏离中道往往赋予文本以时代特色,展示译者的个性和追求。

以《四书》英译为例。韦利的《论语》、陈荣捷的《大学》《中庸》、林语堂的《大学》《论语》《孟子》接近适度释译。辜鸿铭的《论语》《大学》《中庸》、浦安迪的《大学》《中庸》似可归类为深度释译。理雅各的《四书》、林戊荪的《论语》、安乐哲、罗思文的《论语》《中庸》、刘殿爵的《孟子》《论语》都可以归属为浅度释译。

同一文本释译的差异,不仅表现在内容上诠释的差异,更具体显在地体现在篇幅字数上。因为诠释扩展较多深度释译,通常篇幅较大,字数较多。而浅度释译则反之。以《中庸》的辜鸿铭和理雅各译本为例。辜鸿铭的译本为11145英文词,而理雅各的译文只有7341英文词。因此,评判一个译者或一个译本的翻译方法,篇幅字数是重要的指标。

受制于中国传统译论的惯性,研究者们常常使用直译和意译去标示《论语》暨中国古代思想典籍的翻译方法。例如,人们常常称理雅各的翻译方法为直译,韦利、辜鸿铭的翻译方法为意译。王国维干脆主张辜鸿铭不是在翻译。因为术语概念的含糊,建基于直译意译二元对立的讨论必然缺乏学理的说服力和翻译方法的区分度。理雅各的译文其实并不"直译"。为了句义的完整和表达的地道流畅,理雅各在翻译过程中增插了许多词汇。为了句意的明晰和逻辑的严谨,他使用了许多英文连接词。他专门用斜体标明这些增插的成分。去掉这些增插的成分,他的译文将不复可读。事实上,除了已经标识的增插部分之外,在译文的其他部分,理雅各也做了大量的诠释工作,做了大量的增删改的翻译操作。基于上述释译理论,我们可以知道虽然辜鸿铭作了深度诠释,但是他的译文与原文句子对等,基本遵循一句还一句的原则。他仍然在翻译,而他的方法属于深度释译。

四、扩展与缩减的释译操作

具体到释译的翻译操作,可以分为扩展(amplifying)和缩减(diminishing)。扩展指译者张扬主体性,发挥主观能动性进行的有节制的言语扩张。在词和句子层面,为了目的语的正确流畅地道,目的语读者阅读和接受的方便,译者进行原作的再诠释和意义层面的深化,具体体现为译作字数的增加和篇幅的扩张。缩减的目的和扩展相同,但操作方式刚好相反,指译者对原作某些冗余成分的删改。释译具体操作会同时涉及扩展与缩减,以何种为主决定了释译的种类——是深度、适度还是浅度。

对于《论语》暨中国古代思想典籍而言,释译的翻译操作主要体现为扩展上。这是因为先秦文言极度俭省,意蕴又极度丰厚。非扩展性释译无法成文敷章,也无法保证文本的可读性和流畅性。关于扩展,我们在前文所举的《泰伯篇》8.8的英译可以看得很清楚。对于《四书》的英译无论理雅各、安乐哲、韦利、林戊荪、许渊冲,还是辜鸿铭、浦安迪都运用了不同程度的扩展。值得注意的是,即使是高度俭省的先秦文本,在外译时也有需要缩减的地方。例如,先秦文本中有许多对偶、对仗、排比的平行句。原作的平行句式意味着实词和功能词的重复出现。为了英语的表述习惯和修辞上的简洁要求,译者常常采用缩减的方法。浦安迪就注意到了这一方面,他对此有所论述并付诸实践。这样的缩减不但不是浅显化,反而可能是深化或美化的操作。

释译同样适用于思想类之外的其他类型文本,尤其是宋元明清的白话小说和现当代小说。中国传统白话小说有很多程式化的表达方式,而现当代小说繁缛冗余之处所在多有。对于这些文本,逐字逐词的翻译往往会导致译文不流畅、不地道的文本。成功的译者大多偏向使用缩减的翻译操作,而以扩展性的操作为辅(对于富有中国文化意蕴的词语,仍然必须做扩展性释译）。缩减的翻译操作可以使译文更简洁有力，更地道流畅，更利于目的语读者的阅读和接收。中国小说域外接受的成功与释译的方法有很大的关系。赛珍珠译《水浒》、大卫·霍克斯译《红楼梦》、芮效卫译《金瓶梅》、闵福德译金庸武侠小说、葛浩文译莫言的小说，这些译者无不采用了缩减性的释译。在英语文学汉译的另一端，林纾以文言翻译狄更斯、哈葛德的英国小说获得了巨大的成功，也与其缩减的释译操作有关。钱钟书、韦利都认为林译小说更加简洁有力，字净句省，比原文更佳。

释译（paraphrase）原意是"用其他词复述"（say something in other words）。这容易让人觉得这是一个文本浅显化转换过程。这不无道理，许多中文著作的英文译本的确比原语文本更浅显易懂。反之亦然。但是释译也可以是深化的过程。许渊冲的三美、三化、三之的翻译论本质上就是释译的深化论。

为了更好地说明释译的必要性和合法性，我们翻译了林语堂的《论释译》和浦安迪论中国古代思想典籍翻译的短文，作为单元的翻译专题。这两位翻译名家的观点可为本文作佐证。

Unit Fourteen
The Doctrine of the Mean (2)

This part of *The Doctrine of the Mean* dwells on the concept of filial piety and politics, highlighting in particular the great gains that filial piety can bring to the individual. To illustrate this point, Shun, an ancient sage king is used as a typical example, whose political exaltation was achieved mainly due to his filial piety. A similar situation is seen with a number of other ancient political figures. It is one of the important Confucian traditions that filial piety leads to a good political order. Specifically, politics based on filial piety revolves around two central concepts. First, the implementation of good politics depends on a good ruler, whose death may mean the end of his policies. Second, the key to politics is to cultivate oneself. Based on this idea, *The Doctrine of the Mean* proposes nine fundamental courses of action for governing the state. And to achieve this goal, one needs to follow the Way of Heaven, which will enable the ruler to achieve a state of sincerity and ultimately a good political life.

The Doctrine of the Mean(2) and Notes

The Master said, 'How greatly filial① was Shun! His virtue was that of a sage; his dignity was the imperial throne; his riches② were all within the four seas. He offered his sacrifices in his ancestral temple, and his descendants preserved the sacrifices to himself. Therefore having such great virtue, it could not but be that he should obtain the throne, that he should obtain those riches, that he should obtain his fame, that he should attain to his long life. Thus it is that Heaven, in the production of things, is sure to be bountiful to③ them, according to their qualities. Hence the tree that is flourishing, it nourishes, while that which is ready to fall, it overthrows. In the Book of Poetry, it is said, "The admirable, amiable prince displayed conspicuously his excelling virtue, adjusting his people and adjusting his officers. *Therefore*, he received from Heaven the emoluments of dignity. It protected him, assisted him, decreed him the throne; sending from Heaven these favours, *as it were* repeatedly." *We may say* therefore that he who is greatly virtuous will be sure to receive the appointment of Heaven.'

The above is the seventeenth chapter.

① "孝",理雅各译作 filial(孝顺的)。辜鸿铭译作 pious(虔敬的)。安乐哲译作 fidelity(忠诚;忠贞)。浦安迪译作 filiality(孝)。【编者按语】在随文的评点中,辜鸿铭说:"the word 孝 in the text above does not mean merely a filial son, but has the meaning of the Latin '*pius*'-pious in its full sense, reverential to God, dutiful to parents, good faithful and orderly in all the relations of life"(上文中的"孝"不仅仅指孝顺的儿子,而是含有拉丁文 pius 的全部意思——对上帝虔敬,对父母尽责,在生活中的所有关系中都保持友善、守信和有序)。

② "禄",理雅各译作 riches(财富)。辜鸿铭译作 great prosperity(巨大的繁荣)。安乐哲译作 emoluments(酬金)。浦安迪译作 recompense(报酬)。

③ "笃",理雅各和辜鸿铭译作 be bountiful to(对……慷慨)。安乐哲译作 be in response to(回应;适应)。浦安迪译作 shed its grace upon(将恩泽施予)。

子曰:"舜其大孝也与! 德为圣人,尊为天子,富有四海之内。宗庙飨之,子孙保之。故大德必得其位,必得其禄。必得其名,必得其寿,故天之生物,必因其材而笃焉。故栽者培之,倾者覆之。《诗》^①曰:'嘉乐^②君子,宪宪^③令德^④。宜民宜人,受禄于天,保佑命之,自天申之。'故大德者必受命。"

* 右第十七章。

① 《诗》:指《诗·大雅·假乐》。
② 嘉乐:今本《诗经》中作"假乐"。一般认为,"假"通"嘉",意为善;乐,意为喜悦。
③ 宪宪:今本《诗经》中作"显显",意为明显、盛大。
④ 令德:美好的德行。

The Master said, 'It is only King Wăn of whom it can be said that he had no cause for grief! His father was King Chî, and his son was King Wû. His father laid the foundations of his dignity, and his son transmitted it①. King Wû continued the enterprise of King T'âi, King Chî, and King Wăn. He once buckled on his armour②, and got possession of the kingdom. He did not lose the distinguished personal reputation which he had throughout the kingdom. His dignity was the royal throne. His riches were the possession of all within the four seas. He offered his sacrifices in his ancestral temple, and his descendants maintained the sacrifices to himself. It was in his old age that King Wû received the appointment to *the throne*, and the duke of Châu completed the virtuous course of Wǎn and Wû. He carried up the title of king to T'âi and Chî, and sacrificed to all the former dukes above them with the royal ceremonies. And this rule③ he extended to the princes of the kingdom, the great officers, the scholars, and the common people. If the father were a great officer and the son a scholar, then the burial was that due to a great officer, and the sacrifice that due to a scholar. If the father were a scholar, and the son a great officer, then the burial was that due to a scholar, and the sacrifice that due to a great officer. The one year's mourning was made to extend *only* to the great officers, but the three years' mourning extended to the Son of Heaven. In the mourning for a father or mother, he allowed no difference between the noble and mean."

The above is the eighteenth chapter.

① "述",理雅各译作 transmitted(传承)。辜鸿铭译作 carried it on(继承)。安乐哲译作 continued along the proper way(继续沿着正确的路前行)。浦安迪译作 carrying forward of their undertakings(继承弘扬他们的事业)。

② "壹戎衣",理雅各和辜鸿铭译作 buckle on his armour(系好盔甲)。安乐哲译作 in slaying the Great Yin(在毁灭强大的殷的过程中)。浦安迪译作 cut down the mighty Yin (推翻了强大的殷)。

③ "礼",理雅各和辜鸿铭译作 the rule(规则)。安乐哲译作 the use of these same rites (同样礼仪的运用)。浦安迪译作 the ritual system(礼仪体系)。

子曰:"无忧者,其惟文王乎! 以王季①为父,以武王为子,父作之,子述之。武王缵②大王、王季、文王之绪,壹戎衣而有天下。身不失天下之显名,尊为天子,富有四海之内。宗庙飨③之,子孙保之。武王末受命,周公成文、武之德,追王大王、王季,上祀先公以天子之礼。斯礼也,达乎诸侯大夫,及士庶人。父为大夫,子为士,葬以大夫,祭以士。父为士,子为大夫,葬以士,祭以大夫。期之丧,达乎大夫。三年之丧,达乎天子。父母之丧,无贵贱一也。"

右第十八章。

① 王季:姬姓,名历。季指排行,即第三子,一般称季历,尊称公季、王季等。王季在商王文丁时为西方诸侯之长,后为商王软禁而死。

② 缵:继承。

③ 飨:祭祀。

The Master said, 'How far-extending was the filial piety of King Wu and the duke of Châu! Now filial piety is seen in the skilful carrying out of the wishes of our forefathers, and the skilful carrying forward of their undertakings. In spring and autumn, they repaired and beautified the temple-halls of their fathers, set forth their ancestral vessels, displayed their various robes, and presented the offerings of the several seasons①. By means of the ceremonies of the ancestral temple, they distinguished the imperial kindred according to their order of descent. By ordering the parties present according to their rank, they distinguished the more noble and the less. By the arrangement of the services, they made a distinction of talents and worth②. In the ceremony of general pledging, the inferiors presented the cup to their superiors, and thus something was given the lowest to do③. At the *concluding* feast, places were given according to the hair, and thus was made the distinction of years. They occupied the places of their forefathers, practised their ceremonies, and performed their music. They reverenced those whom they honoured, and loved those whom they regarded with affection. Thus they served the dead as they would have served them alive; they served the departed as they would have served them had they been continued among them. By the ceremonies of the sacrifices to Heaven and Earth they served God, and by the ceremonies of the ancestral temple they sacrificed to their ancestors. He who understands the ceremonies of the sacrifices to Heaven and Earth, and the meaning of the several sacrifices to ancestors, would find the government of a kingdom as easy as to look into his palm!'

The above is the ninteenth chapter.

① "时食",理雅各译作 the offerings of the several seasons(各季的祭品)。辜鸿铭译作 the appropriate offering of the season(当季的祭品)。安乐哲译作 the newly harvested crops(新收获的谷物)。浦安迪译作 the sacrificial foods of the season(当季的祭祀食物)。

② "辨贤",理雅各译作 made a distinction of talents and worth(辨别才干和价值)。辜鸿铭译作 as a recognition of distribution in moral worth(辨认道德价值的差异)。安乐哲译作 distinguishing those most worthy(突显最有价值的人)。浦安迪译作 distinguishing the moral worth of the celebrants(彰显礼仪主持人的道德价值)。

③ "逮贱",理雅各译作 something was given the lowest to do(让最低微的人分担一些

任务)。辜鸿铭译作 show that consideration is shown to the meanest(显示最卑贱的人也受到照顾)。安乐哲译作 reaching down to include the lowliest(屈尊关注地位最低的人)。浦安迪译作 granting equal participation to those of lower status(给与下位者平等的参与机会)。

子曰:"武王、周公,其达孝矣乎! 夫孝者,善继人之志,善述人之事者也。春秋修其祖庙,陈其宗器①,设其裳衣②,荐③其时食。宗庙之礼,所以序昭穆④也。序爵⑤,所以辨贵贱也。序事⑥,所以辨贤也。旅酬⑦下为上,所以逮贱⑧也。燕毛⑨,所以序齿⑩也。践其位⑪,行其礼,奏其乐,敬其所尊,爱其所亲,事死如事生,事亡如事存,孝之至也。郊社⑫之礼,所以事上帝也。宗庙之礼,所以祀乎其先也。明乎郊社之礼、禘尝⑬之义,治国其如示诸掌乎!"

* 右第十九章。

① 宗器:宗庙祭祀之器具。
② 裳衣:郑玄认为,"裳衣,先祖之遗衣服也。"
③ 荐:祭献。
④ 序昭穆:序,意为排定或排序。昭穆,针对的是宗庙或墓地的辈分。古代将父的庙或墓称为昭,子的庙或墓称为穆。
⑤ 爵:本意为饮酒之器具,古代饮酒根据个人的阶位不同而所用饮酒器具不同,因此用什么样的爵也就代指一个人的身份之贵贱。
⑥ 序事:此处的事特指用乐之事,序事即陈列乐器以及安排如何奏乐的次序。
⑦ 旅酬:宾客与主人之间互相敬酒的仪式。
⑧ 逮贱:主人回敬酒时,先从地位低下人开始,显示恩惠及于一切人。
⑨ 燕毛:燕,通"宴",意为根据年纪之长幼定位次。
⑩ 序齿:齿,指牙齿之数目,代指年纪之长幼。然"毛"与"齿"不同的是,"毛"主要是对年纪长的人之间的座次排定,而"齿"特指年幼的人的座次的排定。
⑪ 践其位:践,本意为履,指踏上或登上,此处指在宗庙之中,每个人站到自己应该站的位置。
⑫ 郊社:周代祭祀的两种仪式。在冬至日,天子祭天称郊,夏至日,天子祭地称社。
⑬ 禘尝:禘礼和尝礼的并称,都属于祭祀祖先的仪式。《礼记·王制》:"天子诸侯宗庙之祭,春曰礿,夏曰禘,秋曰尝,冬曰烝。"

The Duke Âi asked about Government. The Master said, 'The government of Wăn and Wû is displayed in *the records*, —the tablets of wood and bamboo①. Let there be the men and the government will flourish; but without the men, their government decays and ceases. With the *right* men the growth of government is rapid, just as vegetation is rapid in the earth; and, moreover, *their government might be called* an easily-growing rush②. Therefore the administration of government lies in *getting proper* men. Such men are to be got by means of *the ruler's own* character. That character is to be cultivated by his treading in the ways *of duty*. And the treading those ways of duty is to be cultivated by the cherishing of benevolence. Benevolence is the *characteristic element of* humanity, and the great exercise of it is in loving relatives. Righteousness is *the accordance of actions with what is right*, and the great exercise of it is in honouring the worthy. The decreasing measures of the love due to relatives③, and the steps in the honour due to the worthy, are produced by *the principle of* propriety④. When those in inferior situations do not possess the confidence of their superiors, they cannot retain the government of the people. Hence the sovereign may not neglect the cultivation of his own character. Wishing to cultivate his character, he may not neglect to serve his parents. In order to serve his parents, he may not neglect to acquire a knowledge of men. In order to know men⑤, he may not dispense with a knowledge of Heaven. The duties of universal obligation are five, and the virtues wherewith they are practised are three. The duties are those between sovereign and minister, between father and son, between husband and wife, between elder brother and younger, and those belonging to the intercourse of friends. Those five are the duties of universal obligation. Knowledge, magnanimity, and energy, these three, are the virtues universally binding. And the means by which they carry *the duties* into practice is singleness.

Some are born with the knowledge *of those duties*; some know them by study; and some acquire the knowledge after a painful feeling of their ignorance. But the knowledge being possessed, it comes to the same thing. Some practise them with a natural ease; some from a desire for their advantages; and some by strenuous effort. But the achievement being made, it comes to the same thing.

① "方策",理雅各译作 the records—the tablets of wood and bamboo(竹木板条的文档)。辜鸿铭译作 the records preserved(保存的文档)。安乐哲译作 the wooden slats and bamboo strips(木条和竹片)。浦安迪译作 the wooden tablets and the bamboo strips(木条和竹片)。【编者按语】辜鸿铭的翻译是泛化的诠释。其他译法比较忠实。

② "蒲卢",理雅各译作 an easily-growing rush(快速生长的灯芯草)。辜鸿铭译为 a

fast growing plant(快速生长的植物)。安乐哲译作 the silkworm wasp(细腰蜂)。浦安迪译作 a quick-growing reed(快速生长的芦苇)。【编者按语】关于"蒲卢",郑玄与朱熹有不同的诠释。前者释为"细腰蜂",后者释为"蒲苇"。辜译据朱训又做了泛化的诠释。

③ "亲亲之杀",理雅各译作 the decreasing measures of the love due to relatives(对亲疏有别的亲戚表现的差等的爱)。辜鸿铭译作 the relative degrees of natural affection we ought to feel for those who are nearly related to us(人们对近亲体会到的自然感情的相对程度)。安乐哲译作 the degree of devotion due different kin(对不同亲戚程度有别的爱)。浦安迪译作 the maintenance of proper gradation in the affectionate treatment of one's kin(对亲疏有别的亲戚表现的差等的爱)。

④ "礼",理雅各译作 the principle of propriety(礼的原则)。辜鸿铭译作 the forms and distinctions in social life(社会生活的形态和差异)。安乐哲和浦安迪译作 ritual propriety(礼仪)。

⑤ "知人",理雅各译作 know men(知人)。辜鸿铭译作 understand the nature and organization of human society(知晓人类社会的性质和组织)。安乐哲译作 realizing human conduct(了解人的行为)。浦安迪译作 appreciate the subtleties of human relations(了解细微的人际关系)。

哀公①问政。子曰:"文武②之政,布在方策。其人存,则其政举;其人亡,则其政息。人道敏③政,地道敏树。夫政也者,蒲卢④也。故为政在人,取人以身,修身以道,修道以仁。仁者人也。亲亲为大;义者宜也。尊贤为大。亲亲之杀⑤,尊贤之等,礼所生也。在下位不获乎上,民不可得而治矣!故君子不可以不修身;思修身,不可以不事亲;思事亲,不可以不知人,思知人,不可以不知天。天下之达道五,所以行之者三。曰:君臣也,父子也,夫妇也,昆弟也,朋友之交也,五者天下之达道也。知,仁,勇,三者天下之达德也,所以行之者一也。或生而知之,或学而知之,或困而知之,及其知之,一也。或安而行之,或利而行之,或勉强而行之,及其成功,一也。"

① 哀公:指鲁哀公。春秋时鲁国的国君。
② 文武:文指周文王,武指周武王,文、武为他们的谥号。
③ 敏:勤勉、竭力。
④ 蒲卢:郑玄认为是一种细腰的土蜂,朱熹认为是芦苇。不论何者解释合理,此处都以某种事物比喻政治教化。
⑤ 杀:等级。

The Master said, 'To be fond of learning is to be near to knowledge. To practise with vigour is to be near to magnanimity. To possess the feeling of shame[①] is to be near to energy. He who knows these three things, knows how to cultivate his own character. Knowing how to cultivate his own character, he knows how to govern other men. Knowing how to govern other men, he knows how to govern the kingdom with all its States and families. All who have the government of the kingdom with its States and families have nine standard rules to follow[②];—viz., the cultivation of their own characters; the honouring of men of virtue and talents; affection towards their relatives; respect towards the great ministers; kind and considerate treatment of the whole body of officers[③]; dealing with the mass of the people as children; encouraging the resort of all classes of artizans; indulgent treatment of men from a distance; and the kindly cherishing of the princes of the States. By the ruler's cultivation of his own character, the duties *of universal obligation* are set forth. By honouring men of virtue and talents, he is preserved from errors of judgment. By showing affection to his relatives, there is no grumbling nor resentment among his uncles and brethren. By respecting the great ministers, he is kept from errors in the practice of government. By kind and considerate treatment of the whole body of officers, they are led to make the most grateful return for his courtesies. By dealing with the mass of the people as his children, they are led to exhort one another to what is good. By encouraging the resort of all classes of artizans, his resources for expenditure are rendered ample. By indulgent treatment of men from a distance, they are brought to resort to him from all quarters. And by kindly cherishing the princes of the States[④], the whole kingdom is brought to revere him.'

① "知耻",理雅各译作 to possess the feeling of shame(拥有羞耻感)。辜鸿铭译作 sensitiveness to shame(对羞耻保持敏感)。安乐哲译作 having a sense of shame(有羞耻心)。浦安迪译作 a sense of shame(羞耻心)。

② "经",理雅各译作 standard rules to follow(必须遵循的规矩)。辜鸿铭译作 cardinal directions(根本的指南)。安乐哲译作 guidelines(指南)。浦安迪译作 cardinal principles(原理)。

③ "体群臣",理雅各译作 kind and considerate treatment of the whole body of officers(体贴宽待所有的公务人员)。辜鸿铭译作 identifying himself with the interests and welfare of the whole body of public officers(认同所有公务人员的利益和福利)。安乐哲译作 be inclusive of the whole assembly of ministers(包容全体大臣)。浦安迪译作 empathizing with the concerns of the official rank and file(照顾全体普通公务员的种种关切)。

④ "怀诸侯",理雅各译作 the kindly cherishing of the princes of the States(善待各国的诸侯)。辜鸿铭译作 taking interest in the welfare of the princes of the Empire(关心帝国诸侯的利益)。安乐哲译作 cherish the various nobles(爱护各类别的贵族)。浦安迪译作 embracing the Lords of All the States under one' sway(将各国诸侯置于自己影响之下)。

子曰:"好学近乎知,力行近乎仁,知耻近乎勇。知斯三者,则知所以修身;知所以修身,则知所以治人;知所以治人,则知所以治天下国家矣。凡为天下国家有九经,曰:修身也。尊贤也,亲亲也,敬大臣也,体①群臣也。子②庶民也,来③百工也,柔④远人也,怀⑤诸侯也。修身则道立,尊贤则不惑,亲亲则诸父昆弟不怨,敬大臣则不眩,体群臣则士之报礼重,子庶民则百姓劝,来百工则财用足,柔远人则四方归之,怀诸侯则天下畏之。"

① 体:体察或亲身经验。
② 子:子女。
③ 来:通"徕",意为招徕。
④ 柔:安抚。
⑤ 怀:眷顾。

'Self-adjustment and purification, with careful regulation of his dress, and the not making a movement contrary to the rules of propriety: —this is the way for the ruler to cultivate his person. Discarding slanderers, and keeping himself from *the seductions of* beauty①; making light of riches, and giving honour to virtue: —this is the way for him to encourage men of worth and talents. Giving them places *of honour* and large emolument②, and sharing with them in their likes and dislikes: —this is the way for him to encourage his relatives to love him. Giving them numerous officers to discharge their orders and commissions: —this is the way for him to encourage the great ministers. According to them a generous confidence, and making their emoluments large: —this is the way to encourage the body of officers③. Employing them only at the proper times, and making the imposts light: —this is the way to encourage the people. By daily examinations and monthly trials, and by making their rations in accordance with their labours: —this is the way to encourage the classes of artizans. To escort them on their departure and meet them on their coming; to commend the good among them, and show compassion to the incompctcnt: —this is the way to treat indulgently men from a distance. To restore families whose line of succession has been broken, and to revive States that have been extinguished; to reduce to order States that are in confusion, and, support those which are in peril; to have fixed times for their own reception at court, and the reception of their envoys; to send them away after liberal treatment, and welcome their coming with small contributions: —this is the way to cherish the princes of the States. All who have the government of the kingdom with its States and families have the above nine standard rules. And the means by which they are carried into practice, is singleness.'

① "远色",理雅各译作 keeping himself from *the seductions of* beauty(抵御美女的诱惑)。辜鸿铭译作 keeping away from the society of women(不要女性的陪伴)。安乐哲译作 distracting enticing faces(远离娇美迷人的脸蛋)。浦安迪译作 keeping sensual temptation at a safe distance(远离声色的诱惑)。

② "重禄",在本段落里二现。理雅各译作 large emoluments(丰厚慷慨的酬劳)。辜鸿铭分别译作 bestowing ample emoluments(赐给丰富的财物)和 allowing a liberal scale of pay(支持丰厚慷慨的工资)。安乐哲译作 being generous in emoluments(慷慨地给予薪水)。浦安迪译作 granting liberal recompense(给予慷慨的酬劳)。

③ "劝士",理雅各译作 encourage the body of officers(鼓励全体官员)。辜鸿铭译作 give encouragement to men in the public service(鼓励公务人员)。安乐哲译作 encourage scholar-officers(鼓励学者-官员)。浦安迪译作 provide incentives to the untitled officers(为普通公务员提供激励)。【编者按语】浦安迪将"士"译作 the untitled officers,以区别于上文的"大臣"(the greater officers)。

齐明盛服,非礼不动。所以修身也;去谗远色,贱货而贵德,所以劝贤也;尊其位,重其禄,同其好恶,所以劝亲亲也;官盛任使,所以劝大臣也;忠信重禄,所以劝士也;时使薄敛,所以劝百姓也;日省①月试,既廪②称事,所以劝百工也;送往迎来,嘉善而矜不能,所以柔远人也;继绝世,举废国,治乱持危。朝聘以时,厚往而薄来,所以怀诸侯也。凡为天下国家有九经,所以行之者一也。

① 省(xǐng):检查。
② 既廪:"既"通"饩",孔颖达认为,"既廪谓饮食粮廪也"。

'In all things success depends on previous preparation, and without such previous preparation there is sure to be failure. If what is to be spoken be previously determined, there will be no stumbling. If affairs be previously determined, there will be no difficulty with them. If one's actions have been previously determined, there will be no sorrow in connexion with them. If principles of conduct have been previously determined, the practice of them will be inexhaustible. When those in inferior situations do not obtain the confidence of the sovereign[①], they cannot succeed in governing the people. There is a way to obtain the confidence of the sovereign;—if one is not trusted by his friends, he will not get the confidence of his sovereign. There is a way to being trusted by one's friends:—if one is not obedient to his parents, he will not be true to friends. There is a way to being obedient to one's parents;—if one, on turning his thoughts in upon himself, finds a want of sincerity, he will not be obedient to his parents. There is a way to the attainment of sincerity[②] in one's self;—if a man do not understand what is good, he will not attain sincerity in himself. Sincerity is the way of Heaven. The attainment of sincerity is the way of men[③]. He who possesses sincerity, is he who, without an effort, hits what is right, and apprehends, without the exercise of thought;—he is the sage who naturally and easily embodies the *right* way. He who attains to sincerity is he who chooses what is good, and firmly holds it fast. To this attainment there are requisite the extensive study of what is good, accurate inquiry about it, careful reflection on it, the clear discrimination of it, and the earnest practice of it. The superior man, while there is anything he has not studied, or while in what he has studied there is anything he cannot understand, will not intermit his labour. While there is anything he has not inquired about or anything in what he has inquired about which he does not know, he will not intermit his labour. While there is anything which he has not reflected on, or anything in what he has reflected on which he does not apprehend, he will not intermit his labour. While there is anything which he has not discriminated, or his discrimination is not clear, he will not intermit his labour. If there be anything which he has not practised, or his practice fails in earnestness, he will not intermit his labour. If another man succeed by one effort, he will use a hundred efforts. If another man succeed by ten efforts, he will use a thousand. Let a man proceed in this way, and, though dull, he will surely become intelligent; though weak, he will surely become strong.'

The above is the twentieth chapter.

① "在下位,不获乎上",理雅各译作 When those in inferior situations do not obtain the confidence of the sovereign(如果居于下位者不能获得君主的信任)。辜鸿铭译为 If those in authority have not the confidence under them(如果在权位者没有获得下属的信任)。安乐哲译作 When those in inferior situations do not gain the support of their superiors(如果居于下位者不能获得上级的支持)。浦安迪译作 As long as those in inferior positions are unable to gain the support of those above them(只要居于下位者不能获得居上位者的支持)。【编者按语】辜鸿铭理解为"在上位,不获乎下"。这可能是他故意误读,表示了西方主权在民的思想。

② "诚",理雅各译作 sincerity 或 the attainment of sincerity in one's self(诚实或对自己诚实)。辜鸿铭译作 truth 或 to be true to oneself(真实或对自己真实)。安乐哲译作 creativity 或 being creative in one's person(创生或自主创生)。浦安迪译作 integral wholeness(整全)。

③ "诚之者,人之道",理雅各译作 the attainment of sincerity is the way of men(诚心是人之道)。辜鸿铭译作 acquired truth is the law of man(后天习得的真实是人的法则)。安乐哲译作 creating is the proper way of becoming human(创生是成人的正当方法)。浦安迪译作 the process of making oneself whole is, however, within the province of the Way of Man(但是使自己整全的过程属于人道的范围)。

凡事豫①则立,不豫则废。言前定则不跲②,事前定则不困,行前定则不疚,道前定则不穷。在下位不获乎上,民不可得而治矣。获乎上有道,不信乎朋友,不获乎上矣;信乎朋友有道,不顺乎亲,不信乎朋友矣;顺乎亲有道,反诸身不诚,不顺乎亲矣;诚身有道,不明乎善,不诚乎身矣。诚者,天之道也;诚之者,人之道也。诚者不勉而中,不思而得,从容中道,圣人也。诚之者,择善而固执之者也。博学之,审问③之,慎思之,明辨之,笃行之。有弗学,学之弗能,弗措④也;有弗问,问之弗知,弗措也;有弗思,思之弗得,弗措也;有弗辨,辨之弗明,弗措也;有弗行,行之弗笃,弗措也。人一能之己百之,人十能之己千之。果能此道矣。虽愚必明,虽柔必强。"

＊右第二十章。

① 豫:通"预",意为预备、预先考虑。
② 跲:本意为绊倒,此处引申为不顺畅、不流利。
③ 审问:详尽地询问。
④ 弗措:弗,不;措,放置、安置。弗措,意为不放弃。

Exercises

1. Put the following passage into English.

中庸何为而作也？子思子忧道学之失其传而作也。盖自上古圣神继天立极,而道统之传有自来矣。其见于经,则"允执厥中"者,尧之所以授舜也;"人心惟危,道心惟微,惟精惟一,允执厥中"者,舜之所以授禹也。尧之一言至矣,尽矣！而舜复益之以三言者,则所以明夫尧之一言,必如是而后可庶几也。

盖尝论之:心之虚灵知觉,一而已矣,而以为有人心、道心之异者,则以其或生于形气之私,或原于性命之正,而所以为知觉者不同,是以或危殆而不安,或微妙而难见耳。然人莫不有是形,故虽上智不能无人心,亦莫不有是性,故虽下愚不能无道心。二者杂于方寸之间,而不知所以治之,则危者愈危,微者愈微,而天理之公卒无以胜夫人欲之私矣。精则察夫二者之间而不杂也。一则守其本心之正而不离也。从事于斯,无少闲断,必使道心常为一身之主,而人心每听命焉,则危者安,而微者著,而动静云为无过不及之差矣。

2. Debate the following topic.

According to Confucianism, filial piety is closely related to good politics. Do you agree or disagree. Please use evidence to support your argument.

Supplementary Reading: Andrew Plaks on Paraphrase as a Translation Method for Chinese Philosophical Classics

浦安迪论中国古代思想典籍的"释译"

浦安迪(Andrew Plaks, 1945—),著名汉学家,普林斯顿大学东亚系和比较文学系荣休教授、以色列希伯来大学东亚系教授,他通晓十几种语言。其中包括汉语、日语、俄语、法语、希伯来语。研究领域广泛,包括中国古典小说、叙事学、中国传统思想文化、中西文化文学比较。代表性译著有《大学》《中庸》《左传》。本书《大学》《中庸》采用了他的译本作为参照文本。

关于《中庸》《大学》的英译,浦安迪写作了较长的《简论翻译》,论述他的翻译方法。他把他的翻译方法概括为等值话语(equivalent utterances)或创造性调整(creative adjustment)。他不主张原文和译文词汇单位的严格匹配,反对干巴巴的逐字逐句的翻译。为了语义的完整和英文表达的地道,他主张可以插补一些英文词——实词和连词等语法功能词。同时删去原文的冗余的词和表达方式。在句式层面,他主张译者享有较大的自主裁量权。句序的颠倒、句式的调整、句子的长短调节、语域的确定,都可由译者自主决定。

浦安迪的翻译方法可以概括为"释译"。在《大学》《中庸》的翻译中,他对原文的各个层次都进行了拓展性的诠释。译文篇幅不仅远超过中文原文,也超过了大多数译者的译本。例如,《大学》开场白的三句话:大学之道,在明明德,在亲民,在止于至善。共16个汉字,浦安迪的译文共46个英文词里。理雅各的译文共21个词。林语堂译文共30个词。陈荣捷的译文共25个词。

浦安迪的中国古代思想典籍的翻译实践和翻译主张,为本书倡导的释译方法提供了有力的佐证。以下译文选自浦安迪翻译的《大学》和《中庸》绪论中的《简论翻译》。

"此处提供的新译本基于三个主要的翻译原则。在最一般的层面上,我的目标是生成可能被称为'等值话语'的译文,即提供上下文中语义和句法值的近似,而不是词汇单位的严格匹配。考虑到这一点,我经常在我的表述中给自己留出相当大的余地。例如,在我觉得用英语通常应当这样表达的时候,插入额外的词来传达意义丰富的中国概念,或者将中国文体冗余合并成单个命题。仅举一个最显著的例子,我翻译的《大学》的'三句话'开场白:

The Way of self-cultivation, at its highest level, is a three-fold path:
It lies in causing the light of one's inner moral force to shine forth,
in bringing the people to a state of renewal,
and in coming to rest in the fullest attainment of the good.

(修身之道的最高境界是三重道路:
在于使人内在道德力量的光芒闪耀,
在使人民进入更生的状态,
并安顿于最充分扩展的善。)

这是从原语经典文本仅仅16个字翻译而来。我这里的目的是利用丰厚的中国学术资源,包括传统的注疏和现代的评注,努力表现出原作富含的多层意涵。而干巴巴的逐字逐句的翻译在我看来严重不足。且看熟悉的译文:

The Way of the Great Learning lies in
shining with one's bright virtue,
in renovating the people,
and in resting in the highest good
(大学之道在于:
照亮明洁的德行,

改造人民,
安顿于至善。)

在进行这种类型的词语插补时,我尝试在相关点的注释和附录一对关键术语作较长篇幅的解释和说明。但鉴于这么做是以冗长为代价的,我经常在相同短语的后续重复时进行缩略。例如,to set straight the seat of their emotive and cognitive faculties(将他们的情感和认知能力的位置摆正),在下一行我将之缩略为 to set these faculties straight(将这些能力摆正)。在中文文本分句之间的逻辑连接要么含糊不清,要么没有表现出来的地方,我也援用了这个翻译原则。我添加了 by definition(根据定义)和 so to speak(可以这么说)之类的短语,以使论点更加清晰。在一系列平行从句中,如果一个中文术语一成不变地重复,我经常选择一组不同的同义词,以避免单调。我也特别注意原文中连词和从属标记的使用,例如'故(therefores)'和'若(if-then)'结构。我致力于调整我的英语用法,以表现在它们每次出现时的修辞冲击力。

本着同样的精神,我试图在句子结构的层次上最大限度地提高语法和句法的灵活性,以此作为寻找汉语表达方式对等的手段。例如,反问句可以转化为否定句,断言句转化为反问句;汉语情态助词的意义可以用括号短语来表示(I fear, long may we),或者用其他方式。对于连词'而'(通常译为 moreover,或干脆译作 and)联结的并列句的常规汉语结构,我通常更喜欢以方式或条件状语从句的方式来处理其中一个分句。比如《大学》的首篇中的'其本乱而末治',翻译时我颠倒了语序:For one to put the peripheral 'branches' of one's behaviour into order, while the 'roots' at its core are yet in a state of chaotic entanglement(一个人行为的外在'枝节'有序,而其核心的'根本'处于混乱纠缠状态)。我认为这么做比字面翻译更准确地表达了原意:When the roots are entangled and the branches are in order(当根系纠缠,而枝干有序时)。

最后,我试图捕捉中文原文的多种'声音':圣人的智慧教诲、证明文本的使用(即引用据称是古代经典的语句来证明一个观点)、哲学论证的博学的话语。我会使用不同语域的表达方式。在这样做的时候,我可能偶尔会在英语中使用一种故意学究式或伪古代风格。在我看来,经典文本的雍容风格似乎需要这种的处理方式。虽然'创造性调整'的许多例子可能会让熟悉原语语言的读者觉得是不必要的自由,但是每一个例子都是大量研究、思考的结果,每一个例子还代表了在作最终选择时译者不可避免体会的大量痛苦。"

Unit Fifteen
The Doctrine of the Mean (3)

This unit presents the last part of *The Doctrine of the Mean*, which is the most obscure part of the book. It concentrates on the metaphysics of Confucianism, which holds that only when a person reaches the state of absolute sincerity does his nature fully reveal itself, and only when he can fully reveal the nature of external objects, can he then appreciate all things and be in harmony with heaven and earth. In this part, sincerity is particularly emphasized, as it is considered an important way of communication between man and the heavenly path. And if a person finally achieves the state of complete sincerity, he is considered a sage who is able to fully comprehend the way of Heaven and give good order to the whole world, realizing the political state envisioned by Confucianism.

The Doctrine of the Mean(3) and Notes

When we have intelligence resulting from sincerity, this condition is to be ascribed to nature[①]; when we have sincerity resulting from intelligence, this condition is to be ascribed to instruction. But given the sincerity, and there shall be the intelligence; given the intelligence, and there shall be the sincerity.

The above is the twenty-first chapter. Tsze-sze takes up in it, and discourses from, the subjects of 'the way of Heaven' and 'the way of men,' mentioned in the preceding chapter. The twelve chapters that follow are all from Tsze-sze, repeating and illustrating the meaning of this one.

It is only he who is possessed of the most complete sincerity that can exist under heaven, who can give its full development to his nature[②]. Able to give its full development to his own nature, he can do the same to the nature of other men. Able to give its full development to the nature of other men, he can give their full development to the natures of animals and things. Able to give their full development to the natures of creatures and things, he can assist the transforming and nourishing powers of Heaven and Earth. Able to assist the transforming and nourishing powers of Heaven and Earth, he may with Heaven and Earth form a ternion.

The above is the twenty-second chapter.

Next to the above is he who cultivates to the utmost the shoots *of goodness* in him③. From those he can attain to the possession of sincerity. This sincerity becomes apparent. From being apparent, it becomes manifest. From being manifest, it becomes brilliant. Brilliant, it affects others. Affecting others, they are changed by it. Changed by it, they are transformed. It is only he who is possessed of the most complete sincerity that can exist under heaven, who can transform.

The above is the twenty-third chapter.

It is characteristic of the most entire sincerity to be able to foreknow. When a nation or family is about to flourish, there are sure to be happy omens; and when it is about to perish, there are sure to be unlucky omens. *Such events are* seen in the milfoil and tortoise, and affect the movements of the four limbs. When calamity or happiness is about to come, the good shall certainly be foreknown by him, and the evil also. Therefore, the individual possessed of the most complete sincerity is like a spirit.

The above is the twenty-fourth chapter.

① "自诚明,谓之性",理雅各译作 When we have intelligence resulting from sincerity, this condition is to be ascribed to nature(来自真诚的才智应该归结到天性)。辜鸿铭译作 The intelligence which comes from the direct apprehension of truth is intuition(来自对真理直接的领会的才智是直觉)。安乐哲译作 Understanding born of creativity(*cheng* 诚)is a gift of our natural tendencies(*xing* 性)(源于诚的理解力是人们天性的馈赠)。浦安迪译作 When one's path of cultivation proceeds from integral wholeness to conscious understanding, this can be attributed to the predisposition of inborn nature(当修身之路从整全过渡到有意识的理解力,这可以归结为先天的性质)。

② "尽其性",理雅各译作 give its full development to its nature(充分扩展人类的本性)。辜鸿铭译作 get to the bottom of the law of his being(洞察人类生存法则)。安乐哲译作 make the most out of their natural tendencies(充分利用人类的自然倾向)。浦安迪译

作 have the capacity fully to realize their inborn nature(有充分的能力实现自己的天性)。

③"致曲",理雅各译作 cultivates to the utmost the shoots *of goodness* in him(最充分培育善的根苗)。辜鸿铭 attain to the comprehension of a particular branch of learning(洞悉某一特定知识领域)。安乐哲译作 cultivate these processes and events with discretion(审慎地培育这些过程和事件)。浦安迪译作 achieve fulfilment within the realm of concrete particulars(在具体的知识领域有所成就)。

自诚明谓之性。自明诚谓之教。诚则明矣,明则诚矣。

* 右第二十一章。子思承上章夫子天道、人道之意而立言也。自此以下十二章,皆子思之言,以反复推明此章之意。

唯天下至诚,为能尽其性;能尽其性,则能尽人之性;能尽人之性,则能尽物之性;能尽物之性,则可以赞①天地之化育;可以赞天地之化育,则可以与天地参②矣。

* 右第二十二章。

其次致曲。曲能有诚,诚则形,形则著,著则明,明则动,动则变,变则化。唯天下至诚为能化。

* 右第二十三章。

至诚之道,可以前知。国家将兴,必有祯祥;国家将亡,必有妖孽。见乎蓍龟,动乎四体。祸福将至,善必先知之;不善必先知之。故至诚如神。

* 右第二十四章。

① 赞:佐助。
② 参:通"三",意为人与天地并列为三。也有学者解释为参与。两种解读皆通。

Sincerity is that whereby self-completion is effected①, and *its* way is that by which man must direct himself. Sincerity is the end and beginning of things; without sincerity there would be nothing. On this account, the superior man regards the attainment of sincerity as the most excellent thing. The possessor of sincerity does not merely accomplish the self-completion of himself. With this quality he completes *other men and* things *also*②. The completing himself *shows his* perfect virtue. The completing *other men and* things *shows his* knowledge. *Both these are* virtues belonging to the nature, and *this is* the way by which a union is effected of the external and internal. Therefore, whenever he—*the entirely sincere man*—employs them,—*that is, these virtues,—their action will* *be right*③.

The above is the twenty-fifth chapter.

① "诚者自成",理雅各译作 sincerity is that whereby self-completion is effected(是诚,使得人的自我完善得以实现)。辜鸿铭译作 truth means the realization of our being(真理意味着人存在的领悟)。安乐哲译作 creativity is self-consummating(创生是自我圆满的)。浦安迪译作 the term 'integral wholeness' refers to a process of becoming complete through one's own agency("整全"这一术语指通过自己的力量变得完整的过程)。

② "所以成物",理雅各译作 with this quality, he complete *other men* and things *also*(因为有这个特质,他同时完成了其他人和物)。辜鸿铭译成 it is that by which things outside of us have an existence(由此,我们之外的物得以存在)。安乐哲译作 it is what consummates events(它使得事件得以圆满)。浦安迪译作 it constitutes the ground for bringing to completion all things with which one interacts in the phenomenal world(它为把人与现象世界互动的万物完成奠定了基础)。【编者按语】"物"在中国传统哲学中既可指称物,也可指称人。理雅各这样译,有其道理。

③ "故时措之宜也",理雅各译作 Therefore, whenever he—*the entirely sincere man*—employs them,—*that is*,—*these virtues*,—*their action will be* right(因此,只要至诚之士运用了这些美德,他们的行为无不正确)。辜鸿铭译作 Therefore with truth, everything done is right(因此,掌握了真理,做的一切事情都是正确的)。安乐哲译作 Thus, whenever one applies excellence, it is fitting(因此,人们无论何时行德,无不恰如其分)。浦安迪译作 And so, it behoves one to put it into practice unceasingly(因此,人们理应不停歇地运用它)。【编者按语】理雅各在儒学经典翻译中强调忠实于原文。但有时候,不添加语词,译文意义不足或不清。他的做法是用斜体标记添加的语词。

诚者,自成也。而道,自道也。诚者物之终始,不诚无物。是故君子诚之为贵。诚者非自成己而已也,所以成物也。成己仁也;成物知也。性之德也,合外内之道也,故时措之宜也。

* 右第二十五章。

Hence to entire sincerity there belongs ceaselessness. Not ceasing, it continues long. Continuing long, it evidences itself①. Evidencing itself, it reaches far. Reaching far, it becomes large and substantial. Large and substantial, it becomes high and brilliant②. Large and substantial:—this is how it contains *all* things③. High and brilliant:—this is how it overspreads *all* things. Reaching far and continuing long:—this is how it perfects *all* things. So large and substantial, *the individual possessing it* is the co-equal of Earth. So high and brilliant, it makes him the co-equal of Heaven. So far-reaching and long-continuing, it makes him infinite. Such being its nature, without any display, it becomes manifested; without any movement, it produces changes; and without any effort, it accomplishes its ends. The way of Heaven and Earth may be completely declared in one sentence.—They are without any doubleness④, and so they produce things in a manner that is unfathomable. The way of Heaven and Earth is large and substantial, high and brilliant, far-reaching and long-enduring.

① "征",理雅各译作 it evidences itself(它显现自身)。辜鸿铭译作 self-existent(自存的)。安乐哲译作 effective(有效的)。浦安迪译作 it is subject to objective verification(它可以进行客观的论证)。

② "高明",理雅各和安乐哲译作 high and brilliant(高明灿烂)。辜鸿铭译作 transcendental and intelligent(超越与聪明的)。浦安迪译作 loftiness and brilliance(高远灿烂)。

③ "载物",理雅各译作 it contains *all* things(它包容万物)。辜鸿铭译作 it contains all existence(它包容了万物)。安乐哲译作 bear up everything(承载一切)。浦安迪译作 all things are borne up from below(万物由下托举着)。

④ "为物不贰",理雅各译作 they are without any doubleness(它们独一无二)。辜鸿铭译作 it exists for its own sake without any doubt or ulterior motive(它为自身而存在,没有疑问或隐藏的动机)。安乐哲译作 since events are never duplicated(既然事件永远无法复制)。浦安迪译作 a seamless state of non-dualism(严丝合缝,浑然一体)。

故至诚无息,不息则久,久则征;征则悠远,悠远则博厚,博厚则高明。博厚所以载物也;高明所以覆物也;悠久所以成物也。博厚配地,高明配天,悠久无疆。如此者不见而章,不动而变,无为而成。天地之道,可一言而尽也。其为物不贰,则其生物不测。天地之道,博也,厚也,高也,明也,悠也,久也。

The heaven now before us is only this bright shining spot①; but when viewed in its inexhaustible extent, the sun, moon, stars, and constellations of the zodiac, are suspended in it, and all things are overspread by it. The earth before us is but a handful of soil; but when regarded in its breadth and thickness, it sustains mountains like the Hwâ and the Yo, without feeling their weight, and contains the rivers and seas, without their leaking away. The mountain now before us appears only a stone; but when contemplated in all the vastness of its size, we see how the grass and trees are produced on it, and birds and beasts dwell on it, and precious things which men treasure up are found on it. The water now before us appears but a ladleful; yet extending our view to its unfathomable depths, the largest tortoises, iguanas, iguanodons, dragons, fishes, and turtles, are produced in them, articles of value and sources of wealth abound in them②. It is said in the Book of Poetry, 'The ordinances of Heaven, how profound are they and unceasing!' The meaning is, that it is thus that Heaven is Heaven. *And again*, 'How illustrious was it, the singleness of the virtue of King Wăn!' indicating that it was thus that King Wăn was what he was. Singleness likewise is unceasing.

The above is the twenty-sixth chapter.

① "今夫天,斯昭昭之多",理雅各和辜鸿铭译作 The heaven before us is only this bright, shining spot(人们面前的天只是明亮灿烂的一块天)。安乐哲译作 Now, the firmament(*tian* 天)is just an accumulation of light(现在,天只是光线的积聚)。浦安迪译作 it consists, in effect, of a multiplicity of single points of luminescence(从视觉上看,它是一束束光点)。

② "货财殖焉",理雅各译作 articles of values and source of wealth abound in them(各种奇珍异宝存乎其中)。辜鸿铭译作 all useful products abound in them(各种各样的有用的东西充斥其间)。浦安迪译作 goods and products of every description are increased by traders plying their lanes(商人穿行于各海道,各种各样的货物和商品大大增加)。【编者按语】浦安迪增译了 traders plying their lanes,因为他认为原文太单薄了。

今夫天,斯昭昭之多,及其无穷也,日月星辰系焉,万物覆焉。今夫地,一撮土之多。及其广厚,载华岳而不重,振河海而不泄,万物载焉。今夫山,一卷石之多,及其广大,草木生之,禽兽居之,宝藏兴焉,今夫水,一勺之多,及其不测,鼋、鼍、蛟龙、鱼鳖生焉,货财殖焉。《诗》①曰:"惟天之命,于穆不已!"盖曰天之所以为天也。"于乎不显,文王之德之纯!"盖曰文王之所以为文也,纯亦不已。

* 右第二十六章。

①《诗》:指《诗经·周颂·维天之命》。

How great is the path proper to the Sage! Like overflowing water, it sends forth and nourishes all things, and rises up to the height of heaven. All-complete is its greatness! It embraces the three hundred rules of ceremony, and the three thousand rules of demeanour. It waits for the proper man, and then it is trodden. Hence it is said, 'Only by perfect virtue can the perfect path, in all its courses, be made a fact①.' Therefore, the superior man honours his virtuous nature, and maintains constant inquiry and study②, seeking to carry it out to its breadth and greatness, so as to omit none of the more exquisite and minute points which it embraces, and to raise it to its greatest height and brilliancy, so as to pursue the course of the Mean. He cherishes his old knowledge, and is continually acquiring new. He exerts an honest, generous earnestness, in the esteem and practice of all propriety. Thus, when occupying a high situation, he is not proud, and in a low situation, he is not insubordinate. When the kingdom is well-governed, he is sure by his words to rise; and when it is ill-governed, he is sure by his silence to command forbearance to himself. Is not this what we find in the Book of Poetry, —'Intelligent is he and prudent, and so preserves his person?'

The above is the twenty-seventh chapter.

① "苟不至德,至道不凝",理雅各译作 Only by perfect virtue can the perfect path, in all its courses, be made a fact(只有凭借完美的德性,人们才能在条条道路中选择最完美的路径)。辜鸿铭译作 Unless there be highest moral power, the highest moral law cannot be realized(除非有最高的道德力量,最高的道德法则不会实现)。安乐哲译作 If persons are not of the utmost excellence(*zhide* 至德), the utmost path (*zhidao* 至道) will not take shape under their feet(如果人们不具备终极德行,终极的道路不会在他们的足下形成)。浦安迪译作 Absent the utmost moral power, the fullest attainment of the Way will never take on concrete form(缺少了终极的道德力量,大道的最充分的实现永远不会完成)。

② "故君子尊德性而道问学",理雅各译作 Therefore, the superior man honours his virtuous nature, and maintain constant inquiry and study(因此,君子尊重道德本性,并保持不懈的探寻和研究)。辜鸿铭译作 Whereof the moral man, while honouring the greatness and power of his moral nature, yet does not neglect inquiry and pursuit of knowledge(因此有德行的人在尊重道德本性的伟大和伟力的同时,不忽视知识的探寻和追求)。安乐哲译作 Thus exemplary persons (*junzi*) prize their natural tendency towards excellence(*dexing* 德行), and go the way of study and inquiry(因此作榜样的人珍视德行的天性,走上研究和探寻之路)。浦安迪译作 For this reason, the man of noble character places the highest value upon his inborn moral value, and takes the path of enquiry and cultivation as his guide(因为这个原因,品行高贵的人最珍视天生的道德价值,走上探寻和修身之路)。【编者按语】安乐哲和浦安迪将"道"的意象移植到译文。

大哉,圣人之道! 洋洋乎,发育万物,峻极于天。优优大哉! 礼仪三百,威仪三千。待其人然后行。故曰:苟不至德,至道不凝焉。故君子尊德性而道问学。致广大而尽精微。极高明而道中庸。温故而知新,敦厚以崇礼。是故居上不骄,为下不倍①;国有道,其言足以兴;国无道,其默足以容。《诗》②曰:"既明且哲,以保其身。"其此之谓与!

* 右第二十七章。

① 倍:通"背",背叛。
② 《诗》:指《诗经·大雅·烝民》。

The Master said, 'Let a man who is ignorant be fond of using his own judgment; let a man without rank be fond of assuming a directing power to himself; let a man who is living in the present age go back to the ways of antiquity:—on the persons of all who act thus calamities will be sure to come.' To no one but the Son of Heaven does it belong to order ceremonies, to fix the measures, and to determine the written characters. Now, over the kingdom, carriages have all wheels of the same size; all writing is with the same characters; and for conduct there are the same rules①. One may occupy the throne, but if he have not the proper virtue. he may not dare to make ceremonies or music②. One may have the virtue, but if he do not occupy the throne, he may not presume to make ceremonies or music. The Master said, 'I may describe the ceremonies of the Hsiâ dynasty, but Chî cannot sufficiently attest my words. I have learned the ceremonies of the Yin dynasty, and in Sung they still continue. I have learned the ceremonies of Châu, which are now used, and I follow Châu.'

The above is the twenty-eighth chapter.

① "行同伦",理雅各译作 for conduct there are the same rules(在行为规则中,规则相同)。辜鸿铭译作 in all the relations of life, all recognise the same established principles(在所有的社会关系中,人们遵循同样的既定原则)。安乐哲译作 in our conduct we accept the same norms(在行为规范中,我们遵守同样的规则)。浦安迪译作 all customary practices follow uniform ethical standards(所有习俗都遵循统一的道德标准)。

② "作礼乐",理雅各译作 make ceremonies or music(制作仪式或音乐)。辜鸿铭译作 make changes in the established moral and religious institutions(对既定的道德和宗教制度进行改革)。安乐哲译作 initiate ceremonies and music for the court(为宫廷创制仪式和音乐)。浦安迪译作 institute rituals and music(创制仪式和音乐)。【编者按语】对"礼乐",辜鸿铭进行了阐释式诠释。

子曰:"愚而好自用,贱而好自专,生乎今之世,反古之道:如此者,灾及其身者也。"非天子,不议礼,不制度,不考文。今天下车同轨,书同文,行同伦。虽有其位,苟无其德,不敢作礼乐焉;虽有其德。苟无其位,亦不敢作礼乐焉。

子曰:"吾说夏礼,杞①不足澂也。吾学殷礼,有宋②存焉。吾学周礼,今用之,吾从周。"

* 右第二十八章。

① 杞:古国名,为夏代后人所分封地,在今河南杞县。
② 宋:古国名,为商代后人所分封地,在今河南商丘。

He who attains to the sovereignty of the kingdom, having *those* three important things, shall be able to effect that there shall be few errors *under his government*. However excellent may have been the regulations of those of former times①, they cannot be attested. Not being attested, they cannot command credence; and not being credited, the people would not follow them. However excellent might be the regulations made by one in an inferior situation, he is not in a position to be honoured. Unhonoured, he cannot command credence; and not being credited, the people would not follow his rules. Therefore the institutions of the Ruler are rooted in his own character and conduct②, and sufficient attestation of them is given by the masses of the people. He examines them *by comparison* with those of the three kings, and finds them without mistake. He sets them up before heaven and earth, and finds nothing in them contrary to their mode of operation. He presents himself with them before spiritual beings, and no doubts about them arise. He is prepared to wait for the rise of a sage, a hundred ages after, and has no misgivings. His presenting himself *with his institutions* before spiritual beings, without any doubts arising about them, shows that he knows Heaven. His being prepared, without any misgivings, to wait for the rise of a sage a hundred ages after, shows that he knows men. Such being the case, the movements of such a ruler, *illustrating his institutions*, constitute an example to the empire for ages. His acts are for ages a law to the kingdom. His words are for ages a lesson to the kingdom. Those who are far from him, look longingly for him; and those who are near him, are never wearied with him. It is said in the Book of Poetry, —'Not disliked there, not tired of here③, from day to day and night to night, will they perpetuate their praise.' Never has there been a ruler, who did not realize this description, that obtained an early renown throughout the kingdom.

The above is the twenty-ninth chapter.

① "上焉者",理雅各译作 the regulations of those of former times(先前时代的规则)。辜鸿铭译作 a system of moral truths appealing to supernatural authority(诉诸超自然权威的一套道德真理)。安乐哲译作 the ritual observances that are practiced by those who came before the Zhou Kings(周王之前施行的礼仪规范)。浦安迪译作 of greatest weight(分量最重的)。【编者按语】理雅各和安乐哲这里的翻译依据朱熹注(上焉者,谓时王以前,如夏商之礼)。

② "本诸身",理雅各译作 be rooted in his own character and conduct(根植于自己的品德和言行)。辜鸿铭译作 be based upon the man's own consciousness(基于人们自己的意识)。安乐哲译作 be rooted in his own person(根植于人自身)。浦安迪译作 be grounded in his own individual character(基于自己的品性)。

③ "在此无射",理雅各译作 not tired of here(这里人们也不厌弃他)。辜鸿铭译作 Here they ever welcome him(在这里人们永远欢迎他)。安乐哲译作 Here no one tires of him(这里呀,没有人厌弃他)。浦安迪译作 here in our court...there are none that weary of his presence(在这里的宫廷,没有人对他的出现表示厌烦)。

"王天下有三重焉,其寡过矣乎！上焉者虽善无征①,无征不信,不信民弗从;下焉者虽善不尊,不尊不信,不信民弗从。故君子之道:本诸身,徵诸庶民,考诸三王而不缪,建②诸天地而不悖,质诸鬼神而无疑,百世以俟圣人而不惑。质诸鬼神而无疑,知天也;百世以俟圣人而不惑,知人也。是故君子动而世为天下道,行而世为天下法,言而世为天下则。远之则有望,近之则不厌。《诗》③曰:'在彼无恶④,在此无射⑤。庶几夙夜,以永终誉！'君子未有不如此,而蚤⑥有誉于天下者。"

右第二十九章。

① 征:应验。
② 建:确立。
③《诗》:指《诗经·周颂·振鹭》。
④ 恶:音 wù,厌恶。
⑤ 射:音 yì,《诗经》中本作"斁",意为厌弃、懈怠。
⑥ 蚤:通"早"。

Chung-nî handed down the doctrines of Yâo and Shun, as if they had been his ancestors, and elegantly displayed the regulations of Wăn and Wû, taking them as his model. Above, he harmonized with the times of heaven①, and below, he was conformed to the water and land. He may be compared to heaven and earth in their supporting and containing, their overshadowing and curtaining, all things. He may be compared to the four seasons in their alternating progress, and to the sun and moon in their successive shining. All things are nourished together without their injuring one another. The courses *of the seasons, and of the sun and moon,* are pursued without any collision among them. The smaller energies are like river currents②; the greater energies are seen in mighty transformations. It is this which makes heaven and earth so great.

The above is the thirtieth chapter.

① "上律天时",理雅各译作 Above, he harmonized with the times of heaven(在上,他与天时保持和谐)。辜鸿铭译作 they harmonise with the divine order which governs the revolutions of the seasons in the Heaven above(在上,它们与上天掌控的季节交替的神圣秩序保持和谐)。安乐哲译作 He modeled himself above on the rhythm of the turning seasons(在上,他以上天掌控的季节交替的节奏为自己的典范)。浦安迪译作 he took his regulating precepts from the seasonal cycles in the heavens above(他的管理准则基于上天季节交替循环)。

② "小德川流",理雅各译作 The smaller energies are like river currents(较小的能量像河水一样)。辜鸿铭译作 the lesser forces flowing everywhere like river currents(较薄弱的力量恰如河水一样四处流动)。安乐哲译作 The lesser excellences are to be seen as flowing streams(较小的德性应当被视作流动的河流)。浦安迪译作 Their lesser forces flow like a mighty river(它们较小的力量像浩荡的河水一样流淌)。

仲尼祖述①尧舜,宪章②文武:上律③天时,下袭水土。辟如天地之无不持载,无不覆帱④,辟如四时之错行⑤,如日月之代明⑥。万物并育而不相害,道并行而不相悖,小德川流,大德敦化,此天地之所以为大也。

* 右第三十章。

① 祖述:效法承袭。

② 宪章:宪,此处引申为动词"效法"。章,通"彰",意为彰显。

③ 律:效法。

④ 覆帱:帱与覆同意,该词表示覆盖。

⑤ 错行:交替运行。

⑥ 代明:日月交替照明。

It is only he, possessed of all sagely qualities that can exist under heaven, who shows himself quick in apprehension, clear in discernment, of far-reaching intelligence, and all-embracing knowledge, fitted to exercise rule①; magnanimous, generous, benign, and mild, fitted to exercise forbearance; impulsive, energetic, firm, and enduring, fitted to maintain a firm hold; self-adjusted, grave, never swerving from the Mean, and correct, fitted to command reverence②; accomplished, distinctive, concentrative, and searching, fitted to exercise discrimination③. All-embracing is he and vast, deep and active as a fountain, sending forth in their due seasons his virtues. All-embracing and vast, he is like heaven. Deep and active as a fountain, he is like the abyss. He is seen, and the people all reverence him; he speaks, and the people all believe him; he acts, and the people all are pleased with him. Therefore his fame overspreads the Middle Kingdom, and extends to all barbarous tribes. Wherever ships and carriages reach; wherever the strength of man penetrates; wherever the heavens overshadow and the earth sustains; wherever the sun and moon shine; wherever frosts and dews fall; —all who have blood and breath unfeignedly honour and love him. Hence it is said: —'He is the equal of Heaven.'

The above is the thirty-first chapter.

① "足以有临",理雅各译作 fitted to exercise rule(有统治的资格)。辜鸿铭译作 qualities necessary for the exercise of command(具有统治民众的品格)。安乐哲译作 needed to oversee the empire(掌控帝国必需的)。浦安迪译作 sufficient to watch over all things with a providential view(居高临下,监察万物)。

② "足以有敬",理雅各译作 fitted to command reverence(具有令人肃然起敬的品格的)。安乐哲译作 needed to command respect(获得敬重所必需的)。浦安迪译作 sufficient to evince deep reverence(足以令人敬畏)。【编者按语】辜鸿铭漏译,可补译为 qualities necessary to command respect(具有令民众敬重的品质)。

③ "文理密察",理雅各译作 accomplished, distinctive, concentrative, and searching, fitted to exercise discrimination(有成就的、显著的、专注的、探索性的,具有高度辨别能力的)。安乐哲译作 have the culture and discernment needed to be discriminating(具有进行判别的文化素养和辨别力)。浦安迪译作 refined correctness and minute perception(精致而正确、细密而洞察)。【编者按语】辜鸿铭漏译,可译为 culture, discipline, attention to details and acumen, qualities necessary for critical judgement(文化素养、专业训练、关注细节和敏锐的判断力——这些品质是做出批判性判断所必需的)。

唯天下至圣为能聪明睿知,足以有临①也;宽裕温柔,足以有容也;发强刚毅,足以有执②也;齐庄③中正,足以有敬也;文理密察,足以有别也。溥博渊泉,而时出之。溥博如天,渊泉如渊。见而民莫不敬,言而民莫不信,行而民莫不说④。是以声名洋溢乎中国,施及蛮貊⑤。舟车所至,人力所通,天之所覆,地之所载,日月所照,霜露所队⑥,凡有血气者,莫不尊亲,故曰配天。

* 右第三十一章。

① 临:居上而俯瞰下。
② 执:决断。
③ 齐庄:齐,意为恭肃;庄,意为庄重。
④ 说:通"悦",愉悦。
⑤ 蛮貊:蛮,中国古代对南方少数民族的称谓;貊,中国古代北方少数民族的称呼。该词于此代指除去中原地域之外的一切少数民族地区。
⑥ 队:朱熹认为此字音"坠",为坠落之意,如此解释合乎文意。

It is only the individual possessed of the most entire sincerity that can exist under heaven, who can adjust the great invariable relations of mankind①, establish the great fundamental virtues of humanity, and know the transforming and nurturing operations of Heaven and Earth; —shall this individual have any being or anything beyond himself on which he depends?② Call him man in his ideal, how earnest is he! Call him an abyss, how deep is he! Call him Heaven, how vast is he! Who can know him, but he who is indeed quick in apprehension, clear in discernment, of far-reaching intelligence, and all-embracing knowledge, possessing all heavenly virtue?

The above is the thirty-second chapter.

① "经纶天下之大经",理雅各译作 adjust the great invariable relations of mankind(调节根本的不变的人际关系)。辜鸿铭译作 order and adjust the great relations of human society(确定和调适人类社会的重大关系)。安乐哲译作 separate out and braid together the many threads on the great loom of the world(将世界的大织布机上的丝线分拆,然后编织在一起)。浦安迪译作 putting into perfect order the great cardinal principles of the universe(把宇宙的根本原则完美地调和)。【编者按语】安乐哲将"经纶"做了意象化处理。相对于一般翻译的"浅化",这里是"深化"的一种方式。

② "夫焉有所倚?",理雅各译作 Shall this individual have any being or anything beyond himself on which he depends?(除了他自己,这样的个体还能依赖任何人或任何东西么?)。辜鸿铭译作 Now where does such a man derive his power and knowledge except from himself? (除了他自己,这样一个人的力量和知识还能来自哪里呢?)。安乐哲译作 How could there be anything on which they depend? (他们还能依赖于其他任何东西么?)。浦安迪译作 On what power, pray, need such a one rely for support? (请告诉我,这样一个人需要依仗什么力量呢?)。

唯天下至诚,为能经纶天下之大经,立天下之大本,知天地之化育。夫焉有所倚? 肫肫[①]其仁! 渊渊其渊! 浩浩其天! 苟不固聪明圣知达天德者,其孰能知之?

*右第三十二章。

[①] 肫肫:肫,音 zhūn。本意为面颊,该词引申为诚恳貌。

It is said in the Book of Poetry, 'Over her embroidered robe she puts a plain, single garment,' intimating a dislike to the display of the elegance[①] of the former. Just so, it is the way of the superior man to prefer the concealment *of his virtue*, while it daily becomes more illustrious, and it is the way of the mean man to seek notoriety, while he daily goes more and more to ruin. It is characteristic of the superior man, appearing insipid, yet never to produce satiety; while showing a simple negligence, yet to have his accomplishments recognized; while seemingly plain, yet to be discriminating. He knows how what is distant lies in what is near. He knows where the wind proceeds from[②]. He knows how what is minute becomes manifested. Such a one, we may be sure, will enter into virtue. It is said in the Book of Poetry, 'Although *the fish* sink and lie at the bottom, it is still quite clearly seen.' Therefore the superior man examines his heart, that there may be nothing wrong there, and that he may have no cause for dissatisfaction with himself. That wherein the superior man cannot be equalled is simply this, — his *work* which other men cannot see. It is said in the Book of Poetry, 'Looked at in your apartment, be there free from shame as being exposed to the light of heaven.'

① "文之著也",理雅各译作 the display of the elegance(文采的外露)。辜鸿铭译作 the loudness of its colour and magnificence(色彩和奢华之外露或刺目)。安乐哲译作 make a display of refinement(炫耀优雅)。浦安迪译作 all display of refinement(各种炫耀优雅的方式)。【编者按语】loud 在此意味着 vulgarly obtrusive(恶俗地刺目)。辜鸿铭的翻译极为传神。

② "知风之自",理雅各译作 He knows where the wind proceeds from(他知道风从哪里来)。辜鸿铭译作 He knows that great effects are produced by small causes(他知道重大的效果源自细小的原因)。安乐哲译作 know the source of what is customary(知道习见事物的来源)。浦安迪译作 know from whence fresh winds are bound to blow(知道新起的风从哪里刮来)。

《诗》^①曰:"衣锦尚絅^②",恶其文之著也。故君子之道,闇然^③而日章;小人之道,的然^④而日亡。君子之道:淡而不厌,简而文,温而理,知远之近,知风之自,知微之显,可与入德矣。《诗》^⑤云:"潜虽伏矣,亦孔之昭!"故君子内省不疚,无恶于志。君子之所不可及者,其唯人之所不见乎!《诗》^⑥云:"相在尔室,尚不愧于屋漏。"

① 《诗》:指《诗·卫风·硕人》。
② 絅:通"褧",套在外面的单衣。
③ 闇:幽暗。
④ 的:音 dí,其本字为旳,意为明显的。
⑤ 《诗》:指《诗·小雅·正月》。
⑥ 《诗》:指《诗·大雅·抑》。

Therefore, the superior man, even when he is not moving, has *a feeling of* reverence, and while he speaks not, he has *the feeling of* truthfulness. It is said in the Book of Poetry, 'In silence is the offering presented, and *the spirit* approached to; there is not the slightest contention.' Therefore the superior man does not use rewards and the people are stimulated *to virtue*. He does not show anger, and the people are awed more than by hatchets and battle-axes. It is said in the Book of Poetry, 'What needs no display is virtue. All the princes imitate it[①].' Therefore, the superior man being sincere and reverential[②], the whole world is conducted to a state of happy tranquillity. It is said in the Book of Poetry, 'I regard with pleasure your brilliant virtue, making no great display of itself in sounds and appearances.' The Master said, 'Among the appliances to transform the people, sounds and appearances are but trivial influences. It is said in another ode, "His virtue is light as a hair." Still, a hair will admit of comparison *as to its size*. "The doings of the supreme Heaven have neither sound nor smell". —That is perfect virtue.'

The above is the thirty-third chapter. Tsze-sze having carried his descriptions to the extremest point in the preceding chapters, turns back in this, and examines the source of his subject; and then again from the work of the learner, free from all selfishness, and watchful over himself when he is alone, he carries out his description, till by easy steps he brings it to the consummation of the whole kingdom tranquillized by simple and sincere reverentialness. He farther eulogizes its mysteriousness, till he speaks of it at last as without sound or smell. He here takes up the sum of his whole Work, and speaks of it in a compendious manner. Most deep and earnest was he in thus going again over his ground, admonishing and instructing men:—shall the learner not do his utmost in the study of the Work?

① "百辟而刑之",理雅各译作 all the princes imitate it(所有的诸侯王都效仿)。辜鸿铭译作 all the princes follow in his steps(所有的诸侯王都跟随他的脚步)。安乐哲译作 the various vassals model themselves after him(不同的爵爷都以他为典范)。浦安迪译作 all the noblemen of the realm take him as their model(诸侯国的所有的贵族都以他为榜样)。

② "笃恭",理雅各译作 sincere and reverential(诚挚而恭敬)。辜鸿铭译作 living a life of simple truth and earnestness(过着朴素、真实而认真的生活)。安乐哲译作 earnest and reverential(诚挚而恭敬)。浦安迪译作 behave with integrity and respect(行为正直而恭敬)。

故君子不动而敬,不言而信。《诗》①曰:"奏假②无言,时靡有争。"是故君子不赏而民劝,不怒而民威于鈇钺③。《诗》④曰:"不显⑤惟德!百辟其刑之⑥。"是故君子笃恭而天下平。《诗》⑦云:"予怀明德,不大声以色。"子曰:"声色之于以化民。末也。"《诗》⑧曰:"德輶如毛。"毛犹有伦,"上天之载,无声无臭"⑨,至矣!

* 右第三十三章。子思因前章极致之言,反求其本,复自下学为己谨独之事,推而言之,以驯致乎笃恭而天下平之盛。又赞其妙,至于无声无臭而后已焉。盖举一篇之要而约言之,其反复丁宁⑩示人之意,至深切矣,学者其可不尽心乎!

① 《诗》:指《诗·商颂·烈祖》。
② 奏假:奏,进奉;假,朱熹认为同"格",该词意为通过进奉而感动神明。
③ 鈇钺:鈇,指斫刀;钺,指大斧。此二者属于砍腰和杀头的刑具,此处代指一切刑具。
④ 《诗》:指《诗经·周颂·烈文》。
⑤ 不显:不,通"丕",意为大,显,为显示。
⑥ 百辟其刑之:辟,音 bì,指官员。刑,通"型",指法式,典范。
⑦ 《诗》:指《诗经·大雅·皇矣》。

⑧《诗》:指《诗经·大雅·烝民》。

⑨ 上天之载,无声无臭:此文句出自《诗经·大雅·文王》。

⑩ 丁宁:通"叮咛"。

Exercises

1. Put the following passage into Chinese.

The idea that the *Ta Hsieh* and the *Chung Yung* stand at the very centre of traditional Chinese thought may be understood in a number of more specific ways. The first of these is a simple matter of textual chronology. Though the precise dating of the original composition of these works remains a subject of scholarly dispute, there is little question that this must fall somewhere between about 300 and 100 BC—that is, within the core period of the 'classical age' of early Chinese thought spanning the three or four centuries from the late Warring States period through the first half of the Han Dynasty. They also stand at the epicentre of early Chinese writings by virtue of the web of intertextual links that tie them to so many of the other seminal texts of the ancient philosophical tradition. In one direction they look back to the venerable foundational texts of the canonic corpus—notably the *Shih Ching* (*Book of Songs*) and the *Shu Ching* (*Book of Documents*) from which they present a variety of scriptural citations in support of their own primary arguments, as well as to the primary fountainheads of the Confucian textual heritage: *the Analects* and *the Mencius*. A large portion of their teachings are framed as pronouncements—some real and some fabricated—purportedly heard from the mouth of Confucius, the 'Master' himself (though it is uncertain whether or not our own received text *of the Analects* would have been in circulation by the time these works were composed), and a number of formulations unmistakably reproduce or paraphrase passages in *the Mencius*. Still other passages clearly echo a variety of Warring States writings notably those compiled under the names of Kuan Tzu, Mo Tzu and, most visibly, Hsun Tzu—despite the fact that some of these thinkers' ideas are commonly held to at sharp variance with those of Mencius. There are also a number of expressions suggesting notions of quietism, inaction and spiritual cultivation that may strike modern readers as decidedly Taoist in tone.

2. Discussion and composition.

The Doctrine of the Mean has been highly valued because it presents Confucian metaphysics. How do you understand this metaphysics? Please compare it with the metaphysics of the Western tradition.

Suplementary Reading: Lin Yutang on Paraphrase as a Translation Method for Chinese Philosophical Classics

林语堂论中国古代思想典籍的释译

　　林语堂(1896—1976),中国现代著名作家、学者、翻译家,长于英文著述,英文作品有《吾国与吾民》《生活的艺术》《苏东坡传》《京华烟云》等。他对中国古代思想典籍的译介主要是《孔子的智慧》。其中七篇选自《礼记》(包括《中庸》《大学》。《中庸》主要采用了辜鸿铭的英译),还有《论语》《孟子》节译。全书有长篇导言,每章另有较长篇幅的导读。本书采用了林译《大学》作为参照文本。本文译自《孔子的智慧》第一章导言的第四节《论翻译方法》。

　　关于本书的翻译方法,还必须多说几句。我认为这种情况的翻译与释意(paraphrase)没有区别,并相信这是最好和最令人满意的方法。

　　情况是这样的。古文在用词上极为俭省,这当然是由于在竹简上刻字的方法。涵盖一整类特质的最重要概念和术语,大多是用单音节词来表达的,同时按照汉语语法的一般性质,用句法或词序来表示意思,而不是用通常的英语连接词来表示。以下是中文文言的两个极端例子:"子绝四:毋意,毋必,毋固,毋我"(Confucius completely cut-off four—no idea—no must—no ku—no I),"辞达而已矣"(Language expressive only)。很明显,除非译者提供连接词,否则译文实际上是不可读的。连接词和扩展解释性短语必须由译者自行决定,为此译者除了自己对孔子智慧的洞察之外别无他法,当然还有注疏家的帮助。

　　首要的工作当然是确定一个术语经典用法中的范围和内涵,其次是确定它在特定句子中的特定含义。在上面"固"这个词的例子中,这个词有几个意思:"坚强""顽固""坚持""心胸狭窄""庸俗""知识有限""有时也"。译者必须从这些不同的可能含义中做出选择。这就是赋予中国古代文本翻译者"可怕"的责任和自由。而且很明显,选择不同的词会彻底改变该行的含义。我将这句话翻译如下:Confucius denounced (or tried completely to avoid) four things: arbitrariness of opinion, dogmatism, narrow-mindedness and egotism。当然,这句话"毋必"是否应该译为 don't insist upon a particular course, don't be persistent, don't be insistent, or don't assume that you must be right (or don't be dogmatic)都是可以讨论的。这些翻译中的任何一个都涉及与其他翻译一样多的释意。在翻译短语"毋意"时,我已将其释意为"不要从先入为主的观念开始"或"不要主观专断"。"意"的这个含义或微妙的意义的认知源于我对汉语中"意"字的一般意义的理解,还源于我对孔子思想整体特点的洞察。但是,"不要从先入为主的观念开始"或"不要主观专断"都只是汉语"意"隐含的意义。至多如此。

对于几个核心概念,比如"礼""仁""信""中",我采用了一种方法,在脑海中将这些概念临时翻译出来,然后检索包含这些词的篇章,看看哪一个英语概念在大多数情况下最充分地涵盖其意义领域。当然,不排除一个词有多种含义。由此我得出结论,在孔子的一般社会哲学中,通常译作 ritual 或 ceremony 的"礼"必须译为 the principle of social order。在某些涉及个人言行的篇章中必须译为 moral discipline。我也得出结论,"仁"这个词翻译成 kindness, charity, 或 benevolence 是完全不够的。这个词代表了孔子 the true man, the great man 或 the most complete man 的理想人格。同样,"信"不能译为 honesty 或 keeping one's promise,因为后者是孔子相当鄙视的,实际上自己的言行并不在意这一点。有时"信"在英语中意味着 mutual confidence in the state,有时候意味着 faithfulness。

在实际的翻译中,译者在掌握了句子的意思后,面临着两个工作。首先,他面临着从多个同义词中选择一个的问题。如果不能找到准确的词,就完全无法让读者明白这句话的意思。例如,我发现不可能总是把"德"这个字翻译成 virtue 或 character,否则它的意义对读者来说将无可救药地失去。因此,子曰:"骥不称力,称其德也。"(Thoroughbred, don't praise its strength, praise its character)只有当我们将其翻译如下时才清楚:In discussing a thoroughbred, you don't admire his strength, but admire his temper。在另一篇同样的字出现了。子曰:"有德者必有言,有言者不必有德。"(One having virtue must have words: one having word not always has virtue)只有当我们将"德"这个字翻译为"soul",而不是 virtue 或 character,其含义才变得清晰。我的译文如下:Confucius said, A man who has a beautiful soul always has some beautiful things to say, but a man who says beautiful things does not necessarily have a beautiful soul。又如,在短语"德音"中出现相同的字。如果将其翻译为 virtuous sounds,可以给人一种学术忠实的印象,但只是掩盖了学者兼翻译家缺乏理解力,它其实意为 sacred music。又如,子曰:"奢则不孙,俭则固。与其不孙也,宁固。"(Extravagant than not humble; frugal than vulgar or stubborn, etc. Rather than not humble, be ku)。奢侈和不逊之间的联系一定是相当模糊的。只有当我们意识到生活奢侈的人容易自负时,意思才会变得清晰。因此,一个完全清晰和充分的翻译必然涉及词的选择。我认为上一句应译为:Confucius said: The people who live extravagantly are apt to be snobbish (or conceited), and the people who live simply are apt to be vulgar. I prefer vulgarity to snobbery—or I prefer the vulgar people to the snobs)。

其次,译者无法避免将思想置于现代语言更精确的概念中。译者不仅要提供连接词,还必须提供更精细的思想定义,否则英语会非常单调乏味。因此上面给出的例子——"辞达而已矣",现代译者只能翻译为 Expressiveness is the only principle of language, 或者 Expressiveness is the sole concern, or aim, or principle, of rhetoric。很明显,无论如何这句话至少有十几种翻译方式。但不可避免的是,译者不得不悄悄插入 principle, aim, concern 或 standard 之类的词。如果不想让翻译变得不可卒读,只能这么做,别无他法。

括号的使用。在以下译文中,为了避开了上述困难,我不得不求助于括号的使用。括号有两个用途。第一,用于提供替代翻译,通常用(或……)表示。这种情况通常出现在没有人可以确定特定解释是唯一正确的解释的情况下。第二,括号仅用于必要的解释性文字。读者不参考脚注,就可以清楚地理解文本。不这么做,解释性参考文字将是无止境的。在这种情况下,使用括号的唯一目的是提供最少的解释,使读者能够流畅地阅读段落,毫无困难地理解它的含义。所以,我把脚注留给我的评论和引用其他参考材料。

Unit Sixteen
Mencius on "Benevolent Government"—Selected Readings of *Mencius* (1)

Mencius has seven chapters and more than 35,000 characters, and it is the largest of *Four Books*. The core ideas of Mencius did preserve many of Confucius' ideas, but Mencius advanced Confucius' ideas in many ways. There are three important aspects in *Mencius*: the root of benevolence and righteousness, the advocacy of benevolent government, the goodness of human nature. This unit focuses on Mencius' idea of benevolent government. This idea is both an inheritance of Confucius' political ideas and an elaborate response of Mencius to the specific political problems of his time. Mencius argued forcefully that the key of benevolent government is not the construction of institutions per se, but the establishment of a good political order triggered by the good nature of human beings, which constitutes the characteristic of Mencius' idea of benevolent government. This thought had a fundamental impact on Confucianism since the Song Dynasty.

The following text is based on the translation of D.C. Lau, coupled with the translations of James Legge, Irene Bloom and David Hinton.

Selected Readings of *Mencius* (1) and Notes

1.7 King Hsüan of Ch'i asked, 'Can you tell me about the history of Duke Huan of Ch'i and Duke Wen of Chin?'

'None of the followers of Confucius,' answered Mencius, 'spoke of the history of Duke Huan and Duke Wen. It is for this reason that no one in after ages passed on any accounts, and I have no knowledge of them. If you insist, perhaps I may be permitted to tell you about becoming a true King.'[①]

'How virtuous must a man be before he can become a true King?'

'He becomes a true King by tending the people. This is something no one can stop.'

'Can someone like myself tend the people?'

'Yes.'

'How do you know that I can?'

'I heard the following from Hu He:

The King was sitting in the hall. He saw someone passing below, leading an ox. The King noticed this and said, 'Where is the ox going?' 'The blood of the ox is to be used for consecrating a new bell.' 'Spare it. I cannot bear to see it shrinking with fear, like an innocent man going to the place of execution.' 'In that case, should the ceremony be abandoned?' 'That is out of the question. Use a lamb instead.'

'I wonder if this is true?'

'It is.'

'The heart behind your action is sufficient to enable you to become a true King. The people all thought that you grudged the expense, but, for my part, I have no doubt that you were moved by pity for the animal.' ②

'You are right,' said the King. 'How extraordinary that there should be such people! Ch'i may be a small state, but I am not quite so miserly as to grudge the use of an ox. It was simply because I could not bear to see it shrink with fear, like an innocent man going to the place of execution that I used a lamb instead.'

'You must not be surprised that the people thought you miserly. You used a small animal in place of a big one. How were they to know? If you were pained by the animal going innocently to its death, what was there to choose between an ox and a lamb?'

The King laughed and said, 'What was really in my mind, I wonder? It is not true that I grudged the expense, but I *did* use a lamb instead of the ox. I suppose it was only natural that the people should have thought me miserly.'

'There is no harm in this. It is the way of a benevolent man. You saw the ox but not the lamb. The attitude of a gentleman towards animals is this: once having seen them alive, he cannot bear to see them die, and once having heard their cry, he cannot bear to eat their flesh. That is why the gentleman keeps his distance from the kitchen.' ③

The King was pleased and said, 'The *Odes* say,

The heart is someone else's

But it is I who have surmised it.

This describes you perfectly. For though the deed was mine, when I looked into myself I failed to understand my own heart. You described it for me and your words struck a chord in me. What made you think that my heart accorded with the way of a true King?'

'Should someone say to you, "I am strong enough to lift a hundred *chün* but not a feather; I have eyes that can see the tip of a new down but not a cartload of firewood," would you accept the truth of such a statement?'

'No.'

'Why should it be different in your own case? Your bounty is sufficient to reach the animals[4], yet the benefits of your government fail to reach the people. That a feather is not lifted is because one fails to make the effort; that a cartload of firewood is not seen is because one fails to use one's sight. Similarly, that the people have not been tended is because you fail to practise kindness. Hence your failure to become a true King is due to a refusal to act, not to an inability to act.'

'What is the difference in form between refusal to act and inability to act?'

'If you say to someone, "I am unable to do it," when the task is one of striding over the North Sea with Mount T'ai under your arm, then this is a genuine case of inability to act. But if you say, "I am unable to do it," when it is one of making an obeisance to your elders[5], then this is a case of refusal to act, not of inability. Hence your failure to become a true King is not the same in kind as "striding over the North Sea with Mount Tai under your arm", but the same as "making an obeisance to your elders".

Treat the aged of your own family in a manner befitting their venerable age and extend this treatment to the aged of other families[6]; treat your own young in a manner befitting their tender age and extend this to the young of other families, and you can roll the Empire on your palm.

'The *Odes* say

He set an example for his consort

And also for his brothers,

And so ruled over the family and the state.

In other words, all you have to do is take this very heart here and apply it to what is over there. Hence one who extends his bounty can tend those within the Four Seas: one who does not cannot tend even his own family. There is just one thing in which the ancients greatly surpassed others, and that is the way they extended what they did. Why is it then that your bounty is sufficient to reach animals yet the benefits of your government fail to reach the people?

It is by weighing a thing that its weight can be known and by measuring it that its length can be ascertained. It is so with all things, but particularly so with the heart. Your Majesty should measure his own heart.

Perhaps you find satisfaction only in starting a war, imperilling your subjects and incurring the enmity of other feudal lords?'

'No. Why should I find satisfaction in such acts? I only wish to realize my supreme ambition.'

'May I be told what this is?'

The King smiled, offering no reply.

'Is it because your food is not good enough to satisfy your palate, and your clothes not good enough to gratify your body? Or perhaps the sights and sounds are not good enough to gratify your eyes and sounds and your close servants not good enough to serve you? Any of your various officials surely could make good these deficiencies. It cannot be because of these things.'

'No. It is not because of these things.'

'In that case one can guess what your supreme ambition is. You wish to extend your territory, to enjoy the homage of Ch'in and Ch'u, to rule over the Central Kingdoms and to bring peace to the barbarian tribes on the four borders[7]. Seeking the fulfilment of such an ambition by such means as you employ is like looking for fish by climbing a tree.'

'Is it as bad as that?' asked the King.

'It is likely to be worse. If you look for fish by climbing a tree[8], though you will not find it, there is no danger of this bringing disasters in its train. But if you seek the fulfilment of an ambition like yours by such means as you employ, after putting all your heart and might into the pursuit, you are certain to reap disaster in the end.'

'Can I hear about this?'

'If the men of Tsou and the men of Ch'u were to go to war, who do you think would win?'

'The men of Ch'u.'

'That means that the small is no match for the big, the few no match for the many, and the weak no match for the strong. Within the Seas there are nine areas of ten thousand *li* square, and the territory of Ch'i makes up one of these. For one to try to overcome the other eight is no different from Tsou going to war with Ch'u. Why not go back to fundamentals?'

'Now if you should practise benevolence in the government of your state, then all those in the Empire who seek office would wish to find a place at your court, all tillers of land to till the land in outlying parts of your realm, all merchants to enjoy the refuge of your marketplace, all travellers to go by way of your roads, and all those who hate their rulers to lay their complaints before you. This being so, who can stop you from becoming a true King?'

'I am dull-witted,' said the King, 'and cannot see my way beyond this point. I hope you will help me towards my goal and instruct me plainly. Though I am slow, I shall make an attempt to follow your advice.'

'Only a Gentleman can have a constant heart in spite of a lack of constant means of support. The people, on the other hand, will not have constant hearts if they are without constant means. Lacking constant hearts, they will go astray and fall into excesses, stopping at nothing[9]. To punish them after they have fallen foul of the law is to set a trap for the people. How can a benevolent man in authority allow himself to set a trap for the people? Hence when determining what means of support the people should have, a clear-sighted ruler ensures that these are sufficient, on the one hand, for the care of parents, and, on the other, for the support of wife and children, so that the people always have sufficient food in good years and escape starvation in bad; only then does he drive them towards goodness; in this way the people find it easy to follow him.

'Nowadays, the means laid down for the people are sufficient neither for the care of parents nor for the support of wife and children. In good years life is always hard, while in bad years there is no way of escaping death. Thus simply to survive takes more energy than the people have. What time can they spare for learning about rites and duty?

'If you wish to put this into practice, why not go back to fundamentals? If the mulberry is planted in every homestead of five *mu* of land, then those who are fifty can wear silk; if chickens, pigs and dogs do not miss their breeding season, then those who are seventy can eat meat; if each lot of a hundred *mu* is not deprived of labour during the busy season, then families with several mouths to feed will not go hungry. Exercise due care over the education provided by village schools, and reinforce this by teaching them duties proper to sons and younger brothers[⑩], and those whose heads have turned hoary will not be carrying loads on the roads. When the aged wear silk and eat meat and the masses are neither cold nor hungry, it is impossible for their prince not to be a true King.

① "无以,则王乎?",刘殿爵(D.C Lau)译作 If you insist, perhaps I may be permitted to tell you about becoming a true king(如果你坚持,也许我可以和你说说如何成为真正的王)。理雅各(James Legge)译作 If you will have me speak, let it be about Imperial government(如果你坚持要我说,让我们谈谈王政)。卜爱莲(Irene Bloom)译作 how it would be if I were to speak about being a true king?(如果我要说说如何成为真正的王,我要说什么呢?)。欣顿(David Hinton)译作 You won't learn much about the true emperor from them(从他们那里,你不会学到多少成为真正的皇帝的知识)。

② "臣固知王之不忍也",刘殿爵译作 for my part, I have no doubt that you were moved by pity for the animal(对我来说,我确信你被对那头动物的怜悯打动)。理雅各译作 your servant knows surely, that it was your Majesty's not being able to bear the sight, which made you do as you did(您的仆人确知是您陛下不忍看到这一幕,因此你会这么做)。卜爱莲译作 I know it was surely because the king could not bear to see its suffering(我知道这的确是因为国王不忍看到它受苦)。欣顿译作 I know you just couldn't bear the suffering(我知道是因为你不忍看到它受苦)。

③ "是以君子远庖厨也",刘殿爵译作 That is why a gentleman keep his distance from the kitchen(那是君子远离庖厨的原因)。理雅各译作 Therefore he keeps away from his cook-room(因此他远离庖厨)。卜爱莲译作 And so the noble person stay far away from the kitchen(因此君子远离庖厨)。欣顿译作 That is why the noble-minded stay clear of their kitchen(那是君子远离庖厨的原因)。

④"今恩足以及禽兽",刘殿爵译作 Your bounty is sufficient to reach the animals(你的恩惠大到扩展到动物)。理雅各译作 Now here is kindness sufficient to reach to animals(现在的恩惠大到扩展到动物)。卜爱莲译作 kindness sufficient to extend to animals(恩惠大到扩展到动物)。欣顿译作 You have compassion enough for birds and animals(你的同情心大到扩展到禽鸟和动物)。

⑤"为长者折枝",刘殿爵译作 it is one of making an obeisance to your elders(向长者鞠躬致意)。理雅各译作 breaking off a branch from a tree at the order of a superior(听上级的命令从树上折枝)。卜爱莲译作 If it is a matter of bowing respectfully to an elder(如果是向长者鞠躬致意这类的事)。欣顿译作 breaking up a little kindling for an old woman(为老妇劈一点引火柴)。

⑥"老吾老,以及人之老",刘殿爵译作 Treat the aged of your own family in a manner befitting their venerable age and extend this treatment to the aged of other families(以合适他们高龄的方式对待自己家的老人,并把这种待遇扩展到其他家的老人)。理雅各译作 Treat with the reverence due to age the elders in your own family, so that the elders in the families of others shall be similarly treated(以合适他们高龄的方式恭敬地对待自己家的老人,确保其他家的老人也获得同样的待遇)。卜爱莲译作 By treating the elders in one's own family as elders should be treated and extending this to the elders of other families(通过以合适的方式对待自己家的老人,并把这种待遇扩展到其他家的老人)。欣顿译作 Honor your own elders as befits elders and extend this honor to all elders.(以合适的方式敬重自己家的老人,并把这种敬重扩展到所有的老人)。

⑦"欲辟土地,朝秦楚,莅中国而抚四夷也",刘殿爵译作 You wish to extend your territory and enjoy the homage of Q'in and Ch'u, to rule over the entire Central Kingdom and to bring peace to the barbarian tribes on the four borders(你希望扩展领土,享受秦楚的朝贺,统治整个中国,给四边的蛮夷部落带来和平)。理雅各译作 You wish to enlarge your territories, to have Qin and Chu wait at your court, to rule the Middle Kingdom and to attract to you the barbarous tribes that surround it(你希望扩展领土,让秦楚朝贺,统治中国,并把四边的蛮夷部落吸引过来)。卜爱莲译作 His desire is to expand the territory, to bring Qin and Chu into the court, to rule the Central Kingdom, and to pacify the four Yi(他的欲望是扩展领土,让秦楚朝贺,统治中国,并抚平四夷)。欣顿译作 You dream of more land. You dream of Q'in and Ch'u paying court to you, of ruling over the entire Middle Kingdom and pacifying the barbarian nations on all four borders(你梦想更多的领土,梦想让秦楚朝贺,梦想统治整个中国,并抚平四边的蛮夷部落)。

⑧"缘木求鱼",刘殿爵译作 If you look for fish by climbing a tree(如果你通过爬树求

鱼)。理雅各译作 If you climb a tree to seek fish(如果你爬树求鱼)。卜爱莲译作 When one climbs a tree in search of a fish(当人们爬树求鱼)。欣顿译作 Climb a tree in search of a fish(如果你爬树求鱼,就会……)。

⑨"苟无恒心,放僻邪侈,无所不为",刘殿爵译作 Lacking constant hearts, they will go astray and fall into excesses, stopping at nothing(缺少恒心,他们会犯错误,走极端,无所不为)。理雅各译作 And if they have not a fixed heart, there is nothing which they will not do, in the way of self-abandonment, of moral deflection, of depravity, and of wild license(假如他们没有恒心,他们无所不为——自我放纵,道德败坏,荒淫无度)。卜爱莲译作 when they lack constant minds there is no dissoluteness, depravity, deviance, or excess to which they will not succumb(当他们没有恒心时,他们自我放纵,道德败坏,无所不为)。欣顿译作 the common people will never have constant minds. And without constant minds, they'll wander loose and wild(普通人没有恒心。这时候他们自我放纵,道德败坏,无所不为)。

⑩"谨庠序之教,申之以孝悌之义",刘殿爵译作 Exercise due care over the education provided by village schools and reinforce this by teaching them duties proper to sons and younger brothers(给予乡村学校教育以足够的重视,并用孝悌的责任强化教育)。理雅各译作 Let careful attention be paid to education of schools,——inculcation in it especially of the filial and fraternal duties(给予学校教育以足够的重视,尤其要灌输孝悌的责任)。卜爱莲译作 Attend carefully to the education provided in the schools, which includes instruction in the duty of filial and fraternal devotion(给予学校教育以足够的重视,其中包括孝悌责任的教育)。欣顿译作 Pay close attention to the teaching in villages, and extend it to the child's family responsibilities(给予乡村学校教育以足够的重视,并将之扩展到孩子们的家庭责任)。

1.7 齐宣王问曰:"齐桓、晋文之事可得闻乎?"

孟子对曰:"仲尼之徒无道桓、文之事者,是以后世无传焉。臣未之闻也。无以,则王乎?"

曰:"德何如则可以王矣?"曰:"保民而王,莫之能御也。"曰:"若寡人者,可以保民乎哉?"曰:"可。"曰:"何由知吾可也?"曰:"臣闻之胡龁①曰,王坐于堂上,有牵牛而过堂下者,王见之,曰:'牛何之?'对曰:'将以衅钟②。'王曰:'舍之!吾不忍其觳觫③,若无罪而就死地。'对曰:'然则废衅钟与?'曰:'何可废也?以羊易之!'不识有诸?"曰:"有之。"曰:"是心足以王矣。百姓皆以王为爱也,臣固知王之不忍也。"王曰:"然。诚有百姓者。齐国虽褊小,吾何爱一牛?

即不忍其觳觫,若无罪而就死地,故以羊易之也。"曰:"王无异于百姓之以王为爱也。以小易大彼恶知之？王若隐其无罪而就死地,则牛羊何择焉？"王笑曰:"是诚何心哉？我非爱其财。而易之以羊也,宜乎百姓之谓我爱也。"曰:"无伤也,是乃仁术也,见牛未见羊也。君子之于禽兽也,见其生,不忍见其死;闻其声,不忍食其肉。是以君子远庖厨也。"

　　王说,曰:"诗云:'他人有心,予忖度之。'夫子之谓也。夫我乃行之,反而求之,不得吾心。夫子言之,于我心有戚戚焉。此心之所以合于王者,何也？"曰:"有复于王者曰:'吾力足以举百钧',而不足以举一羽;'明足以察秋毫之末',而不见舆薪④,则王许之乎？"曰:"否。""今恩足以及禽兽,而功不至于百姓者,独何与？然则一羽之不举为不用力焉,舆薪之不见为不用明焉,百姓之不见保,为不用恩焉。故王之不王,不为也,非不能也。"曰:"不为者与不能者之形何以异？"曰:"挟太山以超北海,语人曰'我不能',是诚不能也。为长者折枝,语人曰'我不能',是不为也,非不能也。故王之不王,非挟太山以超北海之类也;王之不王,是折枝之类也。老吾老,以及人之老;幼吾幼,以及人之幼。天下可运于掌。诗云:'刑于寡妻,至于兄弟,以御于家邦。'言举斯心加诸彼而已。故推恩足以保四海,不推恩无以保妻子。古之人所以大过人者无他焉,善推其所为而已矣。今恩足以及禽兽,而功不至于百姓者,独何与？权,然后知轻重;度,然后知长短。物皆然,心为甚。王请度之！抑王兴甲兵危士臣,构怨于诸侯,然后快于心与？"

　　王曰:"否。吾何快于是？将以求吾所大欲也。"

　　曰:"王之所大欲可得闻与？"王笑而不言。曰:"为肥甘⑤不足于口与？轻暖不足于体与？抑为采色不足视于目与？声音不足听于耳与？便嬖⑥不足使令于前与？王之诸臣皆足以供之,而王岂为是哉？"曰:"否。吾不为是也。"曰:"然则王之所大欲可知已。欲辟土地,朝秦楚,莅中国而抚四夷也。以若所为求若所欲,犹缘木而求鱼也。"曰:"若是其甚与？"曰:"殆有甚焉。缘木求鱼,虽不得鱼,无后灾。以若所为,求若所欲,尽心力而为之,后必有灾。"曰:"可得闻与？"曰:"邹人与楚人战,则王以为孰胜？"曰:"楚人胜。"曰:"然则小固不可以敌大,寡固不可以敌众,弱固不可以敌强。海内之地方千里者九,齐集有其一。以一服八,何以异于邹敌楚哉？盖亦反其本矣。今王发政施仁,使天下仕者皆欲立于王之朝,耕者皆欲耕于王之野,商贾皆欲藏于王之市,行旅皆欲出于王之涂,天下之欲疾其君者皆欲赴愬⑦于王。其若是,孰能御之？"

王曰："吾惛,不能进于是矣。愿夫子辅吾志,明以教我。我虽不敏请尝试之。"

曰："无恒产而有恒心者,惟士为能。若民,则无恒产,因无恒心。苟无恒心,放辟邪侈⑧,无不为已。及陷于罪,然后从而刑之,是罔民也。焉有仁人在位,罔民而可为也？是故明君制民之产,必使仰足以事父母,俯足以畜妻子,乐岁终身饱,凶年免于死亡。然后驱而之善,故民之从之也轻。今也制民之产,仰不足以事父母,俯不足以畜妻子,乐岁终身苦,凶年不免于死亡。此惟救死而恐不赡,奚暇治礼义哉？王欲行之,则盍反其本矣。五亩之宅,树之以桑,五十者可以衣帛矣；鸡豚狗彘之畜,无失其时,七十者可以食肉矣；百亩之田,勿夺其时,八口之家可以无饥矣；谨庠序之教,申之以孝悌之义,颁白者不负戴于道路矣。老者衣帛食肉,黎民不饥不寒,然而不王者,未之有也。"

① 胡龁:齐宣王的近臣。
② 衅钟:衅,用血祭祀。该词指用血祭新的钟,此为古代的礼仪。
③ 觳觫:因恐惧而发抖的样子。
④ 舆薪:舆,车；薪,柴。该词指一车柴,比喻显而易见的东西。
⑤ 肥甘:肥,脂肪多；甘,甜,表示美味。该词表示美味可口的食物。
⑥ 便嬖:近臣,宠臣。
⑦ 赴愬:赴,往前走。愬,诉说。
⑧ 放辟邪侈:放,放纵；辟,罪恶,不正当；邪,不正当的行为；侈,放肆,夸大。该词表示肆无忌惮,胡作非为。

Exercises

1. Put the following passage into English.

孟子曰："人皆有不忍人之心。先王有不忍人之心,斯有不忍人之政矣。以不忍人之心,行不忍人之政,治天下可运之掌上。

所以谓人皆有不忍人之心者,今人乍见孺子将入于井,皆有怵惕恻隐之心。非所以内交于孺子之父母也,非所以要誉于乡党朋友也,非恶其声而然也。

由是观之,无恻隐之心,非人也；无羞恶之心,非人也；无辞让之心,非人也；无是非之心,非人也。恻隐之心仁之端也；羞恶之心义之端也；辞让之心礼之端也；是非之心智之端也。人之有是四端也,犹其有四体也。有是四端而自谓不能者,自贼者也；谓其君不能者,贼其君者也。

凡有四端于我者,知皆扩而充之矣,若火之始然,泉之始达。苟能充之,足以保四海；苟不充之,不足以事父母。"

2. Discussion and presentation.

Mencius presented a set of economic policies. Are they feasible? Why?

Supplementary Reading: D. C. Lau as a Translator of Chinese Philosophical Classics (1)

跨越大众导向和精英导向的鸿沟（一）
——刘殿爵翻译《孟子》暨中国古代思想典籍

刘殿爵(D.C.Lau,1921—2010),著名翻译家、语言学家、汉学家。早岁肄业于香港大学,1946年赴英格兰格拉斯哥大学攻读西洋哲学。1950年起任教英国伦敦大学亚非学院。1970至1978年任伦敦大学中文讲座教授,是英国历来首位出任中文讲座教授的华人。1978年起任香港中文大学讲座教授,后任文学院院长。他的翻译代表作有《道德经》《论语》《孟子》。刘殿爵具有中西学术专业和职业背景。他翻译中国古代思想典籍,具有众多先天和后天的优势。这里仅就他的翻译的读者导向以及连带的翻译文体作出简论。他的读者导向具有双重的双重性:一是既针对大众,又针对精英读者,二是既针对国际读者,又针对汉文化圈的读者。

中国古代思想典籍的外译有一个领域不太为人重视,即读者导向。读者导向大致可分为大众导向和精英导向。后者指传统的以汉学家等知识精英为设定读者群。前者指以西方大众读者为设定读者群。以大众导向的译者试图将孔子思想的现代价值传达给西方的普通大众。因此,他的翻译往往更加注重翻译文体的通俗性和文艺性。而传统的精英导向往往更注重译本的学术性,副文本通常会有大量的导言性、注释性的文字。文体也不太顾及读者的感受。

在过去三十年中,中国古代思想典籍外译的大众导向渐成气候。大众导向的形成与两个因素有关。一、世界范围内大众时代的来临。普罗大众逐渐占据了文化、政治舞台的中心。二、20世纪90年代以来,东亚经济腾飞,东亚儒学文化圈崛起,在西方引发了儒学热。西方大众读者对于中国经典也有了了解的兴趣和需求。大众导向的勃兴深刻影响了中国古代思想典籍的外译。除了明确申明为大众翻译如利斯译《论语》外,越来越多的译者有意无意增加了译本的可读性和通俗性。

那么,有没有译者尝试跨越大众导向和精英导向的鸿沟,消弭二者的对立,在译作中融大众导向和精英导向于一体,使大众乐读,专家折服呢?

在历史上,辜鸿铭的儒学典籍翻译兼顾了大众性和学术性,是这方面较早而成功的践履者。在当代,著名翻译家刘殿爵在这方面进行了成功的尝试,达到了很高的境界。下面以刘译《孟子》为例,简论他的做法和启示。刘殿爵的跨越和融汇主要体现在以下几个方面。

首先,译文文体的大众化和译文副文本的专业化。从表面上看,他的用词构句走的是大众化的路子,多用常用的语汇和平常的句式。可用平易晓白去形容其风格。通俗地说,刘殿爵用的是现代英语白话。而《孟子》的副文本则具有高度的学术性。企鹅版《孟子》全书共 402 页,译文正文仅 147 页,副文本共 255 页。由长篇导言和五个附录以及文本注释、人名地名索引组成。除了处处遵循西学规范和处处体现的深厚的西学修养外,刘殿爵的考据、义理、辞章的国学功底相当深厚。附录一《孟子一生大事系年》旁征博引,引用了历代的学者,如司马迁、司马光、钱大昕、魏源、钱穆等人的各种文献。考据精当,殊堪叹服。在辞章方面,在附录五《孟子论辩中类比的使用》考察了先秦类比使用,突出了孟子类比使用的独到处,反驳了韦利对孟子修辞的成见。在义理上,刘殿爵一反惯常认为孟子心学玄奥(Mysticism)的定见,认为孟子学说很接地气。他还是一位很有成就的语言学家。在文本注释(Textual Notes)中,他对《孟子》的关键术语和一般语汇的词源考察、意义流变和英译都有学术含量很高的探讨。

其次,刘氏译文语言表面上浅白,但他有深度的学术考量。这是大众和精英导向的奇妙融合。按照刘殿爵的高足安乐哲的说法,他使用拉丁化、基督教化之前的英语来翻译,以免译文带有西方神学、哲学色彩。这种方法尼采和海德格尔也曾有意识地运用过。他们曾经试图返回苏格拉底前的古希腊的观念中,从而绕开西方二元论和本质化的形而上学传统,实现在欧洲文化圈容纳其他哲学的可能性。刘殿爵使用英语最基质的盎格鲁-撒克逊的言语,惟精惟一,而刻意避开后来融入英语的拉丁语、法语等外来语,去移译古老东方相当复杂有时玄奥的思想,难度极大。因难见巧,成就也高。

刘殿爵的《论语》语体可以概括为现代英语白话。它与标准现代英语从大的方面相像,但又有不同。20 世纪人类的社会、经济、政治、文化都发生了巨大的变化。英语作为国际语言也经历了较大的变化。虽然英语不似汉语经历了由文言到白话的整体性位移,但英语的局部性变化显而易见。每个对英语有感知力的语言学家和普通使用者都不难觉察。一般意义上来说,英语句式从复杂、繁缛、冗赘变化为简洁、爽快、晓畅,语脉更加清晰,逻辑更易于把握。英语的用词也从偏爱拉丁及外来词源的"大词"的使用,到更多的使用盎格鲁-撒克逊本土的英语核心基础语汇;从偏爱使用各种修辞手法,到更多地不兜圈子,直抒己意。概而言之,标准现代英语以口语化的句式和词汇为主体,杂糅以书面正式的句式和拉丁及外来语。对于刘殿爵的现代英语白话,邓仕梁用"秋水文章不染尘"来评论刘译的精练澄澈,言简意赅,确是的评。刘译之后中西以标准的现代英文翻译中国古代思想典籍蔚为潮流,似乎与刘殿爵示范不无关联。而刘氏自己出乎其中,又超乎其外。

Unit Seventeen
Mencius on "Nourishing the Vast, Flowing Passion-Nature" —Selected Readings of *Mencius* (2)

This unit includes the very famous discourse of Mencius on Nourishing the Vast, Flowing Passion-Nature (浩然之气). Nourishing the Vast, Flowing Passion-Nature is the very method of cultivating one's moral determination, which constitutes the essence of the Confucian theory of self-cultivation. Nourishing the Vast, Flowing Passion-Nature, in Mencius' view, is to keep one's conscience growing and not to be overshadowed by undesirable external influences. By nourishing the Vast, Flowing Passion-Nature, a man will eventually become a great man who "is above the power of riches and honours to make dissipated, of poverty and mean condition to make swerve from principle, and of power and force to make bend".

Selected Readings of *Mencius*(2) and Notes

3.2. Kung-sun Ch'ou said, 'If you, Master, were given a position above that of the Chief Minister in Ch'i and were able thereby to put the Way into practice, it would be no surprise if through this you were able to equal the achievement of a leader of the feudal lords or even a true King[①]. If this happened, would it cause any stirring in your heart?'

'No,' said Mencius. 'My heart has not been stirred since the age of forty.'

'In that case you far surpass Meng Pin.'

'That is not difficult. Kao Tzu succeeded in this at an even earlier age than I.'

'Is there a way to bring such success about?'

'Yes, there is. The way Po-kung Yu cultivated his courage was by never showing submission on his face or letting anyone outstare him[②]. For him, to yield the tiniest bit was as humiliating as being cuffed in the market place. He would no more accept an insult from a prince with ten thousand chariots than from a common fellow coarsely clad. He would as soon run a sword through the prince as through the common fellow. He had no respect for persons, and always returned whatever harsh tones came his way.'

'Meng Shih-she said this about the cultivation of his courage. "I look upon defeat as victory. One who advances only after sizing up the enemy, and joins battle only after weighing the chances of victory[3] is simply showing cowardice in face of superior numbers. Of course I cannot be certain of victory. All I can do is to be without fear."'

'Meng Shih-she resembled Tseng Tzu while Po-kung Yu resembled Tzu-hsia. It is hard to say which of the two was superior, but Meng Shih-she had a firm grasp of the essential.'

'Tseng Tzu once said to Tzu-hsiang, "Do you admire courage? I once heard about supreme courage from the Master. If, on looking within, one finds oneself to be in the wrong, then even though one's adversary be only a common fellow coarsely clad one is bound to tremble with fear. But if one finds oneself in the right, one goes forward even against men in the thousands. "Meng Shih-she's firm hold on his *Ch'i* is inferior to Tseng Tzu's firm grasp of essentials.'

'I wonder if you could tell me something about the heart that cannot be stirred, in your case and in Kao Tzu's case?'

'According to Kao Tzu, "If you fail to understand words, do not worry about this in your heart; and if you fail to understand in your heart, do not seek satisfaction in your *Ch'i*." It is right that one should not seek satisfaction in one's *Ch'i* when one fails to understand it in one's heart. But it is wrong to say that one should not worry about it in one's heart when one fails to understand words.'

'The will is commander over the *Ch'i* while the *Ch'i* is that which fills the body[4]. Where the will arrives there the *Ch'i* halts. Hence it is said, "Take hold of your will and do not abuse your *Ch'i*."'

'As you have already said that where the will arrives there the *Ch'i* halts, what is the point of going on to say, "Take hold of your will and do not abuse your *Ch'i*"?'

'The will, when blocked, moves the *Ch'i*. On the other hand, the *Ch'i*, when blocked, also moves the will. Now stumbling and hurrying affect the *Ch'i*, yet in fact palpitations of the heart are produced.'

'May I ask what your strong points are?'

'I have an insight into words. I am good at cultivating my "flood-like *Ch'i*"[5].'

'May I ask what this "flood-like *Ch'i*" is?'

'It is difficult to explain. This is a *Ch'i* which is, in the highest degree, vast and unyielding. Nourish it with integrity and place no obstacle in its path and it will fill the space between Heaven and Earth. It is a *Ch'i* which unites rightness and the Way. Deprive it of these and it will starve. It is born of accumulated rightness and cannot be appropriated by anyone through a sporadic show of rightness. Whenever one acts in a way that falls below the standard set in one's heart, it will starve. Hence I said Kao Tzu never understood rightness because he looked upon it as external. You must work at it and never let it out of your mind. At the same time, while you must never let it out of your mind, you must not forcibly help it grow either[6]. You must not be like the man from Sung. There was a man from Sung who pulled at his seedlings because he was worried about their failure to grow. Having done so, he went on his way home, not realizing what he had done. "I am worn out today", said he to his family. "I have been helping the seedlings to grow." His son rushed out to take a look and there the seedlings were, all shrivelled up. There are few in the world who can resist the urge to help their seedlings grow. There are some who leave the seedlings unattended, thinking that nothing they can do will be of any use. They are the people who do not even bother to weed. There are others who help the seedlings grow. They are the people who pull at them. Not only do they fail to help them but they do the seedlings the positive harm.'

'What do you mean by "an insight into words"?'

'From biased words I can see wherein the speaker is blind[7]; from immoderate words, wherein he is ensnared; from heretical words, wherein he has strayed from the right path; from evasive words, wherein he is at his wits' end. What arises in the mind will interfere with policy, and what shows itself in policy will interfere with practice. Were a sage to rise again, he would surely agree with what I have said.'

'Tsai Wo and Tzu-kung excelled in rhetoric; Jan Niu, Min Tzu and Yen Hui excelled in the exposition of virtuous conduct. Confucius excelled in both and yet he said, "I am not versed in rhetoric." In that case you, Master, must already be a sage.'

'What an extraordinary thing for you to say of me! Tzu-kung once asked Confucius, "Are you, Master, a sage?" Confucius replied, "I have not succeeded in becoming a sage. I simply never tire of learning nor weary of teaching." Tzu-kung said, "Not to tire of learning is wisdom; not to weary of teaching is benevolence. You must be a sage to be both wise and benevolent." A sage is something even Confucius did not claim to be. What an extraordinary thing for you to say that of me!'

'I have heard that Tzu-hsia, Tzu-yu and Tzu-chang each had one aspect of the Sage while Jan Niu, Min Tzu and Yen Hui were replicas of the Sage in miniature[8]. Which would you rather be?'

'Let us leave this question for the moment.'

'How about Po Yi and Yi Yin?'

'They followed paths different from that of Confucius. Po Yi was such that he would only serve the right prince and rule over the right people, would take office when order prevailed and relinquish it when there was disorder. Yi Yin was such that he would serve any prince and rule over any people, would take office whether order prevailed or not. Confucius was such that he would take office, or would remain in a state, would delay his departure or hasten it, all according to circumstances. All three were sages of old. I have not been able to emulate any of them, but it is my hope and wish to follow the example of Confucius.'

'Were Po Yi and Yi Yin as much an equal of Confucius as that?'

'No. Ever since man came into this world, there has never been another Confucius.'

'Was there anything in common to all of them?'

'Yes. Were they to become ruler over a hundred *li* square, they would have been capable of winning the homage of the feudal lords and taking possession of the Empire; but had it been necessary to perpetrate one wrongful deed or to kill one innocent man in order to gain the Empire, none of them would have consented to it. In this they were alike.'

'In what way were they different?'

'Tsai Wo, Tzu-kung and Yu Jo were intelligent enough to appreciate the Sage. They would not have stooped so low as to show a bias in favour of the man they admired⑨. Tsai Wo said, "In my view, the Master surpassed greatly Yao and Shun." Tsu-kung said, "Through the rites of a state he could see its government; through its music, the moral quality of its ruler. Looking back over a hundred generations he was able to appraise all the kings, and no one has ever been able to show him to be wrong in a single instance. Ever since man came into this world, there has never been another like the Master." Yu Jo said, "It is true not only of men. The unicorn is the same in kind as other animals, the phoenix as other birds; Mount T'ai is the same as small mounds of earth; the Yellow River and the Sea are no different from water that runs in the gutter. The Sage, too, is the same in kind as other men.

Though one of their kind

He stands far above the crowd⑩.

Ever since man came into this world, there has never been one greater than Confucius."'

① "虽由此霸,不异矣",刘殿爵译作 it would be no surprise if through this you were able to equal the achievement of a leader of the feudal lords or even a true King(假如你这么做成就不亚于做霸主或者甚至做真正的王,这并不令人吃惊)。理雅各译作 though you should thereupon raise the prince to the headship of all the other princes, or even to the Imperial dignity, it would not be to be wondered at(尽管你由此把王举擢升到霸主的地位,甚至使他有帝王之尊,这都不令人吃惊)。卜爱莲译作 it would not be surprising if the ruler were to become a hegemon or even king(假如统治者成为霸主或者甚至做王,这都不令人吃惊)。欣顿译作 making the Ch'i sovereign an emperor without peer(使齐王成为独一无二的皇帝)。

② "不肤挠,不目逃",刘殿爵译作 by never showing submission on his face or letting anyone outstare him(脸上从不显现屈服的神情,或者让别人瞪倒)。理雅各译作 He did not flinch from any strokes at his body; he did not turn his eyes aside from any thrusts at them(他不躲避对身体的打击;对于他人的直视,他双眼也不回避)。卜爱莲译作 neither to shrink from blows nor to avert his gaze(既不躲避对身体的打击,双眼也不回避直视)。

欣顿译作(Po-kung Yu)never bowed down and never broke off a stare(绝不屈服,双眼也不回避直视)。

③"虑胜而后会",刘殿爵译作 joins battle only after weighing the chances of victory(在掂量了胜利的概率后,才参加战斗)。理雅各译作 to calculate the chances of victory and then engage(掂量了胜利的概率,然后参加战斗)。卜爱莲译作 to engage only after having calculated the prospects for victory(在掂量了胜利的前景后,才参加战斗)。欣顿译作 to calculate your chances of success before fighting(在掂量了胜利的概率后,才参加战斗)。

④"夫志,气之帅也;气,体之充也",刘殿爵译作 The will is commander over the *Ch'i* while the *Ch'i* is that which fills the body(意志主宰气,而气充斥体)。理雅各译作 The will is the leader of the passion-nature. The passion-nature pervades and animates the body(意志是情性的主宰,而情性充斥和激活身体)。卜爱莲译作 The will is the leader of the *Qi*, and it is *qi* that fills the body(意志主宰气,而气充斥体)。欣顿译作 The will guides *Ch'i*, and Ch'i fills the body(意志引导气,而气充斥体)。

⑤"我善养吾浩然之气",刘殿爵译作 I am good at cultivating my "flood-like *Ch'i*"(我善养洪水般的气)。理雅各译作 I am skilful in nourishing my vast, flowing passion-nature(我善养浩大流动的情性)。卜爱莲译作 I am good at nourishing my vast, flowing Qi(我善养浩大流动的气)。欣顿译作 I nurture the *Ch'i*-flood(我善养洪水般的气)。

⑥"心勿忘,勿助长也",刘殿爵译作 while you must never let it out of mind, you must not forcibly help it grow either(绝不能忘却,也不能揠苗助长)。理雅各译作 let not the mind forget its work, but there be no assisting the growth of the nature(心不应忽视性的运作,但不应协助性的成长)。卜爱莲译作 with a mind inclined neither to forget nor to help things grow(心不忘记,也不应协助事物的成长)。欣顿译作 don't let it out of your mind, but don't try to help it grow and flourish either(既不置之脑后,也不应协助成长)。

⑦"诐辞知其所蔽",刘殿爵译作 from biased words, I can see wherein the speaker is blind(从偏颇的言辞,我看得出说话者蒙蔽的地方)。理雅各译作 when words are one-sided, I know how the mind of the speaker is clouded over(从偏颇的言辞,我看得出说话者大脑如何被蒙蔽)。卜爱莲译作 from distorted words, one knows the obscuration(从扭曲的言辞,可以看出蒙蔽的状态)。欣顿译作 I understand what lies hidden beneath beguiling words(我知道谎话后面的东西)。

⑧"冉求、闵子、颜渊则具体而微",刘殿爵译作 Jan Niu, Min Tzu and Yen Hui were replicas of the Sage in miniature(冉求、闵子、颜渊是"小号的夫子")。理雅各译作 Yan Niu, the disciple Min, and Yan Yuan had all the members, but in small proportion(冉求、闵子、颜渊都有夫子的品质,只是程度不及夫子)。卜爱莲译作 Ran Niu, Min Zi and Yan Yuan had all of the qualities, but in slighter degree(冉求、闵子、颜渊都有夫子的品质,只是

程度不及夫子)。欣顿译作 and that Jan Po-niu, Min Tzu-ch'ien, and Yen Hui each embodied all aspects of the sage, but only partially(冉求、闵子、颜渊都有夫子各方面的品质,只是不及夫子全面)。

⑨ "污不至阿其所好",刘殿爵译作 They would not have stooped so low as to show a bias in favour of the man they admire(他们不会为了仰慕的人而屈尊显示偏见)。理雅各译作 even had they been ranking themselves low, they would not have demeaned themselves to flatter their favorites(尽管他们自视颇低,也不至于自降身价讨好自己喜欢的人)。卜爱莲译作 though they had a low opinion of themselves, they could not have come to the point of flattering someone just because they liked them(尽管他们自视颇低,也不至于讨好自己喜欢的人)。欣顿译作 And they would never defile themselves by giving someone they admired undue praise(他们绝不会为讨好自己喜欢的人而自降身价)。

⑩ "出乎其类,拔乎其萃",刘殿爵译作 Though one of their kind, he stands far above the crowd(尽管属于同类,他鹤立鸡群)。理雅各译作 but they stand out from their fellows, and rise above the level(但是他们脱颖而出)。卜爱莲译作 Yet he emerges from among his kind and rises to a higher level(但是他们脱颖而出)。欣顿译作 He stands above them(他脱颖而出)。

3.2 公孙丑问曰:"夫子加齐之卿相,得行道焉,虽由此霸王不异矣。如此,则动心否乎?"

孟子曰:"否。我四十不动心。"

曰:"若是,则夫子过孟贲①远矣。"

曰:"是不难,告子先我不动心。"

曰:"不动心有道乎?"

曰:"有。北宫黝②之养勇也,不肤挠③,不目逃④,思以一豪⑤挫于人,若挞之于市朝。不受于褐宽博⑥,亦不受于万乘之君。视刺万乘之君,若刺褐夫。无严⑦诸侯。恶声至,必反之。孟施舍⑧之所养勇也,曰:'视不胜犹胜也。量敌而后进,虑胜而后会,是畏三军者也。舍岂能为必胜哉?能无惧而已矣。'孟施舍似曾子,北宫黝似子夏。夫二子之勇,未知其孰贤,然而孟施舍守约⑨也。昔者曾子谓子襄⑩曰:'子好勇乎?吾尝闻大勇于夫子矣:自反而不缩⑪,虽褐宽博,吾不惴焉;自反而缩,虽千万人,吾往矣。'孟施舍之守气,又不如曾子之守约也。"

曰:"敢问夫子之不动心,与告子之不动心,可得闻与?"

"告子曰:'不得于言,勿求于心;不得于心,勿求于气。'不得于心,勿求于气,可;不得于言,勿求于心,不可。夫志,气之帅也;气,体之充也。夫志至焉,气次焉。故曰:'持其志,无暴其气。'"

"既曰'志至焉,气次焉',又曰'持其志无暴其气'者,何也?"

曰:"志壹则动气,气壹则动志也。今夫蹶者趋者,是气也,而反动其心。"

"敢问夫子恶乎长?"

曰:"我知言,我善养吾浩然之气。"

"敢问何谓浩然之气?"

曰:"难言也。其为气也,至大至刚,以直养而无害,则塞于天地之间。其为气也,配义与道;无是,馁⑫也。是集义所生者,非义袭⑬而取之也。行有不慊⑭于心,则馁矣。我故曰,告子未尝知义,以其外之也。必有事焉而勿正,心勿忘,勿助长也。无若宋人然:宋人有闵其苗之不长而揠之者,芒芒然归。谓其人曰:'今日病矣,予助苗长矣。'其子趋而往视之,苗则槁矣。天下之不助苗长者寡矣。以为无益而舍之者,不耘苗者也;助之长者,揠苗者也。非徒无益,而又害之。"

"何谓知言?"

曰:"诐辞⑮知其所蔽,淫辞⑯知其所陷,邪辞⑰知其所离,遁辞⑱知其所穷。生于其心,害于其政;发于其政,害于其事。圣人复起,必从吾言矣。"

"宰我、子贡善为说辞,冉牛⑲、闵子⑳、颜渊善言德行。孔子兼之,曰:'我于辞命则不能也。'然则夫子既圣矣乎?"

曰:"恶!是何言也?昔者子贡,问于孔子曰:'夫子圣矣乎?'孔子曰:'圣则吾不能,我学不厌而教不倦也。'子贡曰:'学不厌,智也;教不倦,仁也。仁且智,夫子既圣矣!'夫圣,孔子不居,是何言也?"

"昔者窃闻之:子夏、子游、子张皆有圣人之一体,冉牛、闵子、颜渊则具体而微。敢问所安。"

曰:"姑舍是。"

曰:"伯夷、伊尹何如?"

"不同道。非其君不事,非其民不使;治则进,乱则退,伯夷也。何事非君,何使非民;治亦进,乱亦进,伊尹也。可以仕则仕,可以止则止,可以久则久,可以速则速,孔子也。皆古圣人也,吾未能有行焉;乃所愿,则学孔子也。"

"伯夷、伊尹于孔子,若是班乎?"

曰:"否。自有生民以来,未有孔子也。"

曰:"然则有同与?"

曰:"有。得百里之地而君之,皆能以朝诸侯有天下。行一不义、杀一不辜而得天下,皆不为也。是则同。"

曰："敢问其所以异？"

曰："宰我、子贡、有若㉑智足以知圣人。汙，不至阿其所好。宰我曰：'以予观于夫子，贤于尧舜远矣。'子贡曰：'见其礼而知其政，闻其乐而知其德。由百世之后，等百世之王，莫之能违也。自生民以来，未有夫子也。'有若曰：'岂惟民哉？麒麟之于走兽，凤凰之于飞鸟，太山之于丘垤㉒，河海之于行潦㉓，类也。圣人之于民，亦类也。出于其类，拔乎其萃，自生民以来，未有盛于孔子也。'"

① 孟贲：战国时期秦武王手下著名勇士。
② 北宫黝：齐国著名的勇士，也称北宫子。
③ 不肤挠：挠，本意为烦扰，退却；该词指皮肤被刺，也不会退缩。
④ 不目逃：眼睛被刺也不会躲避。
⑤ 一豪：一根毫毛。
⑥ 褐宽博：褐，粗布。宽博，指宽大。此处用粗布制作的宽大衣服代指贫贱之人。
⑦ 严：尊重。
⑧ 孟施舍：生平不详。
⑨ 约：简约，简易。
⑩ 子襄：曾子的弟子，生平不详。
⑪ 自反而不缩：缩，本意为乱，此处一般注解为义或直。该词指自我反省，自己的行为不正义。
⑫ 馁：泄气。
⑬ 袭：偶然的行为。
⑭ 慊：通"惬"，快意。
⑮ 诐辞：谄媚不正的语言。
⑯ 淫辞：过分修饰之语言。
⑰ 邪辞：偏离正道的语言。
⑱ 遁辞：理屈而强为之辩解的语言。
⑲ 冉牛：孔子弟子，冉氏，名耕，字伯牛，德行出众。
⑳ 闵子：孔子弟子，闵损，字子骞，以孝闻名。
㉑ 有若：孔子弟子，有氏，名若，字子有（一说字子若），后世称"有子"。
㉒ 丘垤：垤，本意为蚂蚁窝前所堆的土堆。该词代指小山丘。
㉓ 行潦：指沟渠中的流水。

Exercises

1. Put the following passage into English.

公都子曰："告子曰：'性无善无不善也。'或曰：'性可以为善，可以为不善；是故文武兴,则民好善;幽厉兴,则民好暴。'或曰:'有性善有性不善;是故以尧为君而有象,以瞽瞍为父而有舜;以纣为兄之子,且以为君,而有微子启、王子比干。'今曰'性善',然则彼皆非与?"

孟子曰:"乃若其情,则可以为善矣,乃所谓善也。若夫为不善,非才之罪也。恻隐之心,人皆有之;羞恶之心,人皆有之;恭敬之心,人皆有之;是非之心,人皆有之。恻隐之心,仁也;羞恶之心,义也;恭敬之心,礼也;是非之心,智也。仁义礼智,非由外铄我也,我固有之也,弗思耳矣。故曰:'求则得之,舍则失之。'或相倍蓰而无算者,不能尽其才者也。《诗》曰:'天生蒸民,有物有则。民之秉彝,好是懿德。'孔子曰:'为此诗者,其知道乎!故有物必有则;民之秉彝也,故好是懿德。'"

2. Discussion and composition.

Mencius put forward the proposition of "not stirring the heart"(不动心). In what ways is it different from "non-action"(无为) of Taoism? Write an essay about 300 words.

Supplementary Reading: D. C. Lau as a Translator of Chinese Philosophical Classics(2)

跨越大众导向和精英导向的鸿沟(二)
——刘殿爵翻译《孟子》暨中国古代思想典籍

刘殿爵的《论语》译本1979年由企鹅出版社初版。1983年香港中文大学出版社再版。再版的唯一改变是增加了《论语》中文文言章句,形成了中英对照的正文格局。虽然我们无法确知这是译者的主意,还是出版社的想法,但客观上开辟了《论语》暨中国古代思想典籍外译的双重读者导向——在针对国际读者的同时,针对中国大众读者。由于这样的版式设计,中国读者可以连带学习中国古代思想典籍的表达方式和翻译技巧,甚至学习文言和英语本身。《论语》中英对照的正文格局其实早已有之。理雅各、苏慧廉译本就有,如是编排目的之一是帮助传教士和外籍人士学习汉语。但是到了西方现代这种双语编排反而少了。这里特别提出是因为《论语》刘译本开了中国本土翻译《论语》中英对照的正文格局的先河。20世纪90年代之后,随着中国综合国力的提升和国际地位的提高,中国的文化自信随之增强。对于中国传统文化,官方和民间都有"送出主义"的冲动和行动。随之迎来《论语》英译的潮流,而目的读者群应该为西方的大众读者。值得注意的是,中国译者同时面向中国大众读者。这与国内大众读者对于《论语》英译本的需求和中国多数出版社的发行渠道有关。随着英语成为中小学的必修课,中国形成了全民学英语的局面。对于《论语》英译的好奇心和用英译表达传播中国文化的意愿驱动了《论语》英译本的出版。另外,中国多数出版社的发行渠道在国内,《论语》英译必须照顾和满足中国大众读者的需求。刘殿爵在这方面做了较早成功的有节制的尝试。这样中西读者各取所需。这是值得肯定的一种翻译导向,具有现代中国的特色。

总括地说,刘殿爵的中国古代思想典籍的翻译深入浅出,举重若轻。其文似浅实深,其论似轻实重。对于读者而言,浅者得其浅,深者得其深。刘殿爵的中国古代思想典籍的翻译在中西学界都赢得了很高的赞誉。《道德经》《论语》《孟子》被誉为当代世界的标准译本和西方汉学的必读入门书。在大众普及的一面,他的译作成为企鹅经典的畅销书。《道德经》销售达到了七十万册。《论语》《孟子》的销售也很可观。

钱钟书评论刘殿爵的《论语》译本时说:"刘先生译《论语》,已快读其序文一过,真深思卓识之通人。其仅移译高手而已。书前未介绍其生年,想极四十时许人;才不可及,年更不可及也。"这里的"通人"大约指刘殿爵学贯中西,贯通古今,用西文把《论语》暨孔子学说阐释得如此通透,让西方大众和学术精英都能通晓儒学奥义吧。

刘殿爵能够跨越大众导向和精英导向的鸿沟,与他的专业职业身份有关。他兼有中国传统学者、语言学家和现代汉学家的复合身份。刘殿爵是一个颇有成就的中国古代思想典籍研究的学者。在这一领域,他用中英文发表过高水平的论著。重回香港,在香港中文大学任职期间,他将大量精力投入到中国古籍整理中,在古籍索引编撰、古籍校勘、古籍数字化方面作出了显著的成绩。对中国传统学术的深厚的学术素养保证了其对原本诠释的权威性。刘殿爵还是个语言学家,对中英文有着高度的感知力。他对文言文和英语语言有独特的见解。这又使其译文别具一格。他还是一个长期在西方从事教学、研究和翻译的汉学家,培养过安乐哲这样的高足,翻译过三部中国古代思想经典。众所周知,西方汉学家的工作除了专业的学术性之外,还兼有在西方普及中国文化和学术的职责。而这一职责在今天的大众化时代越来越重要。他翻译的大众导向无疑与他的现代汉学家身份有关。

刘殿爵的跨越还与赞助人——出版机制有关。中国古代思想典籍在西方的出版主要由大学出版社和常规出版社承担。在很长一段时间里,前者是中国古代思想典籍的主要出版机构,如哥伦比亚大学出版社、哈佛大学出版社。随着大众时代的来临,常规的出版社也积极参与了有关书籍的出版。而后者常常是大众导向。出版刘殿爵译作的企鹅出版社就是一个很好的例子。企鹅出版社是为大众读者服务的出版社,每年出版众多排行榜畅销书。企鹅出版社还有出版经典畅销书的传统。经典必然有学术含量,而要畅销必须对大众的胃口。1946年,企鹅出版社出版了一部经典作品《奥德赛》,成为企鹅的一本畅销书。随后一发不可收拾。刘殿爵为企鹅出版社译作的定位就是经典畅销书,事实上也成了畅销书。刘殿爵的经典翻译正是应企鹅出版社的邀请。他的翻译及翻译文体毫无疑问都与赞助人——出版机制有关系。事实上,刘殿爵的翻译已经成为大众与精英、市场与学术结合的成功范例。

刘殿爵在翻译中既重视大众普及又重视学术提高的翻译路径在当下的中国古代思想典籍的翻译中有典范意义。他的成功经验值得我们总结,这有利于中国文化更快更好地走出去,在保证学术含量的同时走入西方的大众读者群体之中。

References

《四书》英译底本及参照本

《论语》

底本

Waley, Arthur, *The Analects of Confucius,* The Macmillan Company, 1938.

参照本

Legge, James, *Confucian Analects, The Chinese Classics,* Hong Kong University Press, 1963.

辜鸿铭. *The Discourse and Sayings of Confucius.* 辜鸿铭文集.海南出版社,1996.

安乐哲,罗思文.《论语》的哲学诠释.中国社会科学出版社,2003.

林戊荪. *Getting to Know Confucius—A New Translation of The Analects.*《论语》新译.外文出版社,2010.

《大学》

底本

Wing-Tsit Chan, *A Source Book in Chinese Philosophy,* Princeton University, 1963.

参照本

Legge, James, *The Great Learning, The Chinese Classics,* Hong Kong University Press, 1963.

辜鸿铭.辜鸿铭英译经典:《大学》《中庸》.中华书局,2017.

Plaks, Andrew, *Ta Hsueh and Chung Yung,* Penguin Books, 2003.

林语堂. *The Wisdom of Confucius.*湖南文艺出版社,2021.

《中庸》

底本

Legge, James, *The Doctrine of the Mean, The Chinese Classics,* Hong Kong University Press, 1963.

参照本

辜鸿铭.辜鸿铭英译经典:《大学》《中庸》.中华书局,2017.

Plaks, Andrew, *Ta Hsueh and Chung Yung,* Penguin Books, 2003.

安乐哲,郝大维.切中伦常——《中庸》的新诠与新释.中国社会科学出版社,2011.

《孟子》

底本

Lau, D.L., *Mencius*, Penguin Books, 1970.

参照本

Legge, James, *Mencius, The Chinese Classics,* Hong Kong University Press, 1963.

Bloom, Irene, *Mencius,* Columbia University Press, 2009.

Hinton, David, *Mencius,* Counterpoint, 2015.

参考书目:

Andrews, G. 2017. *Thesis Research Proposal: Academic Writing Guide for Graduate Students. Essay and Thesis Writing Series.* Downloaded at https://www.amazon.com/Research-Proposal-Academic-Graduate-Students-ebook/dp/B073W1B2R1.

Brause, R.S. 2001. *Writing Your Doctoral Dissertation: Invisible Rules for Success.* London: Routledge.

Mallette, L & Berger, C. 2011. *Writing for Conferences: A Handbook for Graduate Students and Faculty.* Greenwood.

Swales, J.M. & Feak, C.B. 2012. *Academic Writing for Graduate Students: Essential Tasks and Skills,* 3rd ed. Michigan ELT.

Wallwork, A. 2011. *English for Academic Correspondence and Socializing.* Springer International Publishing, Switzerland.

Wallwork, A. 2011. *English for Writing Research Papers.* Springer International Publishing, Switzerland.

Wallwork, A. 2016. *English for Presentations at International Conferences*, 2nd ed. Springer International Publishing, Switzerland.

Wallwork, A. 2016. *English for Academic Research: Grammar, Usage and Style.* Springer International Publishing, Switzerland.

Wallwork, A. & Southern, A. 2020. 100 *Tips to Avoid Mistakes in Academic Writing and Presenting.* Springer International Publishing, Switzerland.

曹威.当代西方的《论语》哲学诠释研究.中国社会科学出版社,2020.

程树德.论语集释(全四册).中华书局,1990.

陈雅玲.北宋《论语》学研究(上、下册).花木兰文化事业有限公司,2020.
陈群.明清之际的《大学》诠释研究.科学出版社,2017.
从丛,王文宇.学术交流英语教程(第二版).南京大学出版社,2014.
江晓梅.《中庸》英译研究.武汉大学出版社,2016.
姜哲.《论语》英译本研究文选.南京大学出版社,2020.
郎擎霄.孟子哲学.北京理工大学出版社,2020.
林怡玲.《孟子》"志气论"的道德哲学.花木兰文化事业有限公司,2020.
刘宝楠,撰,高流水,点校.论语正义(全二册).中华书局,1990.
刘勇.变动不居的经典:明代《大学》改本研究.生活·读书·新知三联书店,2016.
刘莘.《论语》引导.广西师范大学出版社,2021.
刘瑾辉.清代《孟子》学研究.社会科学文献出版社,2007.
李凯.孟子诠释思想研究.人民出版社,2015.
李凯.孟子伦理思想研究.人民出版社,2016.
李零.去圣乃得真孔子.生活·读书·新知三联书店,2008.
李泽厚.论语今读.生活·读书·新知三联书店,2004.
李纪祥.两宋以来《大学》改本之研究.台湾学生书局,1988.
孟子文献集成编纂委员会,编纂.孟子文献集成.山东人民出版社,2020.
钱穆.论语新解.兰台出版社,2005.
钱穆.论语新解.生活·读书·新知三联书店,2005.
唐明贵.宋代《论语》诠释研究.中国社会科学出版社,2017.
王国轩.大学·中庸.中华书局,2006.
魏忠强.孟子与早期经学研究.燕山大学出版社,2020.
杨伯峻.论语译注.中华书局,2006.
杨伯峻,译注.孟子译注.中华书局,2012.
杨树达.论语疏证.江西人民,2007.
杨颖育.英语世界的《孟子》研究.人民出版社,2015.
杨泽波.孟子性善论研究.中国人民大学出版社,2010.
张卉.朱熹《中庸》学研究.四川大学出版社,2018.
张松辉、周晓露.《论语》《孟子》疑义研究.湖南大学出版社,2006.